KU-547-370

DEMOCRACY, REAL AND IDEAL

Discourse Ethics and Radical Politics

RICARDO BLAUG

State University
of New York
Press

Published by
State University of New York Press, Albany

© 1999 State University of New York

All rights reserved

Production by Susan Geraghty
Marketing by Fran Keneston

Printed in the United States of America

No part of this book may be used or reproduced in any manner whatsoever
without written permission. No part of this book may be stored in a retrieval
system or transmitted in any form or by any means including electronic,
electrostatic, magnetic tape, mechanical, photocopying, recording, or otherwise
without the prior permission in writing of the publisher.

For information, address State University of New York
Press, State University Plaza, Albany, N.Y. 12246

Library of Congress Cataloging-in-Publication Data

Blaug, Ricardo.
    Democracy, real and ideal : discourse ethics and radical politics
  / Ricardo Blaug.
        p.   cm. — (SUNY series in social and political thought)
    Includes bibliographical references and index.
    ISBN 0-7914-4107-5 (alk. paper). — ISBN 0-7914-4108-3 (pbk. : alk.
  paper)
      1. Democracy. 2. Legitimacy of governments. 3. Habermas, Jürgen-
  -Ethics. 4. Habermas, Jürgen—Contributions in political science.
  I. Title. II. Series.
  JC423.B59 1999
  321.8'01—dc21   98-7751
                                                                      CIP

10 9 8 7 6 5 4 3 2 1

CONTENTS

To my father, Mark

INTRODUCTION

People who get Alzheimer's disease do not immediately lose their minds. Rather the onset is gradual, so that between health and complete dysfunction is a heartbreaking period where short-term memory and internal behavior controls are progressively eroded yet the person retains sufficient insight to be aware that they are changing. During this period, they are a spectator at their own deterioration.

It's hard to imagine what this might feel like. Probably, one would forgive oneself the first mistakes, but as they increased, and formerly simple activities became more difficult, one would begin to feel concerned. As the illness progressed, one's behavior would become a source of fear. It would become undeniable: you are irritable, volatile, and far too quick to react to even the slightest provocation. You might notice also that whereas before your family argued and made you do things yourself, now they treat you with kid gloves. Finally, someone plucks up the courage to talk to you, and in an awkward exchange, suggests you see a doctor. At first offended, you at last admit that you are behaving badly. You always believed people should be polite and not abuse one another, yet recently you have found yourself losing your temper, forgetting where you are, shouting abuse, and even striking out. You feel better for admitting all this. You visit the doctor, and are referred to a specialist. The specialist asks you lots of questions, and instead of looking at you as you reply, writes your responses down. Trying not to be afraid, you return home.

But you never tell people the strangest thing of all. It's not the tantrums, or the loss of memory; it's those moments *afterwards*, when you suddenly realize that you have just lost control. In an instant, you know what you have done; the way a dreamer sees, quite suddenly, that it is only a dream. In such moments, you judge yourself with past standards, you use the moral principles you have used all your life; only now you are constantly falling short, failing, doing things wrong. Such moments are terrifying, for in them you see how you have changed. And yet still, when something frustrates you, the blind rage returns, you lash out, and such principles are again transgressed.

This disjuncture: between how you think you should behave and how you actually behave, cannot last for long. Having accepted that one is frequently losing control, the moral principle that one should not, say, abuse people, must either be abandoned, or so modified as to allow for your regular lapses. Being a political philosopher, you might spend some evenings rehearsing new qualifications on your moral principle: aggression is permitted when you are attacked, when threatened, when irritated by someone; a threat means such and such, a sufficient irritation means so and so. The principle, thus diluted, now conforms to reality, and you are much comforted.

At last, after some time, the specialist has a long talk with you, in which she uses the word "Alzheimer's." She says you are getting sick. As an example, she refers to the fact that last week you assaulted a member of your family, whereas you would never have done anything like that before you became ill. But to you, this doesn't seem right at all. The specialist is misinterpreting the facts. Angrily, you cite the qualifications that pertained to the assault: how the person behaved badly toward you, how they threatened you, and so on. Though the assault might *look* to be a violation of moral principles, you claim haughtily, it is not in fact a violation at all. So you shout at her. And afterwards, you shout at your family too. You tell them to stop crying. Now you are feeling fine. You no longer get those moments of lucidity and terror.

The point of these imaginings is to focus on the effects of an uncoupling between a notion of what ought to be the case, and what is (repeatedly) experienced to actually be the case. Where the gap is wide, the result is cognitive dissonance, confusion, rationalization. Sooner or later the normative principle itself is revised in order to no longer clash with reality. I want to argue that such an uncoupling, between the normative theory and its empirical institutional embodiment, currently obtains in the area of democratic theory.

We are, as Dunn points out, all democrats now.[1] This is to say we almost all espouse some form of normative belief in democracy, and even tyrants claim the legitimation of the ballot box. But the relation of the normative claim of democracy to its empirical reality is a far more contentious issue. Do the present institutions of democracy have anything to do with popular sovereignty? Are they legitimate in any meaningful sense? Should new institutions be implemented and if so, what would they look like? How might competing institutional designs be evaluated? Does normative democratic theory have anything to do with empirical practice at all? Questions such as these indicate the depth of the gulf that has opened between the "ought" and the "is" of democracy.

Within individuals, this gulf is often observable as a cognitive dissonance. Many of us appear to hold two intuitive assumptions about the making of decisions, and these assumptions are contradictory. The first is that a decision is somehow "more moral" when those affected have participated in its making. This is a normative belief. The second is that human nature and the real constraints of decision-making in fact preclude the possibility of complete participation. This is an empirical assertion.[2]

This contradiction gives rise to both confusion and rationalization. We see, for example, managers in the public and private sectors make faltering attempts to initiate participation in order to legitimate their decisions. Yet these managers are often quite unable to navigate the complexities arising from such attempts, are generally resistant to any serious transfer of power to participants, and eventually fall back on the insistence that greater participation is not a practical possibility.

At the same time, those whose lot it is to be managed are morally outraged when not properly consulted, are profoundly mistrustful of leadership in general, and yet are so overwhelmed by the apparent practical difficulties of participation that the most common response is simple apathy and exhaustion. We are not good at participation, and the brief periods when we were (Athens, Rome, Florence) seem few and far between. Indeed, nowadays, attempts to participate expose individuals to the full force of our collective incapacity to manage moral and value conflicts. Our often disorganized attempts at open debate and cooperative action usually leave us, at best, disenchanted with humanity, and at worst with a tendency to talk about each other (after the meeting) in language more suited to psychopathology than to solidarity.

In political science, the gulf between normative democratic theory and empirical reality has been widely documented and constitutes one of the traditional battlefronts in the critique of liberal democracy, both from the left and the right. Yet the question I want to pursue here is not simply the failure of real institutions to do what they should. Rather, I hope to plumb normative democratic theory, particularly its most vital contemporary strains,[3] for any assistance it can give with the design and evaluation of (empirical) democratic institutions. This is no easy task, for as we shall see, there is, currently, an almost complete uncoupling of normative and empirical theories of democracy. Attempts by political philosophers to move from one to the other are therefore characterized, again, by confusion and rationalization.[4]

Such confusion is particularly apparent around the relation of theory to practice, and this will be a constant theme in our investigation. While it may be naive to follow the recent fashion of insisting that political theory is good only when it is of direct practical use,[5] it nevertheless seems reasonable to hope for a modicum of theoretical assistance with practical decision-making. The attraction of judging all theory in terms of its utility is all too obvious at a time when organized violence is rife in the very heart of Europe and nationalism is once again the predominant applied political theory. The pressure for political answers reaches a crescendo in such chaotic times and though it might seem harsh to blame political theorists for the bad behavior of political actors, there is something fairly shocking about turning from the horror of actual politics to those who think about such problems for a living, only to find those thinkers inspecting their own navels. Of course, some theorists do not want to be seen in such light, and are anxious to provide answers to real problems.[6]

Historically, this is precisely the situation in which Hobbes found himself, and his work is a classic illustration of its dangers. Outside his window raged the English civil war, and the *Leviathan* was a political theory to sort the whole nasty mess out once and for all. It is interesting to note that Hobbes had earlier translated Thucydides' *Peloponnesian War*. In the famous description of civil war in Corcyra, Thucydides uses the telling phrase "human nature revealed itself as insubordinate to the idea of justice."[7] There would be no insubordination to the Leviathan, nor would any truck be given to the human penchant for evil. Hobbes's work stands at the center of an honored tradition in political thought, where humanity is seen as essentially insane, requiring the straightjacket of political authority to solve the problem of coordination. In times of strife then, impatience with theoretical complexity grows, and the most likely outcome of such impatience is an authoritarian "answer."

Any investigation of the proper relationship between the normative theory of democracy and its empirical implications must thread a path between two evils. On the one hand lies the "Lion" of collective oppression.[8] Here, theory is seen as being completely unified with questions of practice. On the other is the blindness of uninformed action, with its dangerous disdain for theory and irritation with moral complexity.

What one needs here is a guide, and for this purpose I turn to the critical theory of Jürgen Habermas. Notwithstanding his occasional turgidity,[9] the methodological self-consciousness of his work, as well as its extraordinary breadth, will help us to focus on our central issue with greater accuracy. In particular, his theoretical position combines a profound belief in the need for relevant theory with an understanding of the dangers of *a priori* answers, and it is this tension that will guide our investigation.

Habermas has articulated a theory of discourse ethics in which he reconstructs a counterfactual ideal of domination-free communication as the grounding for normative validity. I present an account of the reconstruction of this normative position in chapter 1. My concern here is not, as with the vast majority of commentary upon Habermas's thought, to become enmeshed in the complex arguments around the validity of his normative claims. Rather, I will attempt to state his position in such a way as to inform the subsequent inspection of questions surrounding the application of the theory to practical problems. Habermas's normative theory is strongly Kantian in its orientation, yet he has also addressed himself to more Hegelian concerns. Our account of his theory of discourse ethics will, therefore, pay particular attention to Hegel's critique of Kantian ethics, for not only has this important episode in the history of philosophy had significant impact on the development of Habermas's theory, but within it can be found many of the issues that arise when theory proceeds in terms of an application of an ideal to real institutional concerns.

Discourse ethics is, primarily, a theory of morality, yet it also has implications for questions of democratic legitimacy. Coming from the tradition of the Frankfurt School, Habermas makes definite affirmative claims for the implications of his counterfactual ideal in the areas of social criticism and political practice. This has resulted in a careful articulation of the correct relation of theory to practice, and in chapter 2, I explicate what he means by "theory with a practical intent."

Habermas's normative theory has appeared to many to hold great promise, and in chapter 3, I review the various attempts to apply his normative ideal to practical matters, both by himself and by his many commentators. In particular, I concentrate on those affirmative applications in the area of political practice that come closest to addressing the problem of the design and evaluation of real democratic institutions. This review will reveal that there exists considerable confusion as to the political implications of his work, and that all such applications tend to confront a series of recurrent methodological problems. These problems are, in fact, so severe as to disable much of the current research that seeks to realize the democratic promise of his normative ideal.

Chapter 4 proceeds to examine the various sources of both the confusion surrounding questions of application and the recurrent methodological problems encountered by those seeking to mine out the practical implications of Habermasian theory. Focusing particularly on the formal and Kantian character of the normative theory and the care with which Habermas limits its prescriptive scope, I here focus on precisely what he says his theory cannot and should not do. Much of the critique to which Habermas has been subjected turns on these two aspects of his work: the claim that the theory has affirmative uses has prompted some anxiety and even charges of authoritarianism, while the careful negative limitations he places upon his theory have resulted in disappointment and accusations of irrelevance. There is, therefore, at the very heart of Habermas's position, a threatened uncoupling of normative from empirical theory.

In chapter 5 I begin to argue that this uncoupling is not insurmountable, but that the route from one to the other involves an intermediate step: this being a more adequate theory of political judgment. One of the main sources of the methodological problems encountered upon attempting to use Habermas's theory to address problems of design and evaluation of democratic institutions is his understanding of how the faculty of judgment operates. By inspecting the various criticisms to which his description of judgment has been subjected, and particularly the "reflective turn" pursued by many commentators, we are able, in chapter 6, to reformulate an account of the manner in which judgments actually proceed. Here, Wittgenstein's work on the problem of universals is explored in order to render explicit certain assumptions Habermas carries from his theory of normative validity to his theory of judgment. The attempt here is to further our understanding of how a universalist ethics in fact informs the everyday competence to judge the fairness of communicative practices. I then inspect the implications of this reformulated account of judgment for questions surrounding the design and evaluation of democratic institutions.

In order to redeem the political importance of Habermas's thought, however, I argue that it is not sufficient to take his reconstruction of normative validity and his account of the proper relation of theory to practice, and then to show that the recoupling of normative and empirical concerns can be effected with a reformulated theory of judgment. In addition, a shift is required in the object domain to which such theoretical advances are to be applied.

Habermas posits a normative counterfactual ideal of complete participation, and he fully intends this to help us with the empirical problem of how a political order might be made more democratic. Yet though he is able to highlight the importance of the public sphere and to call for the increase in deliberative fora in order to deepen democracy, he never really confronts questions regarding the actual functioning of such fora. Indeed, his most recent work moves rather in the opposite direction, concentrating on the "macro" questions of the normative basis of law and constitutional practices.[10] Chapter 7 seeks to change the object domain to which discourse ethics is applied, to break away from the theorist's perspective that gives rise to the "macro"-orientation, and instead to examine the problems of democracy as they appear from the perspective of participants in real deliberative interactions.

In chapter 8, I focus on this "missing tier," suggesting that Habermasian theory, when augmented with a reformulated account of judgment, can be fruitfully applied to the difficulties encountered by participants as they engage in real participation. With the object domain of application so adjusted, I argue, the possibility of a Habermasian politics re-emerges. Such a recoupling of normative and empirical political theory takes the form of a radical democratic politics that is anti-authoritarian, deliberative, and pragmatic in character. In this way, theory *can* give counsel to participants as they try to make decisions that are both fair and efficient.

If we are to avoid slipping into such an advanced state of collective sickness that we no longer have those chilling moments in which we see what we have lost, we will need to deepen our democratic practice. Habermas, I suggest, gives us the conceptual tools to effect such a project, though not if our understanding of democracy remains constrained to the abstract level of society as a whole. For this reason, our inquiry takes Habermas's extraordinary contribution to democratic theory into places it does not usually go. Only where democracy is conceived as an everyday and real interactive process can we understand what it might mean to truly rule ourselves.

PART 1

Theory and Practice

CHAPTER 1

The Theory of Discourse Ethics

Habermas's project attempts to justify a normative basis for social criticism. As a theory of justification, it seeks to provide the critical power of universalism while avoiding the historical self-righteousness and indefensibility of such positions. At the same time, as a theory of social criticism, it tries to attend to the particular contexts in which we live our lives without degenerating into relativism.

Humankind has always reached for universal truths, and these have often been appealed to in order to justify the oppression and exclusion of those simply different from ourselves. Value pluralism and cultural particularity are more recent discoveries. What began as a way of tempering the critical power of universalism, of resisting the flattening of all difference, has now progressed into an "incredulity towards all metanarratives."[1] In its most recent and postmodern forms, it threatens the removal of all critical power and counsels a kind of clever passivity in the face of human suffering. Postmodernism generally suggests that while relativism may have its drawbacks, it is unavoidable. Yet when asked that most famous (and equally unavoidable) question in political theory—What should we do?—there is silence, or worse, we are ridiculed for asking. Baudrillard, for example, when discussing the morality of the Gulf War, playfully claimed that no such war had ever taken place. His interest was to show that history itself is little more than a "metanarrative," a grand fiction. Similarly, when discussing moral claims, followers of Derrida advocate an ironic stance, a mood of uncertainty, an explosion of laughter.[2]

Most other critical approaches to political science, and certainly those of Marxists, feminists, and Habermasians, are less comfortable with the loss of critical power brought about by relativism. To them, the ironic laughter of the postmodernists, though appealing, is simply not enough. Indeed, as the uninhibited slaughter of innocent people continues, such a hands-off approach hardly suffices. There are real questions to be answered, real sufferings to be addressed, and it seems reasonable to look to political theory for some guidance as to what we should be trying to do about them.

Habermas's difficulty, or perhaps we should say the essential difficulty of the age, is to combine the strengths of universalism with those

3

of cultural relativism. The method by which Habermas navigates the channel between this Scylla and Charybdis is the subject of our first chapter. It is worth noting that Odysseus chose to sail closer to the former, for while Scylla would certainly kill six of his men, Charybdis would take them all. Similarly, Habermas makes a conscious choice between theoretical alternatives. There must, he insists, be a valid moral difference between more and less domination. We must have some universal knowledge if we are to criticize obnoxious positions and guide our political actions. At the same time, he knows that such critical power can only be derived from a universal fulcrum that is abstracted from particular contexts.[3] As he puts it:

> If philosophical ethics and political theory can know nothing more than what is anyhow contained in the everyday norm consciousness of different populations, and cannot even know this in a different way, it cannot then rationally distinguish legitimate from illegitimate domination. . . . If, on the other hand, philosophical ethics and political theory are supposed to disclose the moral core of the general consciousness and to reconstruct it as a normative concept of the moral, then they must specify criteria and provide reasons; they must, that is, produce theoretical knowledge.[4]

Such theoretical knowledge is abstract, disinterested, and objective. It provides an extra-contextual criterion independent of the "everyday norm consciousness of different populations." Yet if such knowledge is to form the basis for social criticism, it must also be applicable to those contexts in which social practices take place. By uncoupling theory from particular contexts, Habermas thus confronts the problem of recontextualization. Yet he would rather face the problem of crossing the gap from universal to particular than to have no recourse to the universal at all.

Social criticism thus becomes, for Habermas, a question of applying a universal criterion to particular situations and practices. The difficulty of formulating a conceptual object that is both independent of contexts and yet sensitive to them, has entertained the human intellect from the beginning. Pocock explicates its history by contrasting the image of the sun with that of the wheel.[5] The former is a perfect sphere, it is outside time and universal. The latter is pitted and imperfect, forever grinding out its particular and time-bound existence. The former is philosophy and logic, the latter, rhetoric and grammar. The former is Plato and rationalism, the latter, Aristotle and empiricism. One can obviously work these categories too far, but they do serve to illustrate what must be brought together if we are to have justified knowledge of practical social issues.

Where social criticism takes the form of an application of a rationally justified universal, we face the danger of becoming ensnared in what Albert has called "Munchhausen's trilemma."[6] Rational justification, according to its critics, must either degenerate into an infinite regress, logical circularity, or the dogmatic acceptance of a first axiom.[7] If this is the case, then there can be no such thing as a theory of justification, no extra-contextual criteria, no grounds. Our examination of Habermas's solution to this trilemma will be in two parts. First (1.1), we will inspect his theory of justification. Second (1.2), we will look at the dilemma his approach generates in regard to questions of application.

1.1 HABERMAS ON JUSTIFICATION

In the face of the "discovery" of contextualism, it is clearly more difficult to generate first axioms or universalist fulcra that overcome our "incredulity to meta-narratives" in such a way as to offer grounds for critical power. Recently, there have been a number of attempts that have revived a loosely Kantian approach to this question, of which Habermas, Rawls, Baier, Dworkin, and Gerwirth are the most notable examples.[8] All have sought to reclaim a fulcrum yet to avoid the pitfalls of foundationalism. Of these writers, perhaps Rawls and Habermas have displayed the greatest methodological transparency in their appropriation of Kant. Certainly, Habermas's theory stands or falls on its Kantian core and by formulating this we can highlight some of the strengths and weaknesses of both Habermas's and Kantian theories generally.

Rather than beginning with a notion of natural rights as does Locke, or with rational death avoidance as does Hobbes, or even with a view that evaluates actions in terms of their consequences, as do the utilitarians, Kant begins with the notion of pure practical reason.[9] The only purely good thing in the world, he asserts, the only thing that is always good, is the human will.[10] The moral worth of an action lies in the principle of volition, the maxim[11] according to which the action is performed. Maxims are therefore to be tested in such a way as to abstract them entirely from all particular outcomes, desires, and intentions. As Kant says:

> Since I have robbed the will of every inducement that might arise for it as a consequence of obeying any particular law, nothing is left but the conformity of actions to universal law as such, and this alone must so serve the will as its principle. That is to say, I ought never to act except in such a way that I can also will that my maxim should become a universal law.[12]

This categorical imperative states the conditions of moral autonomy and pure practical reason. We are here, therefore, treated to a derivation of a procedural test that will ascertain the moral worth of a maxim and that can offer guidance in the evaluation of a particular action. Moral questions are seen as admitting of truth; so the theory is a cognitive one.[13] Truth is here characterized as universalization and provides a foundation for the theory. The categorical imperative functions as a principle much like that of induction in the natural sciences,[14] for it bridges the gap between the abstract universal and the concrete particular, or between the ideal and the real.

Kant extends his notion of moral autonomy into the political sphere by asserting that "a person is subject to no law other than those that he (either alone or at least jointly with others) gives to himself."[15] Kant here borrows heavily from Rousseau[16] and likewise alludes to the notion of a social contract. In this case, the contract is conceived as analogous to the categorical imperative in that it functions as a "standard or test for legislation in the same way that the categorical imperative is a test for the maxims of individual action."[17] Kant is then able to stipulate the conditions for the validity of this public test by again unpacking the content of moral autonomy. The "juridical attributes," as he calls them, of the original social contract, are "freedom, equality and independence."[18]

Kant also offers a deduction for a transcendental principle of publicity: "All actions affecting the rights of other human beings are wrong if their maxim is not compatible with their being made public."[19] We can now see why Baynes asserts that "Kant offers a theory of the social contract that . . . strongly emphasises the idea of a (counterfactual) agreement between free and equal moral persons."[20]

Finally, Kant's moral theory is characterized by an essential distinction between the right and the good. While the categorical imperative provides a procedural moral test, the subject for this test, in other words the scope of morality, is limited to those questions regarding what is right. As long as one does not violate the imperatives of morality, one is free to pursue any conception of the good life one might wish. Kant states the priority of right over good to be *a priori* and again to be deducible from the notion of pure practical reason.

All of these elements are of direct importance in Habermas's conception of discourse ethics. However, though he follows a similar method to Kant, he begins from a different place. It is for this reason that he is able to "detranscendentalize" Kant's moral theory, and thus to take only what is best from it,[21] overcoming its tendency to simply valorize the Lutheran and patriarchal values of Kant's cultural experience.

Instead of beginning with the rational faculties of a monological subject and his/her relation to the objective world, Habermas explicates the concept of communicative reason. What is paradigmatic here is rather the "intersubjective relation that speaking and acting subjects take up when they come to an understanding with one another about something."[22] When Habermas considers the notion of autonomy, therefore, it is understood in dialogic terms.[23] As Benhabib puts it:

> Autonomy no longer means self-legislation as in Kant, self-actualisation as with Hegel or Marx, or mimesis as with Adorno and Horkheimer, but the cognitive competence to adopt a universalist standpoint and the interactive competence to act on such a basis.[24]

Habermas thus derives his discourse ethics and his extra-contextual criterion of fair procedure by way of a reconstruction of the conditions of mutual understanding.[25]

In taking communication as paradigmatic, Habermas is following the "linguistic turn" in twentieth-century philosophy. As in the work of Searle and Austin,[26] however, Habermas is particularly interested in the "*communicative use* of propositionally differentiated language [rather] than in the use of propositions per se."[27] In other words, instead of taking language as a monological capability, as do the dominant schools of linguistics and formal semantics, Habermas seeks to focus on the performative aspects of speech[28] and to "push through the level of accidental contexts to general and unavoidable presuppositions."[29] Here, communication in general is inspected in order to reveal its implicit assumptions.

Habermas's central insight is that speech-acts only work because they occur against a background of assumed meaning.[30] In fact, certain kinds of speech-acts can be shown to raise certain validity-claims, for if they did not, the illocutionary influence that the speaker places upon the hearer would not occur at all.[31] Speech-acts, as communicatives, assert the validity-claim of comprehensibility. Additionally, where the type of speech-act is a constative, the validity-claim is that of truth. Where the speech-act is regulative, the validity-claim is (normative) rightness, where representative, the validity-claim is that of sincerity.[32] (See table 1.)

Communication *as such* therefore relies on specific validity-claims, irrespective of their being raised consciously in the intention of the speaker. These claims also offer ideals against which practical examples of communication can be compared. In other words, they provide a fulcrum for the rational criticism and defense of actual communication.

Now as anyone who has read Edward Lear will know, communication often deploys these claims ironically, or simply violates them in a humorous fashion. Yet it remains the case that, even in ironic and humorous communication, to employ utterances in everyday life entails a communicative competence on the part of speakers and hearers. This

TABLE 1
Dimensions of Habermas's Communications Model

General Functions of Speech	Domains of Reality	Modes of Communication	Types of Speech-Acts	Validity-Claims
Representation of facts	External nature	Cognitive	Constative	Truth
Establishment of legitimate social relations	Intersubjective world	Interactive	Regulative	Rightness
Disclosure of speaker's subjectivity	Internal world	Expressive	Representative	Sincerity

Sources: Adapted from Thompson, Universal Pragmatics, p. 123; Habermas, Communication and the Evolution of Society, pp. 58, 63; and Habermas, Theory of Communication, 1:329.

"knowing how" can be unpacked into a "knowing that" certain validity-claims are being raised.[33] Where Kant derived the categories from the conditions of possible experience, Habermas derives the validity-claims of speech from the conditions of possible communication.[34]

Like Kant, Habermas seeks to generate a fulcrum that will transcend different cultures and times, yet his is not a transcendental argument in the Kantian sense. First, the object from which the derivation is made is, in the case of the communicative use of language, an entirely empirical one, whereas the transcendental aspect of Kantian thought issues from its analysis of the *a priori* concept of the possibility of experience in general. For Habermas, communicative competence is "only the outcome of contingent learning processes."[35] It is from the internal evolution of these contingent processes that we can "cogently reconstruct" a universal pragmatics of communication.[36] Second, the argument by which the universality of the validity-claims are defended is not a deductive justification as it is in the Kantian affirmation of the necessity of the categories. Rather, Habermas, or more particularly Apel,[37] asserts his position by showing that its denial generates an antinomy.

Apel's argument focuses on the unavoidability of validity-claims in successful communication. He seeks to show that when the noncognitivist argues against such claims, they become entrapped in a performative contradiction.[38] Just as a thinker cannot adopt a point of view outside their own consciousness, the skeptic's argument against cognitivism necessarily raises just those validity-claims he is seeking to deny.[39] Watt states that:

The strategy of this form of argument is to accept the skeptical con-clusion that those principles are not open to any proof, being presup-positions of reasoning rather than conclusions from it, but to go on to argue that commitment to them is rationally inescapable because they must, logically, be assumed if one is to engage in a mode of thought essential to any rational human life. The claim is not exactly that the principles are true, but that their adoption is not a result of mere social convention or free personal decision: that a mistake is involved in repu-diating them while continuing to use the form of thought and discourse in question.[40]

In other words, Habermas is not directly pursuing an affirmative argument for a fulcrum upon which he can base his critical power. Instead, he tries to show that one cannot present an argument by which such a fulcrum could be denied. He therefore defends his position by asserting that its negation entails a contradiction.[41] Habermas calls his attempt to reconstruct the species-competence of communication a "reconstructive science," and he points to Kohlberg's theory of moral development, Piaget's theory of cognitive development, and Rawls's reflective equilibrium, as examples of similar activities.[42]

For the most part, validity-claims remain as part of a hidden back-ground consensus, yet where differences between people arise, and therefore particularly around moral and ethical questions, the validity-claims themselves become objects of argumentation. In such situations, referred to by Habermas as "discourses," we momentarily "suspend"[43] our formerly naive beliefs in order for us to call the validity-claims into question. In discourses, validity-claims are treated as hypotheses,[44] whereupon they are subjected to criticism, and reasons are marshalled in their defence.[45] Discourses are thus a "reflective" form of communicative action, and the pragmatic presuppositions of argumentation are "bor-rowed" or "superimposed" on the normative content of communicative action.[46]

A discourse is an argumentative encounter between a number of individuals. It is not, following the notion of "self-reflection" as it appears in the philosophy of consciousness, an activity of an isolated reasoning subject. Habermas takes Toulmin's basic question for ethics: "What kind of argument, of reasoning is it proper for us to accept in support of moral decisions?"[47] and expresses it in terms of a commu-nicative event. To do this, he first outlines a theory of argumentation in general[48] and then derives, from this, the procedures and principles of discourse ethics.[49] In doing so, he again recasts many of the Kantian arguments in communicative terms, particularly the notions of a proce-dural test, generalization as an "inductive" bridge, and the principle of publicity.

Habermas states the formal properties of discourses in terms of an ideal speech situation, or argumentation that is free from domination and constraint. First, building on Mead's notion of "ideal role taking,"[50] and Baier's "moral point of view,"[51] Habermas recasts the impartiality of moral judgment in terms of a principle "that constrains all affected to adopt the perspective of all others in the balancing of interests."[52] The resulting principle of universalization (U) performs the function of Kant's categorical imperative and allows for the discursive redemption of a generalizable interest:[53]

> (U) For a norm to be valid, the consequences and side effects of its general observance for the satisfaction of each person's particular interests must be acceptable for all.[54]

However, in keeping with the general communicative turn, the procedural test (U) cannot be run by an individual, or by a lone theorist.[55] It requires, in addition, the principle of discourse ethics (D):

> (D) Only those norms can claim to be valid that meet (or could meet) with the approval of all affected in their capacity as participants in a practical discourse.[56]

Here, Habermas follows Kant in stressing the need for public discussion in the making of normatively valid decisions. When he uses the phrase "practical discourse," he is making a strong claim for an actual process of argumentation, which he holds to be superior to counterfactual thought experiments (say in the tradition of social contract theory and in Rawls's original position) in a number of ways.

First, he asserts that "the individual is the last court of appeal for judging what is in his best interest" and that an individual's actual participation "prevents others from perspectivally distorting one's own interests."[57] Second, "the descriptive terms in which each individual perceives his interests must be open to criticism by others . . . the revision of the values used to interpret needs and wants cannot be a matter for individuals to handle monologically."[58]

It is worth noting here how different Habermas's conception is from that of Rawls.[59] There is, between the two thinkers, a fundamental divergence as to how the subject is to be characterized. Rawls sees the subject as entering the bargaining game with a finite set of predetermined needs, and it is precisely the rational meeting of those needs (by matching them with a finite and predetermined set of goods) that makes bargaining behavior predictable.[60] Habermas, on the other hand, wants to follow Mead in order to describe an "encumbered"[61] subject who creates and modifies his/her needs in a process of communicative interaction. In this dialogic model, the interpretation of needs cannot be determined by anything other than actual participation.[62] Once again, we see Habermas's insistence that moral theory cannot be a substitute for practical discourse.

In many ways, then, (D) mirrors the Kantian principle of publicity, and it reflects what Benhabib states to be a central assumption for Habermas, this being a "consensus principle of legitimacy."[63] Consensus, here conceived as the discursive redemption of a generalizable interest,[64] can only be said to be rational when the procedures by which it is arrived at are themselves normatively justified.[65] The normative conditions under which consensus is rational can be expressed in terms of pragmatic rules,[66] derived from the presuppositions of argumentation in general.[67]

There are two conditions of ideal speech, these being the symmetry condition and the reciprocity condition. The symmetry condition encompasses two rules for practical discourses, these being first:

> that each participant must have an equal chance to initiate and to continue communication; second, [that] each must have an equal chance to make assertions, recommendations, and explanations, and to challenge justifications.[68]

While the symmetry condition governs the employment of speech-acts, the reciprocity condition refers not to speech-acts but to existing action contexts.[69] It consists of a set of relations that have to obtain between participants. They assert that:

> All must have equal chances as actors to express their wishes, feelings, and intentions; and . . . speakers must act *as if* in contexts of action there is an equal distribution of chances "to order and resist orders, to promise and refuse, to be accountable for one's conduct and to demand accountability from others."[70]

These procedural rules express (D) and are those whereby (U) is achieved. Together these insights comprise what Habermas has called the ideal speech situation (hereafter referred to as the ISS). His assertion is that the ISS is anticipated in every act of actual argumentation.[71] Looming behind the participants is an intuitive ideal of fair argumentation that can be appealed to in order to appraise the legitimacy of norms. Even though it is almost always counterfactual, all discourses "anticipate" it and "approximate" to it, in the sense that they contain the basic presupposition that, given sufficient time and freedom from domination, a rationally motivated agreement could be reached.[72]

The ISS is the extra-contextual fulcrum from which Habermas levers the critical power he requires to evaluate social practices. The validity-claims of speech, and the conditions under which they are legitimately questioned, transcend any local context. Their universal validity is counterfactual, and unsullied by particularity. It is perfect, like the face of the sun.[73] Yet actual communication, and the criticism of social practices, entails the application of this counterfactual ideal to real contexts: the object of justified knowledge is situated not in the heavens but in the world. As we have seen, Habermas is quite clear that only actual participants can provide the content of discourses.[74] The universal validity-claims of speech have to be raised here and now,[75] and by actual participants in a practical discourse.[76]

In processes of mutual understanding such as everyday communication, discourses about moral questions, and criticisms of social practices, fact and counterfact are entwined.[77] It is for this reason that Habermas asserts:

> validity-claims have a Janus face: As claims, they transcend any local context; at the same time, they have to be raised here and now and be de facto recognized if they are going to bear the agreement of interacting participants that is needed for effective cooperation. The transcendent moment of *universal* validity bursts every provinciality asunder; the obligatory moment of accepted validity claims renders them carriers of a *context-bound* everyday practice.[78]

Habermas thus reconstructs his theory of discourse ethics from the possibility of argumentation as such. This theory is procedural, universalist, cognitivist, and formalist. It is intended to provide a fulcrum that offers something more than merely the "moral intuitions of the average, male, middle-class member of a modern Western society,"[79] yet that at the same time remains sensitive to cultural difference and value pluralism. This attempt is profoundly Kantian in its direction, but it also tries to avoid the more troubling aspects of that position. The thin, or procedural, universalism that it generates claims a standpoint for social criticism that is neither transcendental nor relativistic.[80]

Ferrara evaluates the project in this way:

> Habermas has brilliantly rescued the central kernel of Kant's moral theory—the idea of ethical rightness as generalizability—while adapting it to a new cultural situation characterized by . . . the "discovery" of contextuality . . . the irreducible multiplicity of conceptual schemes . . . the linguistic turn . . . and the exhaustion of the philosophy of consciousness.[81]

Habermas's fulcrum for critical power, the ISS, is a counterfactual ideal of complete participation that can be deployed to test the legitimacy of real instances of participation. It is intended to provide critical power, yet at the same time to constrain that power to questions of legitimate procedure in practical discourses, in order to render it applicable to actual contexts in such a way as to avoid the leveling of moral differences.

While his Kantian approach provides universal knowledge that is sufficiently abstracted from particular contexts to enable it to function as a fulcrum for critical power, our attention is now directed to the problem of how, precisely, the ideal is to be applied to the real. Indeed, this has always been a central difficulty with universalist positions, even for Kant. Habermas is quite aware, for example, that Hegel delivered a sustained and penetrating critique of Kantian ethics that essentially accused it of being inapplicable to the real world. This critique effectively recasts Kant's greatest strength—his abstraction from the particular—as his greatest weakness. Habermas's reconstruction of the Kantian project has been profoundly influenced by this critique.[82] Indeed, as the next section will show, we cannot explore the application of Habermas's ideas to questions regarding the design and evaluation of political institutions until we understand the effect this critique has had on the genesis and structure of Habermas's thought.

1.2 DILEMMAS UPON APPLICATION

Where justification is conceived as an appeal to extra-contextual knowledge, legitimate social criticism becomes a matter of applying that knowledge back to particular contexts. The central question for any universalist and formalist moral theory then becomes this moment of application. In the history of philosophy, it is perhaps in the encounter between Hegel and Kant that this issue receives its most thorough explication.[83] Hegel's critique of Kantian ethics opens with the accusation of excessive abstraction.[84] It is charged with being so devoid of content as to be impossible to apply to practical situations.[85] From here, Hegel mounts a number of telling criticisms.

First, Hegel's assertion that Kant's principles yield more than a single possible maxim of action and that the same maxim can admit of different yet equally rational performances effectively shows that universalist ethics is insufficiently discriminative as to its outcomes.[86] Such a theory is thus of questionable value to moral actors, for even if they grasp the moral law, they must still filter out unacceptable performances that nevertheless appear to satisfy it. This raises the problem of some other knowledge being deployed by the actors in addition to the moral law, a problem that becomes still more serious when one considers that a general law must still be applied to a particular situation. The problem of particularization, or correct deployment, suggests that some sort of judging faculty is required if the actors are to contextualize the general law.[87] This would suggest that, by itself, the moral law is insufficient to generate moral action.

A second point of attack for Hegel is to question whether universalizability is intended as a way of testing or generating moral maxims. If Kantian moral theory cannot generate normative content, it appears able to offer itself only as a test for existing content. This criticism is then pressed home by asserting that such a theory cannot even adjudicate between two existing contents in a manner that would allow for their moral differentiation. Hegel's criticism thus points to a "dialectic of form and content in Kantian moral theory."[88] The moral law, which alone was supposed to indicate normative validity, turns out to require both existing moral contents and some knowledge of how to contextualize such law on the part of moral actors.

Third, Hegel goes on to suggest that the moral law is deficient in another area also. According to his own theory, Hegel tries to show that institutions functionally embody normative rules and are both constituted and regulated by contextually meaningful moral laws. One cannot, therefore, use a moral law alone to judge an institution, for institutions exist within an "interdependent totality of social relations and practices."[89] What is at stake here, as with the criticisms looked at above, is the issue of what a Kantian type theory can do and what it cannot. Hegel clearly locates areas where one would need to deploy the moral law yet where the law alone is insufficient.

A fourth criticism, highlighted particularly by Stern, is that Kant gives an account of moral motivation that is so slanted toward the austere requirements of reason as to ignore the question of happiness altogether.[90] This problem relates to the role of a utopian moment in discourse ethics. If happiness is of no importance as a moral motive, then "it would appear reasonable for agents . . . to raise the question of why they should care about morality at all."[91] Here, we face the possibility of a pure virtue unrelated to happiness, just as in discourse ethics we encounter a possible emancipation that may be unrelated to human fulfilment.[92] This deficiency has important implications for how we see our moral interactions with those for whom we have feelings other than, or more than, mere duty. The moral interactions within, say, a family, arise more "as a direct, affective response to the specific interests and needs of the other person."[93] It is this conflation of the moral life to a rational relation with a generalized other that has formed the core of Gilligan's critique of Kantian arguments.[94] In its place she suggests we conceive of the moral relation as being oriented to a concrete other, and that the resulting revalorization of such activities as care, commitment, and loyalty offer a far more realistic view of our moral life.

Fifth, again following Stern, we must notice how Hegel points to a further way in which Kantian ethics is insufficiently related to the real world. Kant's theory, it is argued, "abstracts from a consideration of the agent's prospects for realising his purposes in the objective world."[95] An "ethic of conviction" seems to "focus excessively on the purity of the agent's inner fidelity to principle without affording sufficient consideration to the morally relevant consequences of action."[96] The issue of whether or not to include, in an appraisal of a moral act, the consequences of a moral stance reappears in discourse ethics in terms of the assessment that participants must make of the results of their collective action. Though (U) is designed to incorporate this issue, whether or not the exploration of such consequences is a matter for rational argumentation or intuitive judgment is a question that has concerned Habermas's commentators.[97]

Habermas, as we have seen, takes much from Kant, but he also wants to incorporate these Hegelian insights. Indeed, by stating clearly that the theoretical principles that constitute discourse ethics are not, nor were they ever, intended to be sufficient to determine what is morally right or wrong, what appears in Kant as a theoretical weakness is recast in Habermas as a careful limitation on the scope of application of theory. Habermas is clear that his normative criterion can offer a valid ground for social criticism. This is the affirmative part of his position, in which he asserts that there is a relation of theory to practice that is defensible. Yet he is equally clear that there are things theory cannot do; and this is the negative limit he places upon moral theory generally. As he states, anticipating much of the reaction of those commentators who criticize him for being increasingly divorced from political reality, "my modest opinion about what philosophy can and cannot accomplish may come as a disappointment."[98] He sums up his limitation with the words, "any universalistic morality is dependent upon a form of life that *meets it halfway*."[99] Only participants in a practical discourse can recontextualize the decontextualized normative criteria in order to generate valid social criticism, and it is precisely this preservation of a place for actual participants that ensures his theory remains sensitive to particular contexts.

As we have seen, the normative requirement for practical discourse constitutes a dialogic turn that already renders more concrete the monologic procedure of the Kantian moral law. Habermas wants to build on this by incorporating Hegelian criticisms of Kant. He tries to determine the appropriate scope of theory and, once its necessary limitations have been noted, to show how it is only participants who can carry the contents and contexts required to generate concrete moral validity.[100]

The dialectic of form and content that Hegel located in Kant is therefore moved to the very heart of discourse ethics,[101] and we can see its operation in a number of categories. Moral judgments have content and structure, and in a procedural ethics, these are to be properly distinguished.[102] Habermas thus accepts that discourse ethics is formalistic, yet by claiming that all theory should do is to "explain the moral point of view" (the form), he is able to preserve a space for discourse between participants (the content).[103] His is thus a thin universalism, for it concentrates primarily on form or procedure of a moral decision rather than on its actual content.

This formalism also allows Habermas to take the general primacy of the right over the good that was so prominent in Kantian theory and extend it into his own position. This distinction is itself part of a general debate in contemporary ethics as to the scope of moral theory.[104] Particularly, communitarians and liberals are currently debating whether this distinction can be meaningfully made and whether it is in fact required in order to preserve a value pluralism.[105] Habermas confuses many of those involved with this debate[106] because while he holds to an intersubjective constitution of the self,[107] he borrows the strict separations of right from good and is from ought that Walzer attributes to the liberal position.[108] He disagrees with liberal derivations of natural rights and substantive principles of justice,[109] and upholds the importance of lived contexts of meaning that come to "encumber" individuals via processes of socialization.[110] His straddling of these two positions should not surprise us, for he has borrowed heavily from both Kant and Hegel. Liberals are closer to Kant, yet communitarians, or neo-Aristotelians, owe a greater debt to Hegel. Since the work of Hans Gadamer and Joachim Ritter, neo-Hegelianism is almost indistinguishable from neo-Aristotelianism,[111] for both have come together to form a hermeneutical philosophical ethics that has, as its centerpiece, a notion of *phronēsis* as a "form of contextually embedded and situationally sensitive judgement of particulars."[112]

Once again, Habermas has anticipated both sides of the argument. Where Hegel criticized Kant for his abstraction, indeterminacy in regard to outcomes, inability to generate morality, and for the insufficiency of the moral law alone, Habermas accepts his theory be limited to a procedural test and asserts the importance of processes of socialization in the generation of norms and in the practical discourses to test their validity. His position thus remains Kantian, yet is tempered by the Hegelian critique that, though forcing significant limitations upon his theory, never delivers a *coup de grace*. Nietzsche's dictum: "whatever doesn't kill you makes you stronger," seems to apply here. Once again we can see why Habermas is attacked for being both too Kantian and too Hegelian, and why there is so much confusion about the nature of his assertions. In some senses, his position is better characterized as one that bridges the "formal-rationalist" and "historical-hermeneutic" approaches, rather than, as Stern sees him, being a clear example of the former.[113]

The final example of this tempering of Kant by Hegel occurs when we see Habermas granting that his (and Kant's) focus upon questions of justification indeed leaves questions of application unanswered.[114] In a sense, he agrees, the dilemma which the neo-Aristotelians seek to overcome with *phronēsis* is a real one,[115] for the decontextualized nature of general norms does indeed seem to require a moment of practical judgment in which norms are applied to specific contexts of action.[116] By so distinguishing between the justification of a norm and its contextual application, Habermas has entered the complex area of moral judgment.[117] Yet he resists the neo-Aristotelian solution and instead states that discourse ethics

> is emphatically opposed to going back to a stage of philosophical thought prior to Kant. Kant's achievement was precisely to dissociate the problem of justification from the application and implementation of moral insights. I argue that even in the prudent application of norms, principles of practical reason take effect . . . impartial application . . . is not a prudent but a moral point of view.[118]

Habermas thus seeks to make the application of norms subject to the same procedural test as the norms themselves.[119] Accepting the Hegelian point that application is a problem, he nevertheless resists application becoming something separate, or in addition to, or something of a different nature than, the discursive search for generalizable interests. "Moral judgments," he states, "provide demotivated answers to decontextualized questions."[120] In real discourses, with real participants, questions are always contextualized, and answers always "motivated." The process by which moral judgments move from universal to particular is itself characterized as a discursive and rational task in which participants adopt an impartial moral point of view, both in the exploration of consequences and in the search for generalizable interests.

Habermas sees relativism as a disease that must be cured if we are to have a normative basis for social criticism. His treatment for relativism comes in the form of a discourse ethics that is universalist and formalist. In attempting to reclaim what is best in Kant, he provides us with a decontextualized fulcrum that can legitimate critical power. Yet he also remains acutely aware that precisely this strength of a universalist ethics is also its weakness. As Hegel showed, the treatment for relativism that proceeds by decontextualizing knowledge ushers in a significant problem of its own, for that knowledge must now be recontextualized if it is to form the basis for a critique of real practices.

In medical science, a second symptom that is caused by the attempt to cure the first, is referred to as an iatrogenic effect. Habermas's treatment for relativism thus faces what we might call an iatrogenic dilemma, for in solving the first problem, he has inevitably generated a second.[121] Habermas has consistently shown himself willing to pay this cost. Thus, his theory is not put forward as a solution to all problems, it is seen as limited in its scope of application, and it has struggled, subsequently, to give an adequate account of the nature of moral judgment whereby application is achieved. In particular, he has shown great care to articulate a relation of theory to practice that is sensitive to the limits of theory yet allows for meaningful social criticism. Because our attempt to recouple a normative theory of democracy to empirical questions regarding the design and evaluation of institutions is, in part, an inquiry into the relation of theory to practice, we turn now to Habermas's articulation of this relation.

CHAPTER 2

Theory with a Practical Intent

If we are to use Habermas's normative criteria to address questions surrounding the legitimate design and evaluation of democratic institutions, then the relation between theory and practice must be a substantive one. At the same time, living in the times that we do, it would be quite unrealistic, and perhaps also dangerous, to assume that theory could, or should, be completely unified with questions of practice.

Characterizations of the two extremes of this relation, in other words, total unity or total separation, are clearly presented by Ronald Beiner,[1] who also attempts to describe Habermas's conception of the theory/practice relation. For this reason, we will begin (2.1), by looking at Beiner's argument. Beiner's discussion highlights a number of conceptual difficulties that must be addressed in forming a complete understanding of this relation. In particular, his engagement with Aristotle's distinction between *technē* and *phronēsis* draws our attention to the importance of that distinction in Habermas's own understanding of the relation between theory and practice. Our inspection of this distinction (2.2) is then followed by an attempt to focus on precisely what Habermas means when he characterizes the relation in terms of a "theory with a practical intent" (2.3). In our discussion of the practical intentions of theory, we will also take the opportunity to introduce certain aspects of Habermas's theoretical position, particularly that of "colonization of the lifeworld," which did not arise in our opening chapter and yet which are required for the evaluation of the practical implications of his theory that we undertake in the following chapter.

2.1 THE RELATION OF THEORY TO PRACTICE

Beiner's investigation into the relation of theory to practice takes as its starting point the "canonical statement of the undiluted doctrine of theory-practice unity," which he locates in Lukács's essay "What Is Orthodox Marxism?"[2] Lukács argues that Marx followed Hegel[3] in his conception of theory as the "self-knowledge of history," yet pressed this insight further (beyond Kant) to overcome the duality of thought and being, subject and object, theory and practice. Hegel's retrospective self-knowledge of the philosopher is thus replaced by active self-knowledge in the service of *praxis*.[4] Where the proletariat is, as Marx put it, "gripped" by theory,[5] it is both the subject and object of knowledge. Reality becomes conscious of itself through the emergence of the self-understanding of the proletariat. Oppression thus generates a theoretical consciousness that impels action to remove such oppression. In this way, theory becomes the vehicle for revolution.[6]

Beiner claims that this notion has now been discredited, not because Lukács' argument is logically incoherent, but because it is empirically false. Such "self-conscious" knowledge does not emerge in the proletariat with either the necessity or the clarity claimed by Lukács.[7] Yet it is precisely the necessity of such emergent knowledge within the proletariat, Beiner suggests, that preserves the logic of Lukács's argument. With our realization that the proletariat does not necessarily gain such self-knowledge, the unity of theory and practice breaks down. Beiner suggests that this is what occurs in Adorno's negative dialectics.

The empirical failure to which Beiner alludes, that is, the fact that the proletariat did not in fact do what Lukács thought it necessarily must do, meant that the preservation of theory/practice unity was forced into a long and destructive journey. In order to preserve the philosophy of *praxis*, Lenin argued that Party theoreticians were required to provide correct theory, which could then be acted out by the proletariat. This, Beiner claims, blurred the line between theory and tactics (strategy, propaganda, enforcement of the political line),[8] and it has become a commonplace to assert that this blurring aided the legitimation of vanguardism, thus paving the way for Stalinism.[9]

The first problem for those who assert unity between theory and practice, then, is that it simply does not accord with the facts. "The social situation in the modern world . . . is so overwhelmingly complex that no theory offered . . . will be able to command general assent."[10] In addition, for a necessary actor to be designated, "a massive simplification of social reality" would be required, and theory would effectively be treating the agents of its realization "as children who could be instructed on how to act."[11]

The reduction of such actors to the moral status of children points to a second problem with the unity of theory and practice: that it can serve to legitimate oppression. If all practice requires theory, then "the theorist is in a privileged position," and unity can be seen to be profoundly elitist and antidemocratic.[12] We have already noted that the simple conflation of normative democratic theory with political practice (an example of unified theory/practice) can have dangerously authoritarian tendencies. Indeed, it was precisely as a counter to strong normative theories (with their self-righteous prescriptions of the good life) that liberalism had its greatest and most valuable victories,[13] and against which the "discovery" of contextualism served to argue. Mindful of such problems, Beiner abandons unity, and he does so without regrets. "Theory and practice can each stand on their own two feet," he asserts,[14] and "we honour [them] most by granting each its independence."[15]

Beiner thus warns us against moving too swiftly from the need to do something about the real problems we see in the world to unifying theory and practice in order to derive assistance with those problems. Yet there is a sense in which he is arguing against a strawman here. In asking for assistance with the legitimation of designs and evaluations for democratic institutions, we do not turn like sheep to theory. We do not ask *what* is to be done, so much as *how* we might go about doing it. The "all or nothing" approach that Beiner deploys in order to discredit Marxism does not address the possibility that there might be gray areas in which theory could be useful, and where complete unity between theory and practice is avoided. Brian Fay shows a greater awareness of such areas when he states that:

> One is quite accustomed to seeing sharp divisions being drawn between knowledge and the uses of knowledge, between questions in the philosophy of social science and those in political philosophy . . . between theory and practice.[16]

He then describes such a division as a "piece of common sense" which is at once "misguided,"[17] "implausible,"[18] and in need of "replacement."[19] In fact, "social theory cannot be severed from social practice,"[20] and Fay's book is impressive in its unpacking of the implicit conceptions of the relationship between theory and practice within the various types of social science, and of the effects of such conceptions on practice itself.[21] Where Beiner claims the Marxist union of theory and practice is "a vestige, a left-over,"[22] Fay claims Marxism to have provided the most consistent objection to the pretense that the concerns of social science have no political relevance.[23]

In their respective discussions of Habermas's account of the theory/practice relation, we find again that Beiner, having thrown out the bath water, is unable to locate the baby. Fay describes Habermas as providing an interesting variation of the relationship of theory to practice, yet Beiner claims that Habermas's theory "shackles itself unnecessarily with the impossible duty of contributing to a better practice."[24] To criticize Habermas for conflating theory and practice is not new.[25] Indeed, it is just this accusation that motivates many commentators to locate an inherent authoritarianism within his work.[26] If, as Lyotard suggests,[27] Habermas is in fact espousing a "metanarrative," then his epistemological self-righteousness might indeed tempt him to apply his normative theory in a way that is oppressive. Yet while such a line of criticism might have been applicable to Habermas's early claims for the transcendental interests of reason, it is entirely off the mark with his more recent work. Indeed, there is a competing line of criticism, quite the opposite to the first, that accuses him of dissociating theory from practice.[28] Here the suggestion is that Habermas has become increasingly concerned with metatheoretical issues,[29] which have so little to do with practice that he can be described as having abandoned real problems altogether.[30]

Unfortunately, while criticism is usually a good thing, and is certainly to be expected where a theorist affirms a position rather than merely denying one, that pertaining to Habermas's characterization of the relation of theory to practice seems to be an example of the "damned if you do and damned if you don't" variety of critique.

The fact that Habermas has been accused of making all the mistakes that are possible to make in such a debate might indicate that he is simply wrong (though is it possible to be wrong in all those ways?) and it might indicate that he is being misunderstood. Again, clarity is afforded by Beiner, for his misunderstanding of Habermas's position precisely illustrates the central issue of Habermas's characterization of the theory/practice relation. Focusing on this misunderstanding allows us to anticipate Habermas's position and to place it within the tradition to which it belongs.

Beiner states that:

> all one needs is the ordinary common sense and good judgement of a simple citizen. There is no guarantee that the theorist will be more discerning, more foresightful, or more sensitive to dangers and opportunities in the practical sphere.[31]

Now it is one thing to believe we are all simple citizens, and that none should be privileged because of special knowledge. Yet Beiner, imagining he is following Unger,[32] is so concerned to prevent theorists claiming special knowledge that he ends up asserting that even if the political theorist were to devote a lifetime to inspecting practice, he/she would be unable to offer any useful insights whatsoever. While this may be true of some theorists, say the most studiously obscure or the utterly incompetent, there are, surely, less draconian ways of dealing with bad political theorists than to attempt a complete separation of theory and practice. To deny all responsibility of the theorist, *qua* theorist, simply because complete unity of theory and practice is indefensible, seems too strong. Wanting (quite rightly) to avoid such unity, Beiner can locate only one alternative position, that of total separation.

When Beiner looks at the world, what he sees are practices that are not, primarily, rational. For him, such practices are forged and preserved in traditions, they are expressive of ways of life, they are comprehensible only by hermeneutic inquiry. Above all, they can never be understood, nor therefore improved, by theory. When Habermas looks at the world, he sees practices that, though they anticipate reason in their every fiber, fall short of being rational. Though he does not hold to a unity in the relation of theory to practice, he nevertheless bases his entire *oeuvre* on the emancipatory possibilities afforded by reason. To see how theory might operate in the gray area between unity and separation, we must focus on a recurrent conceptual difficulty that seems to operate behind Beiner's "all or nothing" approach. Only when we understand the *kind* of knowledge that is proper to apply to practice can we see why Beiner is mistaken, both in his appraisal of the role of theory, and in his characterization of Habermas.

2.2 ARISTOTLE'S DISTINCTION BETWEEN *TECHNĒ* AND *PHRONĒSIS*

Beiner's separation is, at its heart, based on the belief that the *type* of knowledge held by the theorist is inapplicable to practice. He is not denying that theorists have knowledge, only that they have the wrong kind. To put this another way, if, as Beiner suggests, "good judgement" is the appropriate knowledge for politics,[33] then he clearly believes that the political theorist has no more of it than any citizen. In his view, the theorist, *qua* theorist, cannot and need not help with practice.

What sort of knowledge, then, does Beiner think the political theorist has? We can say two things in regard to this question: first, that it is a kind a knowledge that is not useful for practice, and second, that it can sometimes be applied by experts in the form of tactics (but it should not be).

In regard to the first point, we have seen how Beiner describes the kind of knowledge held by the theorist to be so abstract as to be of little help to the ordinary citizen.[34] Importantly, he cites with approval Aristotle's "concept of the autonomy of the practical sphere of life vis-à-vis the life of theory."[35] At times then, Beiner clearly sees the kind of knowledge held by the theorist to be (using Aristotle's characterization of the types of knowledge) that of *epistēmē*,[36] this being knowledge that is objective, law-like, and unrelated to practice.

In regard to the second point, the tactical manipulation of politics, this bears a greater resemblance to what Aristotle calls *technē*, or "production under the guidance of true reason."[37] Such a characterization of the knowledge of the theorist seems closer to what Beiner alludes to when he describes the theorist as foisting his special knowledge on the masses.[38] Here, in vanguardism, technical knowledge can be applied to practice, but it is seen as morally objectionable to do so.

Beiner's "all or nothing" argument therefore appears to rest on a conceptual confusion as to the kind of knowledge held by a political theorist. He variously characterizes such knowledge as *epistēmē* and as *technē*. The confusion is compounded when he commends Aristotle for his assertion that "theory and *praxis* each form a distinct and self-sustaining *bios* or way of life."[39] Aristotle does indeed separate theory from practice, but it is *epistēmē* that is so separated. Aristotle's third type of knowledge, *phronēsis* or practical wisdom,[40] is characterized by a unity of theory and practice every bit as "canonical" as that of Lukács. Indeed, as is generally the case with classical political theorists, Aristotle is even happy to acknowledge a direct connection between normative theory and institutional design.[41] This is because *phronēsis* was normatively grounded in the ethos of the polis. Beiner, himself a neo-Aristotelian[42] of the Gadamerian variety, is appreciative of *phronēsis*, and sees ethos as affording a normative ground for critical power where *epistēmē* cannot.[43] In addition, he commends Aristotle's ethics generally for its modesty,[44] in that it leaves a space for "practically reasonable decisions."[45]

A central point of disagreement between Beiner and Habermas therefore concerns the nature of the normative grounds for critical power. As we have seen, for Habermas, critical power requires a universal fulcrum,[46] and we here confront two possible locations for this fulcrum. Either, as Habermas would suggest, it is to be located in universal *epistēmē*, or, following Beiner, it lies within a particular ethos. Beiner rules out the former with his complete separation of theory from practice.

Yet the latter, the grounding of critical power on a contextual fulcrum, is always limited in its application to the boundaries of that context itself. Where such boundaries are indistinct, or there is a value conflict between contexts, critical power becomes disarmed.[47] The danger here is that the appeal to extant values within a political culture can degenerate into a mere approbation of the status quo. While there is nothing *necessarily* conservative about confining moral claims to contexts alone, such a mode of justification certainly holds this danger.[48] Indeed, as Fay points out, this is a weakness of interpretative social science generally.[49]

Beiner's claim, that his separation of theory and practice does not favor the status quo,[50] therefore remains hard to uphold where he has so assiduously ruled out any recourse to extra-contextual fulcra. The difference between Beiner (or perhaps we should say the neo-Aristotelians) and Habermas thus centers on the nature of the universal fulcrum upon which critical power is to be grounded. Habermas holds to a procedural universalism that the neo-Aristotelians claim to be invalid, unnecessary, and morally objectionable.

Beiner's attempt to dispense with an extra-contextual fulcrum results in a simplification of the possible impact that theory can have on practice, and this in turn means that he can provide only a vastly simplified account of Habermas's characterization of the theory/practice relation. In fact, Habermas, using Aristotle's distinctions as to the types of knowledge, and combining this with a notion of theory as critique, is able to open a path for the theory/practice relation that leads between the elitism of tactical thought and the irrelevance of abstract science.

The Aristotelian distinction between *technē* (technical knowledge exhibited in *poiēsis* or making) and *phronēsis* (practical reason informing *praxis*) is one of the fundamental building blocks of Habermas's theory of communicative action. In fact, it is worth noting that Habermas himself is not entirely accurate in his characterization of this distinction, for he tends to counterpose *technē* with *praxis*. Enquiries into the neo-Aristotelian use of *phronēsis* have focused the distinction in the following terms:

Forms of knowledge	*Forms of action*
technē ⟶	*poiēsis*
phronēsiṡ ⟶	*praxis*

Habermas's early inquiries into the relation of theory to practice used this distinction as its "connecting thread,"[51] and his deduction of three "quasi-transcendental" knowledge constitutive interests: the technical, the practical, and the emancipatory, closely followed this same distinction.[52] Keane cites this distinction as being at the heart of the early Habermasian critique of bureaucratic rationality and claims that its importance has been missed in most discussions of Habermas's project.[53] Habermas himself cites the work of Arendt and Gadamer as having "called my attention to [this] fundamental distinction."[54] In his later work, we see it used, *mutatis mutandis*, to generate his theory of communicative rationality, his account of selective rationalization in modernity, and his concept of "colonization."

Habermas's prime interest in the distinction is that it illustrates *technē* to be the wrong kind of knowledge for the political realm. Its inappropriate application is, he suggests, observable in the increasing scientization of politics within the Western tradition, particularly in the work of such thinkers as Machiavelli,[55] Marx,[56] and Hobbes.[57] Here, we see political theory reduced to "logically integrated systems of quantitatively expressed, lawlike statements characteristic of the most advanced natural sciences."[58] While *phronēsis* requires a public space for its enactment,[59] *technē* tends toward an excessively administrative and decisionistic account of politics. Its inappropriate application in this realm thus results in a tendency to substitute discursive interaction in the public sphere with a quite different kind of coordinating activity: that of instrumental action.[60]

The increasing dominance of *technē* results in a removal of values from practical questions. The loss of such classical teleologies as the good and just life, the fulfilment of human nature, the formation of the virtuous character, and the cultivation of political prudence, all signaled the degeneration of the ethos in which the virtues were embedded.[61] Means, not ends, were the proper subject of instrumental reason. Political knowledge, now conceived as the application of scientifically grounded social theory to the technical problem of regulating social intercourse, distinguished between "fact and value" and "is and ought" in ways that classical thinkers never did.[62] So defined, value judgments do not admit of "truth," and normative considerations were therefore to be excluded from the study of social phenomena.[63] Habermas explicates this as a crucial moment in the development of bourgeois rationality. Certainly, where the selection of ends is seen as an irrational activity that can impede the process of rationalization and Enlightenment, reason can claim a victory against dogmatism, superstition, and ignorance. For the most part, however:

> Our civilisation has become increasingly scientific. The relationship of theory to practice can now only assert itself as the purposive-rational application of techniques assured by empirical science.[64]

Such an account of the degeneration of the relation between theory and practice, highlighting as it does the increasing dominance of *technē* in political affairs, clearly illustrates Habermas's inheritance from the Frankfurt School. Particularly in the work of Horkheimer and Adorno,[65] modernity is seen as having an inner logic that is inescapably played out in a process of rationalization. Their extension of Weber's typology of reason resulted in an increasingly aporetic account of the dominance of instrumental reason. So demonised, *technē* appears as something that is impossible to resist.[66]

2.3 PRACTICAL INTENTIONS

Habermas, seeking to reclaim a rational and emancipatory practice, sees his intellectual project as, in part, the recovery of a systematic and theoretically adequate account of the relation of theory to practice. In *Theory and Practice,* Habermas states that the proper theory/practice relation is not that of Lukácsian unification,[67] yet he also affirms his commitment to "a theory of society with practical intent."[68]

Habermas rejects the characterization of the theory/practice relation that he finds in positivistic social science, and he does so by arguing that it gives rise to certain paradoxes. In this way he seeks to reinstate normative considerations and also to indicate some of the ways in which these considerations might cross the gap to empirical concerns; in other words, to show how the increasing dominance of *technē* might be more adequately managed and opposed. For this reason, we will look at these paradoxes in some detail.

First, the interests or ends of positivistic philosophy appear incapable of justification, for a commitment to science and technology, and an opposition to dogmatism, are themselves subjective and beyond the scope of reason conceived in so instrumental a manner.[69] In addition, by ceding the realm of theory to a single type of knowledge, that of *technē,* positivism pretends to a value-neutral relation to practice that implicitly favors increasing rationalization.[70] Yet instrumental reason is no more able to justify this implicit end than it is to justify the explicit ends listed above. The cost of abandoning Aristotle's distinctions between the types of knowledge is, therefore, an "irrational decisionism in the domain of practice" generally.[71]

Second, following Dewey, Habermas seeks to point out that a certain interdependence between fact and value still obtains in modernity, indeed, that it has to obtain if technological progress is to be controlled in a rational manner.[72] Value convictions are dependent on available and imagined techniques for their realization, and changes in techniques in fact cause changes in interest situations, which in turn gives rise to new values. In some ways then, "social interests, as reflected in value systems, are regulated by being tested with regard to the technical possibilities and strategic means for their gratification," and the "development of new techniques is governed by a horizon of needs and historically determined interpretation of these needs, in other words, by value systems."[73] As McCarthy puts it, "from this point of view, the decisionistic separation of questions of fact from questions of value appears abstract; there is a critical interaction between practical orientations and available techniques."[74]

Habermas's accusation is that positivism has failed to entirely separate fact from value, and that once we have realized the many ways in which techniques remain determined by value, we will be more open and careful about the values that inform the ends of our techniques.[75] Technical progress, he asserts, must be brought under the control of the social lifeworld, it must be reflected upon, discussed rationally and investigated in such a way that overcomes the "rigidified value-systems and obsolete ideologies" that have hidden behind the cloak of positivism's pretense of value-neutrality.[76] In other words, technical progress is to be guided by a conscious and rational choice as to the "direction they want to develop their knowledge and capacity in the future."[77] This "rational" choice must (necessarily) be value-laden, and it must be discursive.

Here then, the discursive coordination of human action that takes place within the public sphere is seen as providing the value-laden guidance required for technical progress. Political decision-making must be based on public discussion. This is certainly a strong normative claim, yet stated in this way it is incomplete, for "public discussion" is an indeterminate term; it tells us nothing of the nature of such discussion. Such a critique of positivistic social science would be similarly available to an interpretative social science. What differentiates Habermas's position from contextualist theories is, as we saw earlier, his assertion of a universal fulcrum upon which critical power can be founded. Critical power in this instance allows us to explicate the term "public discussion" and to stipulate its nature. Habermas's counterfactual fulcrum of ideal speech provides a normative grounding for discussion that is free from domination. And it is precisely this ideal that makes his theory a critical one.

With his articulation of the theories of communicative reason and discourse ethics, Habermas is able to oppose the pessimistic diagnosis of modernity found in Horkheimer, Adorno, and Weber, and to assert the selectivity of rationalization in modernity.[78] Weber's rationalization thesis can then be seen, not as an inescapable logic, but as the result of "peculiar restrictions put upon communicative rationalization by the boundary conditions and the dynamics of a capitalist process of production."[79] When communication is revealed as having its own rationality, and where it can be shown to be the primary and appropriate method of coordinating human activity within particular spheres of life, incursion into those spheres by inappropriate forms of coordination can be resisted. Thus, Habermas presents his theory of "colonization,"[80] in which the instrumental and strategic methods by which the differentiated subsystems of the market economy and the administrative state are coordinated are seen to increasingly displace discursive practices within the lifeworld itself.[81] One of the uses for theory then becomes aiding participants in their efforts to resist colonization.

With these conceptual adjustments accomplished, Habermas returns, in his search for a proper account of the relation between theory and practice, to that offered by the Frankfurt School.[82] Early critical theory sought to develop knowledge that could be of direct use to people who sought to overcome oppression.[83] This orientation was, of course, inherited from Marx (especially via Lukács).[84] Fay describes the relation of theory to practice in critical theory as being one of "integration."[85] Critical theory is of practical relevance when it illuminates "structural contradictions"[86] in society in such a way as to lead to "the satisfaction of human needs and purposes."[87]

This emancipatory moment in critical theory is based on its ability to recognize that "a great many of the actions people perform are caused by social conditions over which they have no control, and that a great deal of what people do to one another is not the result of conscious knowledge and choice."[88] As we saw earlier, it is precisely the failure of interpretative social science that it is unable to effect such a recognition, with the result that it "tends to reconcile people to their social order."[89] Critical social science on the other hand, "seeks to uncover those systems of social relationships which determine the actions of individuals and the unanticipated, though not accidental, consequences of these actions."[90] For such theories then, applicability is a necessary (though obviously not a sufficient) test for truth.[91]

The precise nature of this application now comes into view. Theory must show social actors how their experience of discontent is related to certain inherent contradictions in their social order. It must show them, as they come to understand their situation, how they can remove those contradictions by indicating appropriate courses of action by which they might change their social order.[92]

Habermas's normative theory is directed toward elucidating the structural contradictions in modern society. His appropriation of the tools of systems theory, his delineation of the boundaries between lifeworld and system (with their contradictory and competing methods of action coordination), his expression of a normative ideal by which discursive will-formation can be free from domination, are all intended to provide actors with insights that they can use. As he says,[93] "I would expect a critical theory to perform the task of making possible enlightening interpretations of situations, which affect our self-understanding and orientate us in action."[94] The conceptual tools to identify structural contradictions then form a social theory that

> should contribute to the interpretation of conflicts which arise as a result of the over-legalisation and bureaucratisation of areas of life, and it should do so with the intention of assisting those struggling to resist this development to clarify for themselves the conflicts in which they are involved.[95]

Crucial here is the phrase, "for themselves," for it points to the reason Beiner's critique of Habermas is so wide of the mark and also indicates the sophistication of the latter's understanding of the theory/practice relation. Habermas asserts that it is inappropriate for theory to direct political action. Theory should not specify strategies or solutions,[96] for only participants themselves can assess the consequences of their decisions, only participants can evaluate and decide on appropriate goals.[97] As he most famously puts it, "in a process of enlightenment, there can only be participants."[98]

Habermas has argued that an assertion is justified if it can be discursively redeemed under certain communicative conditions (the ISS). This is a normative theory that stipulates the form under which justified assertions emerge, but it does not stipulate the content of such assertions.[99] Another way of putting this is to say that the universalist fulcrum upon which he bases his critical power is not a foundation, nor is it an ethos. Habermas's universalism is, as we have seen, procedural.[100] It is the conditions for discursive will-formation themselves that supply the fulcrum.[101] His normative theory is not, therefore, of a type that can be used for authoritarian ends. Indeed, by rejecting any stipulation of the nature of the good life and by generating a discursive space in which participants can make such determinations "themselves," it in fact sets a "limit to theory."[102]

Now we can see that when Beiner applauds Aristotle's modesty in describing the virtues in "outline" only, he should also extend his approval to Habermas. Aristotle *and Habermas* deploy theory in a way that

> does not intend to invade the proper place of practically reasonable decisions, which are required of the individual in any given situation. All [Aristotle's] sketchy descriptions of the typical are . . . to be understood as oriented towards such a concretisation.[103]

The space for such concretization has been preserved in Habermas's normative theory, and it is for this reason that White asserts that Habermas's theory is deeply incompatible with authoritarianism.[104] Contexts can only be understood by participants,[105] or as Aristotle says, "practical wisdom is concerned with particulars . . . knowledge of particulars comes from experience . . . about which there can be perception but no scientific knowledge."[106] Habermas himself sums up thus:

> The enlightenment of political will can become effective only within the communication of citizens. For the articulation of needs in accordance with technical knowledge can be ratified exclusively *in the consciousness of the political actors themselves.* Experts cannot delegate to themselves this act of confirmation from those who have to account with their life histories for the new interpretation of social needs and for accepted means of mastering problematic situations.[107]

Theory then, is not to be unified with practice, but is nevertheless to have a "practical intent." This intent is not manifest in a particular set of effects, but in a transformed consciousness,[108] which specific actors can translate into change.

Such actors are no longer conceived as a single class however,[109] for once the core category of everyday practice is changed from labor to communication,[110] political practice is no longer to be equated with revolutionary agitation. Now, political practice becomes much more about overcoming systematically distorted communication, both through its identification (using the posited counterfactual of ideal speech) and through its active opposition. Armed with a consciousness that understands the ways in which communication is distorted systemically,[111] actors are able to actively defend the boundaries of the lifeworld from colonization by more appropriate means of sociation.[112] As Bernstein states:

> All the lines of Habermas' investigations converge in emphasising that the most urgent practical problem of our time is to oppose all those intellectual and material tendencies that undermine or suppress practical discourse, and to work toward the achievement of those objective institutions in which such practical discourse can be concretely realised.[113]

Now we begin to see why it is that Habermas is criticized both for separating and conflating theory and practice. On the one hand he upholds the value of abstract theory and expresses distaste for the "devaluation of theory and the overhasty subordination of theoretical work to the *ad hoc* requisites of practice."[114] He also rejects any theoretical imposition on those who participate in practice that is against their wishes or that is unhelpful to them.[115] On the other hand, however, he asserts that critical theory should have a "practical intent," it should be of assistance to participants, it should help them in their struggle to reduce suffering and oppression. Keane alludes to this tension when he suggests that Habermas simultaneously denies and acknowledges the substantive political implications for his theory.[116]

Habermas's recognition of the practical intent of critical theory does not mean that he is attempting, with his account of communicative action, to provide a critical theory of society that will itself have direct practical consequences.[117] Rather his intention is to make a significant contribution to the project of a critical social theory, to provide tools for applied research, and to stimulate an interdisciplinary research program that, he hopes, will have practical implications.[118] Such affirmative claims for his work have been taken up by an extraordinary number of social scientists, and the research arising out of his project will be reviewed and evaluated in the following chapter. Generally, we expect his theory to offer a standard for the evaluation of practice, to help us understand how actions should be coordinated in particular areas of society, to aid in the recognition of distorted communication, and, finally, to assist us in distinguishing between a rational and a merely empirical consensus.

Habermas has therefore sought to provide a normative basis for social criticism, and to delineate an appropriate relation of theory to practice. His theory of communicative action allows him to identify and diagnose the contradictions of modernity in ways that appear useful to actual participants, and the theory of discourse ethics provides a means by which the validity of decision-making processes can be assessed. His concepts of the public sphere and of communication that is free from domination are highly suggestive of practical applications, and in terms of our present concern, particularly in regard to questions surrounding the design and evaluation of democratic institutions.

PART 2

From the Ideal to the Real

CHAPTER 3

The Affirmative Uses of Theory

So far, we have followed Habermas in order to collect a series of theoretical categories that are normative, universalist, and counter-to-fact. We have also identified an appropriate relation of theory to practice. Our task now is to concentrate on the many attempts, by both Habermas and his commentators, to cross over to matters practical, empirical, contextual, and factual.[1]

Our goal is practical: we wish to be able, in a pragmatic and real way, to contribute to the design and evaluation of democratic institutions. In other words, we seek a democratic politics that is both normative and empirical. The requirement that practice be normatively valid means that, though the goal is practical, the method is theoretical. We want to know what theory can do to address the practical matter of a democratic politics; and for this we have chosen Habermas's theory of discourse ethics.

As we have seen, Habermas provides a normative basis for social criticism and a careful articulation of the relation between theory and practice. The resulting critical theory can be characterized as having, first, a reconstructive/synchronic axis (time independent), along which lie the theories of communicative action, rationality, and discourse ethics. Second, it has an empirical/diachronic axis (time dependent), upon which we find the critical theory of society (including theories of colonization, crisis tendencies, and cultural modernity) and the theory of social evolution.[2] The practical intent of theory then expresses a function mapping the synchronic onto the diachronic. As conceived by Habermas, this is no mere conflation of theory with practice. At the same time, this function cannot be adequately described in terms of a simple "application" of theory to practice. Discourse ethics is not a tool to use on, and thus to control, the realm of practice. It does not provide a scientific, empiricist-inductivist[3] set of laws that, once formulated, can be wheeled out to confront an epistemologically independent and pre-existing world where trees make noise as they fall in the forest, even though there is no one there to hear them.

The social world, structured like a language, confronts us as something that is partly pregiven, *and* partly the creation of our own actions.

35

LIVERPOOL JOHN MOORES UNIVERSITY
LEARNING SERVICES

In such a world, to learn is both to make and to discover. The practical intention of Habermas's theory suggests we use it to learn about our social world. With the synchronic aspects of his theory operating as a "relatively permanent interpretative background,"[4] we are urged to carefully inspect the diachronic social world in which we live. The result is a critical-hermeneutical search for learning, a "mutual fit"[5] between universal and particular.

The practical intentions of Habermas's theory should thus be conceived along critical-hermeneutic lines, rather than as an application to reality. Normative theory should help us understand our social world, to penetrate beyond its mere appearances and reveal its hidden structures. Theory should change minds, train eyes, exert a pressure on our intuitions, and help us reclaim our individual and collective authorship of the social world; thus moving us closer to living the lives we wish to live. As we have seen, Habermas not only wants his theory "used" in such ways, but has so constructed it that these practical intentions become components of the validity of the theory itself.

In this chapter, we review the many attempts to fulfil the practical intentions of Habermas's theory. Our concern here is to explore and evaluate such attempts, and then to focus more fully on those that address questions of democratic practice. In this way, the various difficulties encountered by researchers who have attempted affirmative uses of the theory can be seen to coalesce around particular themes. What emerges from this survey is that what we have described as the iatrogenic dilemma at the heart of Habermas's theory now reappears as a series of chronic methodological problems. The argument here is that if normative theory is to inform a democratic politics, these problems will need to be overcome. This chapter highlights and collects these problems; those that follow consider them in greater depth.

Affirmative uses of Habermasian theory constitute a large and growing body of research. I would suggest that since Habermas himself indicated the many ways in which the theory might be used in practical questions,[6] there have been only two attempts to assess this body of research as a whole.[7] Ruane and Todd's article was never a complete survey, and now it is also dated. Additionally, as Strydom's sharp attack so clearly shows, it is seriously misconceived. Parkin takes a different approach to Ruane and Todd, and so is less prone to simply lament the lack of empirical work in the literature. His work is also more systematic and current, though there have been a number of subsequent developments, and he too does not adequately differentiate between the various types of research undertaken. As we consider the various examples of research, we will take up these issues against Ruane and Todd, and against Parkin, as they arise.

In our present survey then, we will distinguish between three types of research. All are attempts to fulfil the practical intentions of critical theory by using it affirmatively; by crossing over from theory to practice. The three types of affirmative use correspond to the different ways in which we learn about our social world: we must understand, we must look with care and clarity, we must consider and act.

First (3.1), we review work in that the normative theory is used as an interpretative tool in order to generate what we might call cultural criticism. This attempt to increase our understanding of the systemic and lifeworld processes at work around us is perhaps the most frequent type of affirmative use of theory, and is certainly the one upon which Habermas has concentrated in his own work.

Second (3.2), we inspect research that uses the theory as an empirical tool with which to look at or inspect our social world, thus forming examples of critical sociological research. Habermas has stated that he intends his theory to generate, and indeed be validated by, such a research program.

Third (3.3), we turn to various attempts to use the theory as a test for legitimacy. This type of affirmative use, wherein we seek to use theory to inform our actions, is the closest to our general concern of articulating a democratic politics.

3.1 AS AN INTERPRETATIVE TOOL—CULTURAL CRITICISM

In regard to affirmative uses of critical theory, much of Habermas's own effort has been directed toward a wide-ranging diagnosis of modernity. His reconstruction of a series of normative categories has been accompanied by an attempt to use them as a basis for a critical theory of society. The theories of communicative action, rationality, and discourse ethics allow him to focus on the differentiations, diremptions, and deracinations of modernity. He has paid particular attention to the selectivity of rationalization processes,[8] colonization of the lifeworld,[9] the fragmentation of consciousness,[10] crisis tendencies of the modern capitalist state,[11] the scientization of politics,[12] the development of moral consciousness,[13] the concept of the system and systems theory,[14] and the philosophical concerns generated by contemporary culture.[15]

In addition, both he and his commentators have attempted to deploy his synchronic categories in interpretative discussions of more concrete practices. Examples are, particularly, New Social Movements,[16] student politics,[17] and international relations.[18] He outlines other applications, particularly in *Legitimation Crisis* and the last two sections of *The Theory of Communicative Action*.[19] Examples are the growth and nature of the welfare state,[20] the development of law,[21] the critique of ideology,[22] child development and socialization,[23] psychopathology,[24] psychiatric service provision,[25] mass media,[26] green politics,[27] and participatory rights in democratic societies.[28] Recently, Habermas has turned his attention to the reconstruction of the normative basis of law and constitutional government.[29]

Other researchers are pursuing interpretative uses of the theory in areas such as public policy analysis,[30] administrative decision-making,[31] economics,[32] counseling battered women,[33] health care,[34] medical intervention in childbirth,[35] care of the elderly,[36] social work practice,[37] information technology,[38] and education.[39] It should be clear from this array that cultural criticism and the diagnosis of modernity is a burgeoning area of research and constitutes a highly successful affirmative use of Habermas's normative categories. Such categories are both revealing of social reality and provocative of further inquiry, and as such, their ability to make sense of the world for its participants is a fine example of the practical intent of critical theory. This, of course, is the traditional strength of critical theory: using its normative basis to draw an appearance/reality distinction within the practices of modernity.

Yet we should notice also the high level of abstraction of such interpretative work. This makes it easy to distinguish from other kinds of "applications." Strydom's critique of Ruane and Todd's survey highlights their failure to adequately distinguish between types of "application." This failure has a number of results. First, they tend to view empirical work as the only valid form of application, thus demeaning cultural criticism, which they describe as using theory "simply as a means of understanding society."[40] Second, by describing such interpretative work as mere "theory production," they tend to accuse it of being insufficiently empirical in its orientation.[41] In fact, as we are here exploring, theory can be used affirmatively in a number of ways, one of which is to interpret culture. Such a use is not just the production of more theory that then, in a separate moment, itself requires empirical application. Cultural criticism is an affirmative use of theory that is not primarily empirical, and it has been a particularly fruitful one for Habermas and his commentators.

3.2 AS AN EMPIRICAL TOOL— CRITICAL SOCIOLOGICAL RESEARCH

Habermas's intellectual ancestry leads directly from the Frankfurt school of the 1930s. The school pursued an interdisciplinary research program in the social sciences, and it is clear that Habermas intends his own theory to operate as a guide for empirical research.[42] White describes the relation between Habermas and the early critical theorists thus:

> [The Frankfurt School's] initial programme foundered . . . because its normative basis was too entangled with an insupportable "objective teleology of history" derived from Marx's view of the dialectical relation between forces of production and relations of production. The communicative model Habermas offers is designed precisely to remedy this normative difficulty in critical theory. With this shift accomplished, Habermas sees the prospects for fruitful social research along some of the same lines taken by earlier critical theorists.[43]

Any assessment of this research program turns on the distinction between cultural criticism and empirical sociology that we are currently pursuing. If we fail to adequately hold to this distinction, we might be tempted to see the plethora of interpretative uses of the theory as fulfilling the promise of a fully fledged research program. Such an error might even be encouraged by the general trend in critical theory toward metatheoretical and normative questions at the expense of empirical and politically transformative ones.[44] John Forester, for example, in introducing a collection of papers that seek to apply the theory to practice, states that Habermas's theory makes possible a "critical and empirical sociological analysis,"[45] yet as Ruane and Todd point out, many of the papers in the Forester volume are in fact "based on very limited empirical data."[46] Parkin, in his comprehensive review of all applications of the theory of communicative action, concludes that in many areas, the applied turn amounts to little more than an assertion of the promise of empirical research suggested by the theory with no actual empirical work being attempted at all.[47] While we have seen that Ruane and Todd are incorrect to accuse cultural criticism of being "based on very limited empirical data,"[48] this would be a far more serious accusation if leveled at affirmative uses of the theory that were expressly empirical in their orientation.

Parkin does highlight certain exceptions to the general absence of empirical work, notably Malhotra's studies with mature women students who are struggling with multiple roles and the pressures of higher education,[49] Forester's work on planning practices,[50] and Young's investigation into the nature of classroom interactions.[51] However, in the case of Malhotra and Young, Parkin notes a weakness in regard to their use of the conceptual innovations offered them by Habermasian theory.[52] One study that combines the use of conceptual innovation with empirical research is Carroll's work on drug dealing in Moss Side and Hulme, though the empirical content only comprises a small proportion of the total work and is not discursive in its construction.[53] Generally, and rather disappointingly, it seems one is offered a choice in the existing literature between the conceptual sophistication of interpretative research and the much rarer empirical substance of sociological studies.

One issue arises in Malhotra's work, however, that seems to hold some promise for future developments. In her study, the research methodology itself was informed by the normative theory of universal pragmatics.[54] In a communicative environment explicitly modeled on the ideal speech situation, a real attempt was made to afford the women equal communicative chances and to remove distortions of power and strategy. In this way, the project was designed to trigger critical self-reflection and encourage attempts by the participants to communicate in similar ways in other areas of their lives.

The requirement to rid the project of methodologically embedded power distortions had significant implications for the role of the researchers themselves. First, at one point in the study, the general excitement and empowerment resulted in changes being initiated by participants to the structure of the experiment itself.[55] Second, Malhotra had a quite different relation to the "subjects of study" than that occupied by most social researchers.[56] Instead of merely interacting with subjects in order to collect data, the analysis of which benefits only the researcher,[57] Malhotra concentrated upon the effects of the study on the participants, as measured by the participants. Malhotra's study therefore raises a further distinction, for it's not just that applications are either interpretative or empirical, the question also arises as to whether the empirical methods themselves are guided by critical theoretic concepts. In this way we can see, for example, that Carroll's work is really interpretative, for its empirical content (generated through questionnaires) is not itself informed by critical theory. We can also see that, irrespective of its alleged conceptual failings, Malhotra's is in fact the *only* example of empirical research where critical theory informs both descriptive concepts and method.

The absence of such research is not due to an inability on the part of researchers to follow the many implications critical theory might have for the methodology of empirical work. On the contrary, building on the notion of "holistic experimentation" outlined by Mitroff and Blankenship,[58] critical theory is able to thematize essential questions in empirical methodology.[59] The suggestion here is that empirical research might view subjects more as participants in a joint communicative venture guided by the notion of ideal speech. It might also attempt to break down the traditional power differential between researcher and subject in order to generate forms of evaluation where participants themselves judge outcomes, write up results, analyze data, and so on.[60] In addition, such a research methodology would remove the need for control groups, for no generalization would ever be attempted from the results.[61]

One methodological development which has been informed by discursive and domination-free notions of opinion formation is that of Q methodology.[62] This research instrument models subjective orientations to social reality in terms of a rated response to a set of statements.[63] Essentially interpretative,[64] it can also be critical[65] and may be "democratizable" for application to small groups.[66] The communicative interaction that produces (not discovers) the "Q sort" between a researcher and an individual effectively deconstructs opinions and meanings in such a way as to bring to light alternatives and to "stimulate a search on the part of the audience for actions that would bring these alternatives into being."[67] One application of Q methodology seeks to "reconstruct" basic democratic beliefs in a large group of respondents in such a way as to assess audience receptivity to various forms of normative democratic theory.[68]

In sum, there is clearly great scope and promise for the affirmative use of critical theory in empirical sociology. The theory seems able to aid our inspection of the social world, both by offering empirical tools and by guiding our choice of practices to study. At present, however, the rarity of such work forces us to conclude that this promise is largely unfulfilled.

3.3 AS A TEST FOR LEGITIMACY— DEMOCRATIC POLITICAL THEORY

As Habermas states, "moral issues are never raised for their own sake; people raise them seeking a guide for action."[69] When we seek such guidance, particularly in the area of politics, we come across perhaps the most contentious type of affirmative use of his theory, for here we confront its practical intent in terms of the possibility of an emancipatory political practice.

Habermas has demonstrated the normative requirement that political decisions involve practical discourse, and he has attempted to describe the conditions under which such a discourse is rational. He therefore addresses what might be seen as two distinct dimensions of democratic legitimacy, for it entails a claim about *who* is to be involved and another about the *manner* of their involvement. In addition, legitimate political decisions must take place *somewhere*, and it is for this reason that democratic theorists have always been concerned with the question of the location of democracy.[70] Habermas and his commentators have addressed this third dimension with an account of autonomous public spheres operating within civil society. Democratic legitimacy can therefore be seen as a three-dimensional conceptual object, raising questions of "who," "how," and "where." We will consider the practical intentions of Habermas's theory along each dimension in turn.

The "Who" of Democratic Legitimacy

As Benhabib has shown, Habermas adheres to the methodological assumption of a "consensus principle of legitimacy."[71] This asserts that rational consensus provides "the only criterion in light of which the legitimacy of norms and normative institutional arrangements can be justified."[72] "Consensus" here expresses the general participatory imperative (D), which calls for a practical discourse involving *all* those affected by a decision.[73] Where constraints are such that this ideal is impractical, the normative theory falls back onto the more realistic requirement that the *maximum possible* number of those affected should be involved, and that those not directly participating should have input via representative or advocatory structures.

Benhabib points out that Habermas shares this assumption with Rawls, but we could extend this and note that she might well have listed almost every democratic theorist, excluding perhaps only the most rabid of realists. Often expressed as an assumption that unanimity confers legitimacy,[74] the principle constitutes the normative core that is a necessary condition for a theory to be called democratic at all. Thus, majoritarian democracy, public choice theory, social contract theory, and the like all adhere to this principle. It is a normative ideal of such distinguished ancestry that it appears to most of us as being intuitively correct and unquestionable. It is, therefore, along this dimension of democratic legitimacy that Dunn is able to assert that "we are all democrats today."[75]

Such a principle can, of course, be instantiated in a variety of ways, and it is this, in part, that accounts for the great range of democratic theories and practices.[76] Indeed, when George Bush can invade Panama, imprison its labor leaders, and rig its elections, all in the name of democracy, it becomes apparent that the empirical mitigation for the application of the normative ideal of consensus can be so great as to render the predicate "democracy" almost meaningless.[77]

The problem we confront here is again one of discrimination. There are simply too many empirical performances that are claimed to satisfy this principle, and it therefore fails to adequately distinguish between positions. To claim, as Habermas's theory does, that the maximum possible number of people be involved in the making of a decision, is therefore, to require of political decision-making "merely" that it be democratic. In terms of the first dimension of democratic legitimacy, the "who," Habermas's theory has the following affirmative use: it shows that democracy is normatively superior to other forms of political order.

The "How" of Democratic Legitimacy

Benhabib describes Habermas as adhering also to a second methodological assumption: that of "methodological proceduralism."[78] This claims that a "rational consensus is to be defined procedurally by specifying strategies and modes of argumentation through which alone such a consensus of norms and normative institutional arrangements can be attained."[79] Habermas has reconstructed, from the presuppositions of argumentation, an ideal procedure that expresses the normative core of democracy. This has two definite implications in regard to the design and evaluation of democratic institutions. First, such institutions should enable the exercise of communicative rationality. They should be deliberative in nature, embody the rationality of the forum rather than that of the market,[80] and seek to transform preferences in rational debate rather than to simply aggregate them.[81] Second, the legitimacy of democratic institutions lies in the degree to which their procedures approximate to the ideal. It is this provision of a normative procedural standard that distinguishes Habermas from most other theorists of discursive democracy. It has also been, as he fully intended it to be, the inspiration for a large body of research.

The normative content of ideal speech, or the inescapable presuppositions of argumentation, can be expressed as a series of pragmatic rules:[82]

1. Every subject with the competence to speak and act is allowed to take part in discourse.

2. Everyone is allowed to question any assertion whatever. Everyone is allowed to introduce any assertion whatever into the discourse. Everyone is allowed to express his attitudes, desires and needs.

3. No speaker may be prevented by either internal or external coercion from exercising his rights as laid down in (1) and (2) above.

These rules of rational discourse describe the conditions of democratic legitimacy. Together, they constitute an ideal of perfect procedural fairness that is inescapably anticipated in the process of discourse, and that can function as a critical standard against which actual discourses can be measured.[83]

Usually, this ideal is raised counterfactually.[84] We do not often meet the ideal in practice. Fairness, or rational consensus, is almost always a practical impossibility.[85] The complexity and scope of the problems we face in modern mass society are such that deliberation must be augmented by representational structures and systemically coordinated activity. Also, there are temporal pressures upon actual deliberation, structural distortions, motivational and cognitive deficits.[86] Generally then, the exigencies of the real world necessitate a retreat from the ideal of fair deliberation. For this reason, Habermas suggests the possibility of legitimate compromises between private interests when consensus is unattainable.[87]

But he also wants to use his theory as a test for the *degree* of fairness of a given deliberative practice. Such a use can be conceived as a "maximal approach" that seeks an asymptotic approximation.[88] Each practice can then be assessed in terms of "degrees of departure from the ideal."[89] The ideal is not to be used simply in order to show that all instances of actual discourse are imperfect,[90] but to illuminate the *degree* of imperfection. Nor should we imagine, as does Dryzek, that the theory "identifies no cut-off point at which approval can be registered."[91] Approval is always historically and culturally situated, and recent theoretical developments have highlighted the context-specific manner in which the ideal might be adequately approximated.[92] A practical discourse can only deploy the state of knowledge available to actual participants at an actual time,[93] and as discursive judgments are always open to re-evaluation in the light of new information,[94] they are essentially fallibilistic in nature. In addition, the growing clarity with which Habermas distinguishes between the justification and the appropriate application of norms admits of an increasingly context-sensitive deployment of the requirement of impartiality.[95] The cut-off point for approval of a discourse is identifiable by the participants themselves who alone can assess the temporal, motivational, and cognitive constraints they face. We might, therefore, say that normative approval is reached when the participants in a discourse can rationally be said to have "done their best."

To use Habermas's theory to address the "how" of democracy is thus to seek institutional designs and practices that reach as closely as possible to the ideal, and to evaluate existing institutions in terms of the success of their approximation. Regarding institutional design, the theory has produced a general approbation of discursive fora, either in the form of autonomous public spheres or, somewhat more concretely, discursive institutional designs. On the one hand, this work is hampered by the level of abstraction of the pragmatic rules of ideal fairness. As such, they simply fail to delimit a particular organizational or institutional form.[96] On the other, the theory itself provides good reasons *not* to provide concrete institutional designs. Habermas is careful to preserve a place, in the process of legitimation, for the culturally specific interpretations, circumstances, needs, and motivations of actual participants. As we saw with the question of a cut-off point for approval, only when a way of life meets the ideal of deliberative fairness "halfway"[97] do we begin to understand the legitimacy of a democratic institution. It is not a matter for a theory or theorist to preselect an organizational form, for to do so would amount to designing a way of life for the participants. His theory is, therefore, purposefully indeterminate when it comes to the questions of institutional design.

In the face of this limitation on the theory, those investigating the political implications of a discourse ethics are increasingly focusing their attention on a somewhat different object. *En masse*, commentators are now turning toward deriving, from the presuppositions of argumentation, a schedule of communicative rights. The insight that drives the various attempts to "say it with rights" is that discursive will-formation is conditional upon the inclusion of communicatively competent subjects. This entirely valid normative assumption is then "cashed in" for the empirical institutional requirements that would enable subjects to gain and maximize such competencies.[98] Rights are thus praised partly, as they are in liberal theory, for their protective ability, here conceived as a protection of the processes of discursive will-formation,[99] as well as for their constitutive ability, in terms of the necessary conditions of agency.[100]

Ingram, acknowledging that the limitations of the theory precludes "the establishment of any particular institutional embodiment of equal democratic rights," goes on to claim that "our communicative commitments . . . favour the adoption of institutions that promote rather than obstruct the equal and effective right of each person to public speech and association."[101] Similarly, Cohen asserts that "discourse ethics . . . provides the basis for a theory of rights,"[102] and draws our attention particularly to those rights that "secure the integrity and autonomy of the person (privacy rights) and those having to do with free communication (assembly, association, expression)."[103] Baynes argues for "constitutionally recognised rights" in order to "secure communicatively structured domains of action against incursions from the market or administrative state."[104] Walzer interprets Habermas as claiming that "his speakers have equal rights to initiate the conversation and to resume it."[105] Cohen, writing with Arato, identifies a bundle of social rights that arise as "claims" whereby the "communicative conditions" of discursive will-formation are "rendered operational and realized as far as possible."[106] Even Benhabib sometimes explicates the normative assumptions contained in the notion of ideal speech in terms of "rights," both to participation and to the deployment of speech-acts.[107]

In fact, the various attempts to embody the normative imperatives of ideal speech in the empirical form of a series of rights turn on a fundamental ambiguity in the way Habermas formalizes his pragmatic rules of fairness. Those who find a grounding of rights in his theory tend to understand these rules as a series of equal *individual entitlements* to use speech-acts.[108] They thus locate, in the normative theory, a grounding for the protection of individual capacities to engage in rational discourse. Yet close inspection of these pragmatic rules suggests that they might be better interpreted in terms of equal *opportunities* to use speech-acts.[109] Such an interpretation changes the object that the rules are seeking to protect. Instead of protecting individual capacities, they would, with this alternative interpretation, be directed more firmly at the conditions of legitimacy of the discourse itself. Thus, while both interpretations of the pragmatic rules call for the inclusion of affected individuals in the discourse, the latter would not express this in terms of an individual right to inclusion. Rather, it would claim that the legitimacy of the discourse turns on the inclusion of individuals. The onus of proof is thus on the institutions of democracy to find ways to include individuals if those institutions want to be legitimate.

In the literature dealing with the institutionalization of the normative requirements, one of the few statements that expresses this issue the right way around is White's discussion of how the First Amendment is (sometimes) understood in American constitutional law:

> It has been considered a "preferred freedom" and attacks upon it or failures to protect it are consequently seen in a special light; the party which has threatened it bears a heavier-than-normal burden of proof in its argument that such infringement is justified. We might think of the two discursive principles in a similar way. With regard to participation, this would mean that the burden of proof would be on the institution . . . to demonstrate why there could not be greater participation in decisions which affect people's lives in important ways.[110]

To interpret Habermas's pragmatic rules as communicative *opportunities* is to point them at a different object. It moves us away from individual entitlements and toward an orientation to the necessary conditions of discursive legitimacy. Such an interpretation does not address, and so does not provide, a grounding for individual rights.

Even if those who seek to "say it with rights" remain unaware of this interpretative ambiguity, there are other difficulties that their project must overcome. Not least among them is the level of abstraction of the rights that the theory putatively picks out. The problem arises because such theorists, having taken on board the need to limit the theory in order to prevent excessive discrimination of institutional design, now find themselves constrained to uttering heart-warming generalities. These usually take the form of a derivation, from the presuppositions of argumentation, of some bundle of rights that would make discursive fairness more meaningful. They are unable to specify precisely what these rights might be, and neither can they indicate their particular institutional embodiment.[111]

This is not to deny that the universal presuppositions of argumentation often take the institutional form, in a specific historical and cultural context, of a schedule of codified rights.[112] Though it can take this form, however, this does not preclude other equally legitimate yet completely different ways of instantiating the universal. Where institutional embodiments of normative validity are ethically patterned,[113] and legitimacy is seen as a culturally specific interpretation of the universal, our attention is turned toward questions of political culture.[114] Here, our orientation changes. Instead of exploring ways to instantiate the universal in this particular context, we now move toward the question of how this particular context instantiates the universal. Such an orientation exerts subtle pressures. It redirects our efforts toward an exploration of the sense in which our existing political order is legitimate. This is, of course, an entirely valid project, and is presently being fruitfully pursued by a number of Habermas's commentators. But the study of a political order's extant legitimacy is a far cry from using the theory affirmatively in order to design legitimate democratic institutions that might be quite different than those we currently have. The various attempts to use the theory to articulate a series of rights therefore moves the question of institutional design to a level of abstraction and generality that threatens to dull the emancipatory edge of the normative theory.

Though increasingly fashionable, attempts to "say it with rights" face significant difficulties that they do not adequately address. Their interpretation of the pragmatic rules is questionable, the limitations of the theory tend to make their attempts highly abstract, and their moral constriction to extant political cultures underestimates the indeterminacy of the theory. Paraphrasing McIntyre's critique of Gewirth,[115] attempts to derive rights from the conditions of (communicative) agency have yet to show that the institutional conditions we *here and now* see as necessary for that agency give rise to a right to just *these* conditions. Rights may constitute a gain in freedom for individuals, and may also be a kind of institutional high-water mark for the normative learning of a particular political culture. Habermas's theory gives us conceptual tools with which to inspect such phenomena. But it does not provide a justification for a series of communicative rights.

We noted above another possible affirmative use of the theory in regard to the "how of democracy." This body of research seeks to evaluate existing institutions in terms of the degree to which their proce-dures approximate to the ideal. The most intriguing and methodologi-cally sophisticated attempts to deploy the ideal in such an assessment of practice take place in the Forester volume.[116] Kemp's paper on the Wind-scale inquiry is particularly instructive, because he sets out to use the ideal in order to "check the 'consensus' that emerged out of a recent example of public participation in the development of nuclear energy in Britain."[117]

Kemp's method is to break the ISS down into its components (his work predates Alexy and Habermas's articulation of the pragmatic rules), and then to take each component and hold it up to the corre-sponding component of the actual practice. This enables him to show that the Windscale inquiry was subject to systematic distortion because "each of the four requirements of distortion-free practical discourse was transgressed in some manner."[118] In other words, in keeping with the promise of Habermas's affirmative claim for his theory, we are here treated to an analysis of a particular practice that shows precisely how and in what ways that practice falls short of rational consensus.

Kemp's work is illuminating in regard to the distortions of the inquiry, yet it also shows the problems encountered with this kind of use of the theory. Actual power distortions are complex and interrelated, and they often involve transgressions of more than one component of the ideal. When we consider the question of how the Windscale inquiry could have been improved, that is to say, how its procedures could have more closely approximated to the ideal, we therefore confront a seem-ingly insurmountable difficulty. This way of using the theory, for all its apparent rigor, turns out to be quite unable to clearly delineate what an improvement would entail.

Kemp unpacks the ideal of rational consensus into four compo-nents, thus providing four axes along which distortions can be said to occur.[119] Paraphrasing, these express the following imperatives:

a. Against Exclusion
b. Against Silencing
c. Against Disempowerment
d. Against Intimidation

As Kemp discovered, the Windscale inquiry transgressed the ideal to some degree along each of the four axes. We might assign a "grading value" to these transgressions, and express them as a_1, b_1, c_1, and d_1. Because these distortions are significant, Kemp rightly questions the legitimacy of the Windscale inquiry, and he then goes on to make some suggestions as to how it might have been improved. Any improvement would here entail some gain along *at least one* of the axes of the ideal. Yet, because power distortions are complex and involve transgressions along *more than one* axis, improvements would be similarly complex. We might, therefore, identify one improvement that drew closer to the ideal along two of its axes, having the form a_1, b_2, c_2, and d_1, and another: a_2, b_2, c_1, and d_1. These possible improvements differ in their transgressions. While the first delivers greater legitimacy along some of the axes, the second has more to offer along others. How would we then decide which was best? How could they be assigned a "ranking value?"[120]

The problem arises whenever we seek to compare and adjudicate between two examples of practice, be they alternatives from which we must select or a practice and its possible improvement. Because the normative argument does not assign a weight to each of the components, or order them lexicographically, gains along individual axes are incommensurable.[121] It would, of course, be normatively preposterous to assign such a weight. Yet nothing short of this would allow us to accurately compare two practices. The theory does not provide the resources to evaluate partial improvements, nor can it evaluate where a gain on one axis requires a trade-off on another. The theory is therefore of limited use in making comparative evaluations.

Only where there is a clear gain along all four axes can we say with any surety that there has been an improvement. It is for this reason that Dryzek, having suggested that we use the theory to enable "comparative evaluations" of practices, gives as his example, the comparison between the American polyarchy and the Third Reich.[122] Here, improvement is obvious along all four axes, indeed, so obvious, that it hardly constitutes a use of theory at all.[123] Most of the choices we face are between alternatives that are of greater similarity. As Habermas puts it, "the typical states are in the grey areas in between."[124]

Clearly, notions such as "critical standards to distinguish degrees of departure from the ideal,"[125] "yardstick," and "measurement,"[126] are misleading. Instead of conceiving of the use of theory as a test for legitimacy, we would do better to see it as a kind of training for our eyes. Having understood the components of rational consensus, one is better able to look for and spot transgressions in the real world. This returns us to the illuminative strength of critical theory, which is so much in evidence in the area of cultural criticism and the diagnosis of modernity. It is certainly the case that:

> There is a "more" [and a] "less" with respect to democratic legitimacy; and the (internal) standard of the "more" or "less" is expressed precisely by the normative idealization which Habermas derives from his notion of communicative rationality.[127]

Yet we are quite unable to extend this insight in order to assert that the idealization can be used as a test to objectively distinguish between instances of distorted communication. As Wellmer puts it, "the structural features of ideal speech situations represent no sufficient or independently applicable criterion for the rationality of discourses."[128]

Here again we find ourselves able only to conceive of the ideal as a regulative one. Wellmer sums up this conception thus:

> I would think that the utopian perspective inherent in the democratic tradition should not so much be considered in analogy to geometrical idealisations, which can never be perfectly embodied in the recalcitrant material of physical bodies (one might rather think of an infinite process of possible approximations), but rather as the center of gravitation of democratic forms of organisation, the attractive force of which becomes proportionately stronger as a relationship of mutual recognition is already embodied in consensual forms of action coordination.[129]

Serious difficulties thus confront any attempt to use the theory as a moral test. In regard to the first two dimensions of democratic legitimacy, we have seen that while the normative theory requires that the maximum number of people be involved and that the procedure they use be as fair as possible, it does not pick out particular institutional arrangements, nor can it adequately adjudicate between practices. As Beauchamp points out, "principles help us see the moral dimensions of . . . problems, but they are too weakened by their abstractness to give us particular duties or to assign any priorities among various assignable duties."[130]

As we move to the third dimension, the "where" of democratic legitimacy, this discriminative failure is exacerbated further still.

The "Where" of Democratic Legitimacy

Communicative rationality involves the public use of reason. Calhoun points out that this "depends upon both the quality of discourse and quantity of participation,"[131] and we have focused on these two dimensions of democratic legitimacy in terms of the "how" and the "who." Now we turn to the question of "where."

Habermas states that "the settling of political questions, as far as their moral core is concerned, depends on the institutionalisation of practices of rational public debate."[132] Such debate takes place (when it does) in the public sphere.[133] As a sociological concept, the public sphere is often inadequately defined,[134] though Habermas has been more careful than most in attempting to explicate the term.[135] First of all, it designates a realm of our social life in which something approaching public opinion can be formed. . . . A portion of the public sphere comes into being in every conversation in which private individuals assemble to form a public body. . . . Citizens behave as a public body when they confer in an unrestricted fashion . . . about matters of general interest.[136]

Habermas charts the historical degeneration of the public sphere and shows how it is variously delineated and supported by legal structures of social rights. He locates its modern form in the "space between the state and civil society,"[137] and, continuing the analogy of space, we might say that the public sphere (or *a* public sphere[138]) opens up wherever citizens participate in a discursive search for understanding of those issues that affect them collectively. It can come into being in a coffee shop, at a constitutional convention or within a New Social Movement.[139] Dryzek cites a good example of the creation of a public space: in rural Canada, Thomas Berger conducted an extensive consultation with local people affected by the building of an oil pipeline by traveling from town to town and holding hearings, discussions, and debates in any venue where he could get them started.[140]

For Habermas then, the public sphere is an appropriate empirical instantiation of the normative requirement of practical and rational discourse. His work on this category, particularly the historical exegesis, has clarified its meaning, and subsequently, further clarification has been attempted along two general lines.

First, writers such as Cohen and Arato have sought greater precision regarding the relation of the public sphere to civil society. In many ways, their work reflects the general rediscovery of civil society by political theorists,[141] though its avowedly Habermasian orientation results in a distinct conception of the category. Against the Marxist view, which distinguishes merely between civil society and the state, and the Hegelian, which sets it against both the state and the private sphere, Cohen and Arato adopt their own trichotomous conception.[142] Here, civil society is contrasted with those two subsystems: the state and the economy, which have been differentiated out of the lifeworld in modernity. Within the lifeworld, some discourses, particularly those "specialized in the reproduction of traditions, solidarities and identities," become institutionalized.[143] These institutions remain coordinated by communicative action oriented to mutual understanding rather than by the purposive-rational steering media of money and power.

Civil society then, is that institutional dimension of the lifeworld wherein the functional requirements of cultural reproduction, social integration, and socialization achieve their institutional facticity.[144] Here we find those institutions that address questions of morality and law, art, science and technology, and education and child-rearing. Importantly, in civil society, we can also locate those political and social institutions that continue to embody forms of discursive will-formation. As we have seen, these are often seen as a structure of rights.

The second area of clarification concerns the mechanisms by which the public sphere has input into the decision-making structures of the state. Habermas has suggested that this input is not to be conceived as an ideal whereby the public sphere takes over the decision-making functions of the state. It can never hope to fully replace the functions provided in late capitalist society by the differentiated subsystems of money and power. The complexity of decisions required in the modern state precludes a Rousseauesque conception of popular sovereignty whereby the moment of deliberation occurs in a single assembly.[145] "Discourses," Habermas points out, "do not govern."[146] For them to do so would entail an unacceptable loss of efficiency, as well as threatening a subsumption of the economy under an administrative bureaucracy. This need for a "separation of powers" is, he claims, the lesson to be drawn from the "experiment" of state socialism.[147]

Instead, he speaks in terms of the Parsonian notion of "influence."[148] The public sphere here feeds the product of its deliberative will-formation into the state's decision-making by exerting a "pressure" upon it,[149] by calling it to account, by keeping a watchful eye upon it. Public spheres are therefore to operate at the periphery of the state, "below the threshold of party apparatuses,"[150] and to exercise a "combination of power and self-restraint."[151] In so acting, they provide the state with normative resources and refrain from imagining that they can operate directly upon the economy and society in such a way as to achieve emancipatory goals.[152]

In supplying the political system with loyalties and legitimations, autonomous public spheres[153] "sensitize the self-steering mechanisms of the state and the economy to the goal-oriented mechanisms of radical democratic will formation."[154] The public sphere thus functions as a kind of superego to the "instinctual" behavior of the political and economic subsystems, and its central concern is to achieve a rational balance between the processes of the system and the lifeworld. It is for this reason that Habermas talks about "democratic countersteering,"[155] boundary disputes, and border conflicts.[156] As the fundamentally different rationalities of the system and lifeworld compete with one another to coordinate human activity, "new frictional surfaces" between them "spark new conflicts."[157] These border conflicts then give rise to New Social Movements that seek to defend the lifeworld from colonization by the system.[158]

If the legitimacy of a political order turns on the degree to which discursive inputs into its decision-making structures are institutionalized, we raise again the question of how closely it approximates to an ideal. Now though, having moved away from the possibility of any kind of "measurement" of legitimacy, we are instead using the theory to inform an analysis of particular political cultures, to ground a critique of liberal democracies and to reveal the normative content of extant constitutional procedures and the law.[159] The project of using the theory as a test for legitimacy and a guide for action thus collapses back into one of interpretative cultural criticism. As Habermas puts it,

> in regard to providing guidance for an emancipatory practice, discourse ethics can acquire a significance for orienting action. It does so, however, not as an ethics, that is, not prescriptively in the direct sense, but indirectly, by becoming part of a critical social theory that can be used to interpret situations.[160]

It is this conception of the affirmative use of theory that dominates Habermas's latest book, which concerns itself with the normative content of constitutional law.[161] Once again, we note a subtle shift in orientation; one that has important implications for questions of political practice. The practical intention of the normative theory, in the area of politics, is no longer to be conceived in terms of guiding emancipatory action (if it ever was), but instead, as helping us to interpret our social world so that we might make decisions with greater understanding. Thus, Benhabib is now able to state that "the deliberative theory of democracy is not a theory in search of practice, rather it is a theory which claims to elucidate some aspects of the logic of existing democratic practices better than others."[162]

To the extent that the theory does provide us with guidance for practice, it articulates a politics of discourse, here conceived as a "proceduralization of the Reausseauean conception of popular sovereignty."[163] The moment of deliberation now occurs in a wide array of self-limiting and institutionalised discourses. These are to be located in "the more or less informal movements and associations in civil society where solidarities are formed, through the various institutions of the public mass media, to the more formal institutions of parliamentary debate and legal argumentation."[164]

This network of discourses (including what Fraser calls "subaltern counterpublics"[165]) would deploy procedures that are, in accordance with Habermas's investigation of the "how" of democratic legitimacy, as fair as circumstance and political culture permit.

In sum, Habermasian attempts to bridge the gap between normative and empirical theory in order to articulate a democratic politics increasingly concentrate on the normative pole. Though empirical questions are by no means ignored, we encounter chronic methodological problems when we try to use the theory as a test for legitimacy. In particular, the abstraction of the normative theory gives rise to various forms of indeterminacy and discriminative failure.

It is for this reason that, having spent tens of pages unpacking the nuances of his normative argument, a quite extraordinary number of books and articles on Habermasian theory end with a somewhat nebulous benediction to its empirical promise. Often, an increase in popular deliberation in the making of political decisions is called for, and general praise is invariably heaped on the public sphere as the appropriate space for such deliberation. Even the most brilliant expositions of Habermas's work seem, on the last page, to stop, as it were, in midair—for no one feels able to bring him or herself to actually address the empirical problem of how the normative insights might be translated into institutional shape.

So, for example, Bohman states that "more democracy . . . is possible . . . so long as citizens find in the public sphere a discursive space for criticism, learning, and new forms of association,"[166] Bernstein claims that "if we do not strive to realise the conditions required for practical discourse—then we will surely become less than fully human,"[167] Benhabib suggests that we form "communities of need and solidarity in the interstices of our societies,"[168] while Baynes calls for "a robust and multifaceted model of the public sphere in which individuals can deliberate about the collective terms and conditions of their common lives."[169]

The point here is not to suggest that these sentiments are incorrect, for they certainly are not. Indeed, they accord with those offered by many other democratic theorists, including those contributing to the present revival of participatory models,[170] and even by those investigating the political implications of postmodernism.[171] Rather, one should simply notice how little actual crossing over from normative theory to empirical institutional design is attempted by Habermas's commentators and how there seems, therefore, to be a kind of missing tier of theory—this being an account of what normatively grounded institutions might look like and how they might actually function.[172]

This apparent lacuna arises from a profound ambivalence regarding the relation of metatheory to substantive political questions. On the one hand, critical theorists generally praise the empirical implications of normative theory. They know that something more than mere critique is required. Yet on the other, any attempt to tell people how to do their politics is anathema. Wanting to provide images of emancipation yet at the same time fearing the coercive power of utopianism, they are left to squeeze themselves into the middle ground, where their knowledge of the consequences of utopianism prevents them from acting, and where their awareness of the suffering in the world serves only to make them miserable.

It is no wonder that Habermas has been accused of both irrelevance and authoritarianism. The mixture of fear and disappointment to which his universalist ethics gives rise is shared by both his adherents and his detractors.

3.4 SUM OF AFFIRMATIVE USES OF THEORY AND ATTENDANT PROBLEMS

Our inspection of the many attempts to fulfil the practical intentions of Habermas's theory has highlighted both successes and failures. In the area of interpretative cultural criticism (3.1), the normative theory offers a conceptual framework that can help participants in a process of enlightenment to make sense of their social environment. For this reason, the diagnosis of modernity has been one of the most fruitful areas of affirmative use of Habermasian theory. Here, the concepts of rationality, communicative action, and colonization are used to inform a hermeneutic investigation of societal processes. Yet the universal character of these concepts renders them highly abstract. There is a great distance between them and the contextual minutiae of our lives as citizens. Seeking a "mutual fit" between theory and reality is not, in itself, a project that can fulfil the practical intentions of a critical theory.

In the area of critical sociological research (3.2), more avowedly empirical work has been attempted. This has given rise to new directions in research methodology, and we still have reason to hope for studies in which the design, organization, and monitoring of outcomes are all conducted by participants in such a way as to "be of use to participants." So far, however, the affirmative use of theory in the area of empirical research has been too thin on the ground.

Regarding work that seeks to use the theory as a test for legitimacy (3.3), we identified a series of discriminative failures, both in questions of design and in the evaluation of democratic institutions. While the ideal of communicative fairness can be used as a tool to interrogate practice, there are limitations on the theory that constrain it to the role of a regulative ideal. As such, it can illuminate the components of fair communication and prompt us to ask the right questions. Yet the ideal remains insufficiently discerning to guide our actions. In this area of affirmative use, the abstraction of the normative position gives rise to discriminative failure, theoretical lacuna, and seemingly insurmountable problems of comparative evaluation.

Despite these difficulties, there is, perhaps, a sense in which the respective gains afforded by the three types of affirmative use of theory can be brought together to fulfill the practical intentions of the theory. Thus, Forester outlines a project wherein the conceptual apparatus of interpretative cultural criticism, the empirical methods of critical sociology, and the understanding of the ideal afforded by the normative critique of practice could all be used to describe and assess the effect of policy decisions on existing communicative structures.[173] Yet still, and particularly in regard to our central question of the implications of the normative theory for a democratic politics, such a combination would also compound the difficulties faced by each type of affirmative use of theory.

It seems unavoidable, therefore, that we must sum up our assessment of the practical intent of Habermasian theory by likening it to a promissory note: fully written, but as yet uncashed. The methodological problems we confront in trying to "apply" the normative theory to practical matters, whether in interpretative critique, empirical observation, or democratic politics, have become chronic and repetitive. Abstraction, lack of empirical work, discriminative failure, and lacuna, all combine to effectively block our crossing over from normative to empirical theory.

We should, perhaps, not be surprised by this. The iatrogenic dilemma we identified at the heart of Habermas's position would suggest that it is precisely the medicine we took to overcome the lack of normative grounds for critique that is now causing our chronic problems in applying the ideal to practice. Once again we are returned to the Hegelian critique of Kant as we encounter a moral theory that is insufficiently discerning, which raises problems of contextualization, and which, if we are tempted to add in any preassigned content at all, threatens authoritarianism.

Yet Habermas is not an authoritarian thinker. He is anti-authoritarian; indeed, so much so that he cannot live in a world in which authoritarianism is normatively indistinguishable from freedom. His dogged insistence that a normative theoretical project is viable began with an attempt to articulate a series of knowledge-constitutive interests. When these were revealed to be indefensible, he turned to a theory of communicative action. Now that this latter attempt has come of age, we find ourselves, with discourse ethics, in possession of the most articulate normative theory currently available. It provides an extra-contextual criterion that can distinguish between authoritarianism and freedom. Yet that criterion must be contextualized if it is to fulfil its practical intentions. Authoritarianism is, after all, a practice. Its eradication thus requires both a counterfactual ideal of participation and an real emancipatory politics. Our assessment of the affirmative uses of the theory indicates that Habermas's concern to preserve the critical power of the ideal gives rise to discriminative failure in questions of practice.

Importantly, Habermas knows this. He has fully accepted this discriminative failure on the empirical side. Perhaps his early experiences of Nazism and of critical theory's retreat from the philosophy of *praxis* accounts for his proclivity to counter the increasing threat of relativism with an attention to normative questions. For whatever reason, his primary concern has remained that of stating the *sense* in which authoritarianism is different from freedom; a project he is not willing to sacrifice for a gain in contextual discrimination. Indeed, as we have seen, he remains highly ambivalent about the prospect of greater discrimination in practical matters, for he holds that such a substantive utopianism itself threatens authoritarianism.

In regard to the practical problems of politics, then, Habermas does not see the discriminative failure of his normative theory as a weakness, or as a "missing bit." While acknowledging that it may be disappointing that the practical problems of politics cannot be so simply solved, he nevertheless continues to insist upon certain limits to his theory. These limits account for the discriminative failure, and it is precisely this failure that preserves a space for actual participants in processes of emancipation to provide contents, contexts, and motivations.[174]

In terms of practical politics, Habermas's project has stalled. Beset by chronic methodological problems, the urgency of defending a viable normative theory has resulted in a turn away from offering guidance for an emancipatory practice. Thus, where we once had "crisis tendencies,"[175] now we have "deficits"[176] and "pathologies." Where we once had a way of evaluating practice, we now have a regulative ideal. Where we hoped for a radical participatory politics, we now have an account of rights, of the normative basis of state power and the law. In these ways, the initial promise of a Habermasian politics gives way to an interpretative sifting through liberal practices for the required "modicum of congruence" between morality and extant political values.[177] With the articulation of a discourse ethics, Habermasian theory was at a crossroads. In choosing to favor a strong universalism, and then to limit the theory in such a way as to preserve a space for participants to contextualize it, we move toward a liberal politics. Now our efforts accord with those of Rawls and Waldron, who seek to account for the ways in which liberal institutions seek to justify themselves.[178]

I do not propose to follow this liberal turn, not because it is incorrect, or because it threatens a possible use of theory in which the status quo is merely offered a justification. Instead, I hope to show that Habermas's theory has definite implications for political practice that remain unexplored. To see what these further implications might be, however, we must first be clear about precisely those aspects of his theory that seem to constrain the move from normative to empirical issues. In the next chapter, we will therefore look more closely at the theoretical sources of the various methodological problems we have encountered in our assessment of the affirmative uses of his theory.

CHAPTER 4

Methodological Problems and the Limits to Theory

Questions surrounding the possibility of a Habermasian politics have received significant attention in the literature. Throughout our inquiry, we have noted how some commentators tend to overestimate the political implications of his theory, and thus view it with a mixture of fear and distaste, while others have been frustrated by the theory's level of abstraction, and so have found it disappointing and of little practical import. Having sifted through these various objections, we can now say with some surety that neither type quite hits the mark. As a theory primarily of *justification*, it confronts inevitable difficulties when it attempts to address questions of emancipatory practice. To this extent, asking it to do more than exert a moral pressure on the facts is simply inappropriate: it constitutes an attempt to use the theory in a manner for which it was never designed.

Yet it is not hard to see why there is so much confusion regarding the political implications of the theory. First of all, Habermas himself has moved his position on the relation of theory to practice[1] in such a way as to distance himself from the heightened expectations raised by his theoretical adjustments to the Frankfurt School's political agenda. Habermas had suggested that the early critical theorists found themselves caught in a political cul-de-sac wherein "the possibility of emancipation appeared only as a critical device or regulative principle."[2] Second, as we have seen, the obvious critical power of his own theory has not been matched by a political project,[3] and has itself backed off some of its early claims, so that now, it too seeks only to operate as a "critical device or regulative principle." Third, in setting out the conditions of democratic legitimacy, his theory is expressly designed to have practical intent and to be of affirmative use in an oppressive social world. As such, it clearly has *some* implications for emancipatory practice, though perhaps, as we have seen, not many. Or should we instead say, "not enough"? Stated thus, we can see that the practical inadequacy of the theory is not just a theoretical problem. There are also political participants who, *requiring emancipation*, look to theory for guidance.

Whenever he has been asked for such guidance, Habermas has given an intriguing reply. He could so easily have followed the French tradition and increased his fame by giving those young political activists who go knocking at the doors of great intellectuals the theoretical package they require to insult and harass the institutions of power. Yet he never did. Indeed, those who sought to use his ideas in this way were often in receipt of a stiff telling-off, a lecture on the difference between the harassment of power and its meaningful challenge, and a series of stern warnings about what should not be tried.[4] Again and again he stresses what his theory cannot do and draws our attention to its limitations.

I want to suggest that the confusion over the question of a Habermasian politics (Should there be one? Is there one? If not, why not?) is partly a result of the complexity and sophistication of the arguments he uses to limit his theory. Only by understanding the intricacies that seem to preclude any extension of the political implications of his normative position can we hope to discriminate between those limitations that are to be honored and those that might be overcome. If discourse ethics is to have *more* to say about democratic practice than we found in the previous chapter, then we must have a more complete understanding of the relation between the limitations of the theory and the chronic methodological problems we encountered there.

We now turn, therefore, to the question of precisely what, in Habermas's theory, prevents us cashing in his normative claims into empirical designs for, and evaluative techniques of, actual democratic institutions. As we shall see, this limitation is not a single thread, but a complex series of arguments plaited around the general distinction between the procedure and the content of a decision-making process. To describe these limitations, we will begin by reviewing the two kinds of arguments Habermas has variously presented to explain why his theory does not permit the design of particular democratic arrangements. These are, first (4.1), that specific institutional designs involve questions of the good life, and that such ethical questions are beyond the remit of a theory of justice. Second (4.2), he argues that using his theory to design institutions involves a category mistake, for such attempts imagine that a normative foundational principle is the same kind of thing as a democratic arrangement. Habermas develops this latter argument via a critique of Rousseau. Following this, we will turn (4.3) to one particular attempt to use the theory to outline a series of political implications, this being the work of John Dryzek. His understanding of the limitation is criticized in order to sharpen our own, and his work is used to highlight the distinction between the *ex ante* design and the *ex post* evaluation of democratic institutions. We will then be able (4.4) to formulate the limit in its full complexity, and to more accurately delimit those implications that are permitted by the theory and those that are not. Finally, we return to the methodological problems we explored in the previous chapter in order to focus (4.5) on one particular direction in which our project might be developed, this being in the area of political judgment.

Habermas's theory offers great critical power, but it operates with a "governor" in the area of democratic practice. This governor is designed to control specific kinds of applications that would, without it, be dangerous. It dampens the effectiveness of the theory in this area, but it also confuses both commentators and activists who look to Habermas's work for its political implications. Our task throughout this chapter is to understand the nature of the governor, the threat posed by its possible removal, and to see whether or not it does what Habermas intends it to do.

4.1 THE DISTINCTION BETWEEN MORALITY AND ETHICS

Discourse ethics, and its constituent principles (U) and (D), express, in formal and procedural terms, the moral point of view. As such, the theory confines itself to questions of right, leaving matters regarding the good life to actual participants. We have already encountered this limitation, first when we inspected Habermas's discussion of whether or not Hegel's critique of Kant was equally effective against discourse ethics, and again when we looked briefly at how an ideal procedure had to meet contextual concerns "halfway." Essentially, formal principles require fleshing out with contextual knowledge, and procedural principles are silent in regard to outcomes. Only actual participants themselves can fill in these gaps and complete the knowledge required to legitimate actual and specific practices. When a theory prescribes a way of life, a particular interpretation of the ideal or a certain outcome, it therefore, inappropriately, inhibits the input of participants.[5]

Habermas is clear that institutional designs involve questions of the good life, that they raise interpretative questions that the theory cannot prejudge, and that they constitute an outcome of discourse about which the theory has little to say. Questions of institutional design are, therefore, beyond the remit of theory.

What is being presented in these arguments is a particular kind of objection to utopian thinking. It is not an instrumental objection, whereby we notice that utopian thinking does not in fact achieve its intended end (though Habermas is quite sure that it does not). It is a normative objection. Habermas is claiming that institutional design constitutes an overextension of theory. It tempts the theorist into areas that are properly avoided and left to participants themselves. When theory attempts to overextend itself, or to operate without a governor, it becomes too powerful, even dangerous, for it then serves to devalue and oppress the participants. It is for this reason that we noted how, for Habermas, discriminative inadequacy in the area of institutional design is both a logical necessity and a moral imperative.

4.2 INSTITUTIONAL DESIGN AS A CATEGORY MISTAKE

Habermas presents a second argument, distinct yet related, in order to address with greater clarity the relationship between normative principles and institutional arrangements. Here, a complication is raised for all those theorists who, since Rousseau, have tried to use normative theory to select particular institutional designs. In this formulation, the limit to theory once again results in a discriminative inadequacy, though this time the objection to crossing from matters normative to empirical places greater stress on the danger of a particular kind of logical mistake.

The most detailed articulation of this argument occurs in the essay entitled "Legitimation Problems in the Modern State."[6] In a section where he attempts to reconstruct the changing concept of justification across history, he introduces the distinction between the "legitimating grounds" of a given order, and the actual "institutionalisations of domination."[7] He then goes on to say that, "Certain systems of institutions are compatible with a given level of justification; others are not." Here then, we are to be treated to a historical reconstruction of the evolving relationship between normative and empirical political theory.

Habermas seeks to trace a phylogenetic movement from "low" levels of justification, such as mythical narrative, through cosmologically grounded religions and classical natural law, to the formal principle of reason. In the writings of Kant and Rousseau, we find that "the formal conditions of justification themselves obtain legitimating force."[8] This "reflective" level of justification reached in the modern period can be described as a "procedural type of legitimacy." First worked out by Rousseau, it holds that legitimacy is determined by "the idea of an agreement that comes to pass among all parties, as free and equal."[9]

Then comes a crucial passage:

> Rousseau did not understand his ideal contract only as the definition of a level of justification; he mixed the introduction of a new principle of legitimation with proposals for institutionalising a just rule. The volonté generale was supposed not only to explicate grounds of validity but also to mark the place of sovereignty. This has confused the discussion of democracy right up to the present day.[10]

These are fighting words,[11] for we are here invited to follow an argument that, if understood, would dispel two hundred years of confusion. Yet the boldness of the claim may well be warranted, for precisely the "mixture" or "confusion" of normative and empirical theory lies at the heart of contemporary democratic thought.[12]

Habermas's distinction is derived from a phylogenetic argument, whereby justification is seen to evolve to a reflective level that is procedural. Such a principle of legitimacy is not the same kind of a thing as a concrete social form of organization—there is a *categorical* difference,[13] and it is because of this difference that Habermas's argument amounts to a restriction on the "cashing in" of the normative theory. Here, then, we confront a somewhat different thread of Habermas's limit to theory. Once again, the argument generates a discriminative inadequacy that, when not properly understood, produces confusion.

Rather than dally in the halfway houses of "greater deliberation," "public spheres," or "incipient discursive designs," Habermas illustrates the confusion with the example of direct or council democracy. The argument is structured in such a way as to suggest something like the following: "You who embrace the normative theory of discourse ethics might well expect that its factual embodiment must be that of direct democracy."[14] Yet the definition of democracy, he states, could simply be "precisely those political orders that satisfy the procedural type of legitimacy."[15] If this is the case:

> Questions of democratisation can be treated as what they are: as organisational questions. For it then depends on the concrete social and political conditions, on scopes of disposition, on information, and so forth, which types of organisation and which mechanisms are in each case better suited to bring about procedurally legitimate decisions and institutions.[16]

The theory of discourse ethics expressed in (U) and (D) thus provides us with a set of normative organizational options. The set itself is called democracy, and the selection of the set is as far as the normative theory can and should carry us. Once the set has been selected, the choice of members, or options within the set, is a matter for individual participants in actual situations. The normative theory is thus indeterminate as to empirical arrangements.[17] This limit on normative theory means that "democratisation cannot mean an *a priori* preference for a specific type of organisation, for example, for so-called direct democracy."[18]

Here then, Habermas is expressing far more than merely moral distaste for utopianism; more even than an instrumental critique of the same. He is also arguing that such thinking amounts to committing a *category mistake.* As he indicates with his allusion to two hundred years of confusion, there are many examples of this kind of logical error, and Habermas is suggesting that clarity regarding this distinction is a necessary condition for a democratic theory to be coherent. In effect, the limit to theory provides a critical tool with which to check whether a theory has a plausible account of the relation between empirical institutional design and grounding normative principle.[19]

So, for example, the reduction of democracy to a method for the selection of elites, which we find in empirical theorists such as Schumpeter, is questionable

> not because, say, this competition of elites is incompatible with forms of basic democracy—one could imagine initial situations in which competitive-democratic procedures would be most likely to produce institutions and decisions having a presumption of rational legitimacy. I find Schumpeter's concept questionable because it defines democracy by procedures that have nothing to do with the procedures and presuppositions of free agreement and discursive will-formation.[20]

In other words, the traditional critique of empirical theories: that they have the "status and character of conservative political ideology,"[21] appears to miss the mark. Democracy is not a question of this but not that organizational arrangement.[22] Nor is the predicate 'democracy' to be identified with a certain percentage of fulfilment of certain predefined methodological categories.[23] Habermas uses Schumpeter to question whether such theories are in fact democratic in any way. Here, the "decisionistic manner"[24] by which elites dominate is so far from the normative theory as to be unable to "borrow" any of its legitimacy at all.[25]

The problem with what are often called normative theories of democracy is, as we have seen, their tendency to confuse the "level of justification of domination with the procedures for the organisation of domination."[26] This results in their being unable ever to locate an empirical example of real democracy, for the normative theory can never be completely and perfectly reflected empirically.[27] It also lays them open to the simple yet powerful criticism that they do not gaze upon a real world.[28]

A proper understanding of the limit to theory thus provides us with certain tools with which we can scrutinize the full array of democratic theories. As such, it is an important contribution, and one that is both widely misunderstood and underestimated. Albrecht Wellmer is one of the few writers who not only seems to comprehend the meaning of the limit[29] but has also added to Habermas's own understanding. Habermas cites an unpublished manuscript by Wellmer[30] in which a direct movement from the "ethic of discourse" to an ideal form of life is described as a "short-cut."[31] The image of a "shortcut" is a good one, for it encapsulates what we have variously called the attempt to overextend theory, to move too quickly from normative to empirical matters and thus to be excessively utopian in one's institutional designs. To criticize a theory as committing a shortcut is to use a tool derived from our understanding of the limit to theory. Specifically, any democratic theory that arrives at a design for democratic institutions via the shortcut is deficient in terms of its rationality. Habermas uses this notion of the shortcut in order to defend himself against his critics. For example, he has claimed that Spaemann's criticism "fails to take account of an essential categorical distinction in [my position]: that between the philosophical problems underlying democratic legitimacy and organisational problems of democratic institutions."[32]

If we now return to the three dimensions of democratic legitimacy that we outlined in the previous chapter, the "who," the "how," and the "where," we can clearly see what Habermasian theory can do and what it cannot. Regarding who should be involved with the making of a legitimate decision, the theory, being democratic, calls for all, or the maximum possible. Regarding how such decisions are to be made, it requires that procedure be deliberative in character, and that such deliberation be as fair as is possible. Thus, the normative theory here begins to circumscribe positions that are of the "forum/public"[33] and "republican"[34] types. General approbations for autonomous public spheres are also members of the permitted set, as are notions such as "strong democracy,"[35] "unitary democracy,"[36] "self-reflective political cultures,"[37] and the "pedagogic" arguments found in Mill and Pateman.[38]

Of course, most democratic theorists sanction wide participatory rights (the first dimension) and then, following a "self-evident" assumption that favors representative over deliberative arrangements, become enmeshed in endless enquiries into the rationality of various aggregation devices (the second dimension). Habermas's normative argument is by no means abstract, irrelevant, and indiscriminate in regard to the second dimension of legitimacy. In a real advance on the liberal conception of democratic procedure, it calls for participation to be deliberative and discursive, and for the fairness of that deliberation to be understood in relation to a fully expressed epistemic criterion.[39] While the theory limits any *further* determination of institutional design, its epistemic core would seem to provide a promising tool with which to approach questions of rational deliberation. We inspected the various efforts to redeem this promise in the previous chapter.

The question as to whether Habermas's criticism of Rousseau is valid is an interesting one, not only because it provides his most focused articulation of the limit to theory, but also because two hundred years of theoretical confusion is a lot, and Habermas attributes all of it to Rousseau. The suggestion is that by committing the mistake that we can now refer to as the shortcut, Rousseau confuses his normative theory with its empirical instantiation. There are certainly places in Rousseau's writings, particularly in *The Social Contract,* where such confusion can be located.[40] But then there are places, as Habermas freely admits, where he himself makes such a mistake.[41] Elsewhere, Habermas does not confuse the two issues, and Rousseau also can show much evidence to support his own ability to keep them separate.

Cohen sums up his own investigation into the allegation against Rousseau by stating that Habermas's criticism does not, on balance, really hold.[42] Certainly, one could read him as the Jacobins did, and find in his words a justification of vanguardism and specific institutional designs, but this does some violence to the texts. Particularly, such a reading would need to show, first, that the normative theory marks the point of sovereignty in such a way as to have direct implications for the design of institutions. Second, it would need to establish that Rousseau was peddling a particular institutional design, or a mistaken belief that his normative theory determined a particular arrangement.

Neither argument seems to work. The first falls because, as all students of Rousseau are aware, he was careful to distinguish between popular government and popular sovereignty, and thus between executive and legislative power.[43] The second fails when it meets the vast disagreement between commentators as to the kind of arrangements Rousseau actually was endorsing,[44] and the wide range of arrangements Rousseau claimed to be compatible with the normative theory.[45]

With regard to Rousseau, Habermas has far more reasons to approve than to criticize. First, Rousseau's general will presents a cognitive core that, like Habermas's, sees the political process as a procedural location of a general interest. Second, there is an attention in Rousseau to normative theory and to the importance of applying it to the real world that Habermas clearly admires. Third, Rousseau attends carefully to the form participation should take if it is to be rational, even if he does understand this in a different way from Habermas.[46]

Rousseau did far more to advance democratic theory than he did to confuse it. Habermas's accusation, that Rousseau commits the mistake of trying to take the shortcut, may have more to do with there being so few complete democratic theories available with which to illustrate this confusion, for most are simply normative, or simply empirical, or see the second dimension of democratic legitimacy as a rational choice problem. Such one-dimensional theories are often guilty of the shortcut, but the criticism is less illustrative if the critic has to work out the other half of the theory before he/she can make the criticism stick. Rousseau is a good target for Habermas, not so much because he is guilty, but because he illustrates the importance of the negative limit to theory so clearly.

The difficult and subtle arguments Habermas adduces to articulate the limit to his theory do not really serve to dispel the confusion that affected Rousseau, many others, and even Habermas himself. Should we imagine that clarity regarding the empirical indeterminacy of normative principles dispels this confusion entirely, we need only return to the recent affirmative uses of Habermasian theory in the area of rights. If rights are to be valid empirico-legal instantiations of the normative principles of discourse ethics, then they must *not* be the result of a shortcut. Certainly, writers such as Ingram are quite aware of the limit to theory,[47] and they often adhere to it in their assertion that such rights can only be of the most general nature; that the normative theory can do no more discriminative work than this. Yet we should not allow this modesty to obscure the fact that, no matter how general and abstract, such rights are empirical arrangements that, if supported by a normative principle, seem to have fallen again into Rousseau's confusion.

Thus, Shelly holds that "despite Habermas's strictures to the contrary, the analytical distinction [between the legitimating grounds and the institutional structures of authority] cannot be adhered to in reality."[48] Rather, he suggests, the problem with Rousseau's position is that he locates legitimacy "in the actual decisions of a concretely assembled group of legislators . . . [and] in the universalistic quality of the actual decision." Against this, Shelly claims that Habermas locates legitimacy "in the *process* whereby the universality is achieved."[49]

Now it may be true that Habermas locates legitimacy in the process rather than the outcome, and that Rousseau occasionally stressed only the outcome. But it is not clear how the indication of an *additional confusion* in Rousseau helps to avoid the original confusion (the shortcut). Shelly's phrase "cannot be adhered to in reality,"[50] is a strange one. Because it is followed by a normative objection rather than an empirical one, it presumably refers to an argument that Shelly holds to be invalid rather than to a set of pragmatic outcomes that "cannot be adhered to." It is only as he develops his argument that we begin to see what is at stake in this phrase, for if the limit to theory excludes *all* institutionalizations of the normative principle, then there can be no empirico-legal rights that can claim normative backing from the theory.

Once again, we find ourselves caught in a twilight world where there are political implications, yet they are severely limited. While no shortcuts are permissible, the fact that the theory calls for the maximum possible deliberation and that this deliberation be as fair as possible would seem to ground a series of rights that are the basic enabling conditions for such deliberation. Yet such a series of rights, no matter how abstractly formulated, always face the threat of overextension, of violating the limit to theory.

Confusion, it seems, is endemic to attempts to cash in Habermasian theory for empirical arrangements. Nevertheless, we have identified an important thread to the limit to theory, and one that goes some way to preventing the theory degenerating into utopianism. Now, in order to further our understanding of the limit, we will consider, in greater detail, one particular attempt to overcome it. With the work of John Dryzek, we once again move from those fearful of the utopian aspect of Habermas's theory to those who are disappointed and feel that the theory is not utopian enough.

4.3 DRYZEK'S ATTEMPT TO OVERCOME THE LIMITS

When it comes to the possibility of a Habermasian politics, Dryzek's *Discursive Democracy*[51] gives us an excellent view of life at the edge of our collective understanding. Here, a bold and scholarly attempt is made to outline a deliberative democratic polity based avowedly on Habermasian normative principles. Dryzek understands that critical theory should do something of pragmatic value, and yet he knows also that theory should not try to do too much. The result is an exploration of an area in which other theorists have not felt comfortable. As he steps in, however, he shows significant ambivalence, and his many nervous asides to other theorists who have not felt able to follow him alert us again to the presence of confusion regarding the proper limits of theory. Dryzek thus combines a somewhat alarming optimism with, finally (and perhaps thankfully), a failure of nerve. Because of this, his work is highly instructive, not so much for its articulation of a Habermasian politics, but for the reasons it is unable to deliver one. As we inspect his attempt, we are able to unpack the limits to theory with greater precision.

Dryzek opens his inquiry with a general disapproval of instrumental rationality and objectivism in human affairs, and contrasts this with communicative rationality and critical theory. He then asserts that "commitment to the procedures of communicative rationality implies approval of certain broad kinds of political institutions."[52] Right away then, the general orientation is to be the question of institutional design. Dryzek's interest in this area is well supported by his knowledge of policy science, planning, and decision theory. Unlike many theorists, he has practical experience in conflict resolution, particularly around environmental issues, and has published extensively in both normative and empirical democratic theory. For these reasons, he seeks ways to expand discursive rationality into social and systemic areas where it can be used to solve human problems.[53] Approbation of the public sphere thus occurs at the beginning of his book, whereas for everyone else it is located at the end. Dryzek is keenly aware of the lack of help so far provided by critical theorists for practical problems. He laments that there is a "constructive dimension which has so far been missing from critical theory,"[54] and, having cited two benedictions for the public sphere (McCarthy and Bernstein) he states,

> Such scattered comments are the closest intimations of a project for the construction of discursive institutions to be found in the literature. . . . Critical theorists have so far failed to generate much in the way of model institutions, still less attempted to apply them to political reality.[55]

Dryzek wants to do better. He knows that our old and indefinite friend "the public sphere" is too often wheeled out as a placeholder for a whole area of democratic theory. He therefore intends to contrast "liberal democracy," which he sees as being dominated by voting, strategy, private interests, bargaining, and exchange, with "discursive democracy," characterized by an orientation to public interest, active citizenship, and debate that is open and face-to-face.[56]

Having stated his intention to design democratic institutions according to the normative theory, the argument then attempts to find a way through a series of objections to such a move. He turns first to the feminist critique of the alleged universalist homogeneity to be found in discourse ethics.[57] There are, he states, three ways in which communicative rationality avoids this conclusion.

First, it admits of an element of local arbitrariness in the determination of consensus, in other words, the ethos in which it occurs is inevitably fragmented.[58] Second, it admits that people can agree upon something for different reasons,[59] so that distinct abstract commitments can coexist with context-specific moral agreement.[60] Third, Dryzek follows Habermas[61] in asserting that communicative rationality can provide only procedural criteria.[62] This allows, indeed requires, a plurality of values, practices, and paradigms of personhood (or gender). Most emphatically, it does not seek to generate a universal theory of human needs.[63] Discourse ethics is, therefore, "minimalist."[64] It can prevent degeneration into a hopeless pluralism yet at the same time allow for a multiplicity of views.

From this, it is clear that Dryzek understands the theory to be limited by its concentration on the procedural conditions of democratic legitimacy and its refusal to stipulate the outcome of a legitimate discourse. He knows that the normative principle of discourse ethics, (D), protects a place for the input of participants who meet the validity-claims of speech "halfway." Because a particular procedure, or an institutional design, is something produced by discourse, it is an outcome. The problem Dryzek faces, then, is to retain the centrality of the participant's input and yet find some validity for his own suggestions as a lone theorist outside their practical discourse. When he suggests that "the design of social and political practices can itself be a discursive process,"[65] he indicates that he has identified this important component of the limit to theory. The question is, has he identified all the components of the limit? One is tempted to suggest that while Habermas might agree that designs *can* be discursive, he might be more comfortable with the stronger statement that they can *only* be discursive.

Next, Dryzek turns to a more common objection to institutional design, this time leveled by critical theorists generally. Confronted with exploitative social relations, critical theory has plied its trade as an illuminator of exploitation. It is thus more suited to the critique of existing social relations than to suggesting what should be erected in their place. As he puts it, "a fear of foisting institutions and practices on already oppressed groups by outsiders who cannot know the true interests of these groups makes critical theorists reluctant to go into specifics."[66]

Stated in this way, we can see that critical theory draws back from utopian thinking because of a healthy fear of instrumental reason, vanguardism, and other secular theodicies. Interestingly, critical theory's historical and recurrent inability to successfully stipulate normative grounds for its social critique has resulted in its objection to utopianism being essentially an empirical one. Following an honest appraisal of the historical evidence, the critical theorist is able to show that utopianism often gives rise to terror. This objection to utopianism thus turns on the empirical observation: *that it does not achieve its stated end*. Here, then, we encounter the second component of the limit to theory: it amounts to a (once bitten) anxiety regarding rational and systematic efforts to control social relations.

Dryzek recognizes this objection to utopianism and seeks, partly, to overcome it. He wants to show that he is "aware of such hazards"[67] and that much of critical theory's anxiety is due to an unnecessarily pejorative understanding of the verb 'design.'[68] Yet this does not capture the full force of Habermas's objection to utopianism. Many critical theorists, devoid of normative criteria upon which to base social critique, are limited to an empirical critique of utopianism. But Habermas is not so constrained. His objection to utopianism is also, as we have seen, strongly normative. What appears in critical theory as a "reluctance to go into specifics" is, in Habermas, a fully developed normative refusal to overextend theory beyond its proper limits. A shortcut, a category mistake, a stipulated form of life: these, for Habermas, are the products of invalid utopian reasoning.

Here then, we should begin to feel uneasy with Dryzek's understanding of the negative limit to theory. Nothing short of a complete refutation of the limit will allow him to proceed with his project of designing democratic institutions. Yet he nowhere attempts such a refutation, mostly because he nowhere formulates it in its full complexity. The limit cannot be summed up merely as a call to honor (D) and an empirical objection to utopianism.

Dryzek, believing he has sufficiently acknowledged the negative limit to theory, now feels he has preserved a place for "constructive critique."[69] Such a critique is characterized, he states, by a theory that, while not providing blueprints, still offers useful and conceivable alternatives to the status quo. The stage is now set for a move from abstract formulations of "authentic public spheres" to real-world institutional designs.[70] Dryzek thus prepares to boldly go where no critical theorist has gone before.

He then proceeds to describe the empirical institutions that, he claims, would reflect the normative theory. First, model institutions would have certain negative characteristics. Hence, any kind of hierarchy, barriers to participation and formal rules are forbidden.[71] More positively, participation requires a level of communicative competence that in turn will require resources and institutional support.[72]

Returning for a moment to our characterization of democratic legitimacy as a three-dimensional conceptual object involving questions of "who" is to be involved in the making of decisions, "how" they are to be made and "where," we can see that Dryzek's proposals address all three. In terms of "who," Dryzek's calls for all (or the maximum) to be able to participate. In terms of "how," his argument calls for participation that is discursive and fair, with the term 'fairness,' being understood according to Habermas's normative articulation. Finally, regarding "where," discourse that is free from domination is to take place in public spheres or discursive fora within civil society, the product of which is then to be fed into the decision-making apparatus of the state.

Yet his attempt to address the second dimension, the manner of participation, begins to alert us to the way in which his argument is overextended. He opens his treatment of this dimension by asserting that the actual manner of the debate must itself be an expression of communicative ethics.[73] To illustrate this, he outlines some characteristics of "principled negotiation" as described by Fisher and Ury.[74] These are: the separation of individual egos from problem-solving tasks at hand, emphasis on interests of parties rather than on bargaining positions, efforts to generate proposals to benefit all actors, and the striving for criteria separate from particular interests of each party—all of which would be scrutinized discursively. Additionally, the decision rule suggested by the ideal speech situation would be that of unanimity,[75] though in instances where this was unattainable, compromise could be rational in so far as it was arrived at under similarly antidominative conditions.[76]

Dryzek also maps out other practical possibilities, such as the legal institutionalization of the principles of discourse, a "holistic" paradigm of social experimentation,[77] and a series of existing institutions and practices in which some aspects of communicative ethics are already instantiated. Examples of the latter are mediation[78] and regulatory negotiation.[79] In addition, he explicates the possibility of comparative evaluation wherein practices are inspected for the degree to which they approximate to ideal speech.

These suggestions are certainly interesting, yet surely, whether or not they actually reflect the normative conditions of communicative ethics, and whether they are the *only* reflections that satisfy those conditions, or even the best, is a more complex question. Perhaps, again, we must accept that exactly which of these arrangements, and how they are to be deployed, are questions more properly addressed by actual participants. If this is the case, we once more confront the limit to theory, and Dryzek's suggestions amount to little more than interesting possibilities for participants to discuss.

The final two thirds of Dryzek's book outlines arguments that purport to indicate how discourse in fact offers a superior method of providing public goods,[80] is more flexible as a decision method,[81] and copes better with complex social problems.[82] While such arguments, if valid, certainly provide reasons to adopt particular practices, they do not fall within our present concern, for the simple reason that they are empirical, even instrumental, in their nature. Empirical arguments can never justify an action, for an evaluative criterion such as efficiency can give rise to morally unacceptable practices. It should be noted anyway that such arguments assert no more than has already been derived from the normative arguments, to wit: deliberation within a public sphere is a good thing. We already know that the counterfactual propositions (U) and (D) constitute a justification. The problem we now face is how to embody this justification in actual practices; in other words, how can empirical institutions derive legitimacy from the normative argument? Though constrained by certain limits, which we are here exploring, we are searching for democratic arrangements that express the epistemic conditions of democratic legitimacy offered us by Habermas's discourse ethics.

One of Dryzek's problems is that he is not entirely pellucid about the nature of this epistemic base. In this sense, his work, though avowedly Habermasian, becomes increasingly similar to that of Benjamin Barber.[83] With both theorists, the lack of focus upon the cognitive core threatens a degeneration into the aporias of relativism.[84] Dryzek states at one point that the only source of authority is, and he uses Habermas's phrase, "the force of the better argument,"[85] and there is a sparse pair of references to "the conditions of communicative ethics." Yet, aside from the general conditions of equality and reciprocity, he nowhere really gets to grips with the cognitivist heart that Habermas has offered him.

At the end of Dryzek's attempt, we find ourselves once more on the outside: in terms of institutional design, he is never able to state more than the most general approbation for deliberation within autonomous public spheres. His discursive designs are either too loosely connected to the normative theory or are not properly empirical at all. This inability to adequately move from ideal to real is well illustrated by his claim that there should be no hierarchy within a democratic institution. For we already know that Habermas's normative theory offers no justification for hierarchy. Yet, given the factual prevalence of hierarchical arrangements,[86] our practical interest centers on the justification of *partial* hierarchies, and on trade-offs between ideal participation and actual arrangements that emerge in response to the pressures of the real world. For example, under what conditions would a partial hierarchy be justified? how? why? and to what extent?

Dryzek's work is at once bold and tentative. He knows what practice needs from theory and his expectations are stimulated by Habermas's discourse ethics. In the end, though, he can only maintain his optimism by effectively changing the subject. What begins as an attempt to stipulate the empirical arrangements that are justified by the normative theory ends in an inspection of extant arrangements using the regulative ideal of discourse free from domination. Once again, democratic theory collapses back into interpretative critique, and yet another theorist fails to emerge from the labyrinth.

Dryzek does not re-emerge because he does not precisely delineate the nature of the Minotaur: the limit to theory. He sees the limit as having two components: that designs are constrained by the principle (D), and that there are empirical reasons to fear utopian blueprints. For Habermas, both these components receive a stronger and more complex formulation, and in addition, the limit has other components. In order to complete our unpacking of the limit, and thus to fully understand why Habermas keeps pointing at the opening of the labyrinth and shaking his head, we should note how Dryzek's efforts to design institutions, though heralded with much fanfare, occupy only a small portion of the book we are presently discussing. By far the larger portion, and arguably the more successful, is the investigation of particular existing practices in the light of the normative theory. This is no accident, and it is a point that rewards greater attention.

First of all, it is clear that the *ex ante* design of an institution is a quite different type of task from an *ex post* evaluation of an institution that already exists. The distinction is drawn by Elster,[87] who, through an investigation of Tocqueville's assessment of American democracy, shows particularly that one can only take into account the consequences of a practice when one evaluates *ex post*. Elster wants to use the distinction to show that one cannot justify a practice *ex ante* by reference to the side-effects or secondary consequences of that practice. Thus, he seeks to criticize the pedagogic arguments put forward by theorists such as Mill and Pateman: that participation is desirable because of its educational side-effects. The argument is an important one, for it blocks off a common justificatory argument for deliberative democracy.[88] Here, though, we are primarily interested in the distinction between two points of view to which Elster's argument alludes.

Once an institution is extant, it already has some positive and negative effects on people's lives that can be described, criticized, and uncovered. We have noted previously that this *ex post* point of view has been, historically, the most comfortable for critical theorists. Thus, Habermas's careful use of the phrase "finding arrangements" in the following quotation indicates the *ex post* evaluative point of view, for the verb "finding" suggests that the practices are already extant:

> [O]ne must think in terms of process categories. I can imagine the attempt to arrange a society democratically only as a self-controlled learning process. It is a question of *finding* arrangements which can ground the presumption that the basic institutions of the society and the basic political decisions would meet with the unforced agreement of all those involved, if they could participate, as free and equal, in discursive will-formation.[89]

Habermas clearly holds the view that discourse ethics can inform the *ex post* evaluation of extant practices. However, the limit he places on his theory amounts to an insurmountable restriction on the *ex ante* design of institutions by anyone other than participants in a situated practical discourse.

4.4 FORMULATING THE LIMITS TO THEORY

We are now able to formulate the limit to theory in its full complexity, to outline its various components, and to relate these to the methodological problems we encountered upon application of the theory to questions of practice. Generally, we have seen how the limit to theory is made up of various threads, all of which address a particular aspect of the relation between the outcome of a decision process and the procedure by which it is achieved. Each thread of the cable also addresses a particular way of approaching the problem of utopian thinking. Having formulated the limit, we will return to the question of what practical implications are not screened out by its restrictions, or, as many theorists have expressed it: What utopian content remains in Habermasian theory?

The Components of the Limit to Theory

1. Moral claims, unlike ethical ones, can be redeemed analogously to a truth claim: they have a cognitive core. Discourse ethics concerns moral questions, leaving ethical ones to the participants themselves.

2. The normative principle of discourse ethics, (D), is procedural only, and does not address the outcome of a decision. It cannot, therefore, be used to preselect a particular arrangement, for such arrangements are themselves, properly an outcome of deliberation among actual participants.

3. History teaches us that utopianism is dangerous and does not achieve its desired end, and that human intention has ironic consequences.

4. Using the normative theory to pick out and design institutional arrangements involves a category mistake. One cannot take such a shortcut from normative to empirical matters. Normative theory picks out the set of deliberative democratic arrangements, but cannot distinguish (and should not) between set members.

5. The limit rules out any *ex ante* designs, except those undertaken discursively by participants. It permits, for the lone theorist, only *ex post* evaluations.

6. Some areas of human activity are, in modernity, *appropriately* (due to the resulting efficiency gains) coordinated by instrumental reason. Just as instrumental reason should be prevented from colonizing areas appropriately coordinated by communicative reason, so *communicative reason should know its place*. This is why Habermas speaks of "self-limiting" public spheres.

7. Discourse ethics is a theory of justification: it articulates the moral point of view. As such it is indeterminate on many practical questions. To fully understand the role of its formal ideal, one must include a moment of application, wherein participants flesh out the universal with particular concerns, motivations, and salient information.

When we sought to use Habermasian normative theory to aid us in the design and evaluation of democratic institutions, we found that a series of recurrent methodological problems seemed to block our way. Now we see that the critical power of the normative theory is, in fact, carefully limited by a series of arguments that prevent it from degenerating into excessive utopianism, or into being used in oppressive ways. Many of the methodological problems we encountered arose from the formal and universal nature of the theory, for the level of its abstraction gives rise again and again to discriminative failure, lacuna, and indeterminacy in comparative evaluation. These problems are further accentuated by the limit to theory. The governor that prevents the slide into utopianism effectively bars theory from certain areas, insisting that only participants can fill them. As such, the methodological problems encountered upon application are not weaknesses of the theory. One cannot criticize the theory for not doing what no theory *should* do. Certainly, it is disappointing that human problems cannot be solved by theory, but this is not the fault of theory. The object of our disappointment should not, therefore, be Habermasian theory, but the human condition itself.

The project of a Habermasian politics has indeed stalled. Yet now we can see that it has done so for some very good reasons. Habermas accepts that his theory cannot preselect the form of either the "processes of enlightenment"[90] or the appropriate political strategies,[91] and we must follow him in this regard. But the growing clarity with which we understand the limit to theory should not cloud our memory. There *are* things it can provide, and it is still intended to be a *critical* theory, one whose practical implications and affirmative uses further emancipation. Once again, we face the difficulty of understanding how to use a theory that provides an "emancipatory ideal which cannot guide emancipatory practice."[92] The sophistication with which Habermas articulates the limit to theory therefore raises the question of whether his theory retains any utopian content at all.

By concentrating on questions of institutional justice and ignoring "those qualities of individual life-histories and collective life-forms which make [lives] fulfilling or unfulfilling,"[93] Habermas has blocked off any possibility of deciding between forms of life, of evaluating the integrity of their values, and of which form of life is the happiest, the most fulfilled, the most joyous. While we would want to follow him when he says that forms of life are not to be stipulated in advance,[94] we are also aware that arguments against modernity that assert a loss of meaning, and a growing anomie have a particular power. Habermas is himself impressed by such arguments.[95] If we are unable to offer anything that might address them, then we are left with a "lingering sense of dissatisfaction with the manner in which Habermas vindicates the project of the Enlightenment."[96] For Habermas "admits the possibility that a free society could be at the same time a meaningless one, or that emancipated individuals could still feel frustrated and alienated."[97]

The problem here is that to ask normative theory to guide the design and evaluation of democratic institutions is, in part, to ask "how do we get somewhere else from here?" Thus expressed, our question assumes a need for substantial political change. Such change entails both the selection of means and ends. While the former raises significant instrumental problems,[98] the latter, even if carefully open-ended, clearly involves a utopian dimension.[99]

Benhabib draws a distinction between change that is the "fulfilment" of the unfinished tasks and cultural promises of the present, and that which is "transfigurational," involving a radical rupture with the present.[100] This allows her to identify the kind of change being asked for by Marx and the early critical theorists. She then goes on to delineate a utopian moment in Habermas's extension of the Kohlbergian scheme of moral development. The stage of "universalised need interpretations has an unmistakable utopian content to it," she says, and "points to a transfigurative vision of bourgeois universalism."[101]

Wellmer also identifies a utopian moment in discourse ethics.[102] Within communicative rationality, he claims, is contained the concept of an "idealised life-world," which he suggests we view less as a "geometric idealisation" to which the real world must infinitely approximate and more as a "centre of gravitation" or as an "attractive force which becomes proportionately stronger."[103] Here then, we encounter again the utopian element in discourse ethics as a regulative ideal, as a criterion for cultural interpretation, and as a moral pressure on the facts. Habermas states his position on this question thus: "Ethical universalism does indeed have a utopian content, but it does not sketch out a utopia."[104]

4.5 CONCERNING JUDGMENT

We have seen that the strength of discourse ethics is in the area of *ex post* evaluation: that it gives theorists in cultural criticism, sociological research, and political theory a standard with which to assess practice. As theorists attempt to apply the moral standard, and thus to contextualize the formal theory and give it content, they encounter a series of recurrent methodological problems. These problems, (of excessive abstraction, of discriminative failure, lacuna, and the difficulty of making comparative evaluations) arise in part from the formal and universal nature of discourse ethics, and in part from the carefully conceived limit to theory, which prevents its utopian element from degenerating into authoritarianism. So constrained, the theorist struggles with these methodological problems in an effort to generate interpretative insights. Such insights, guided by a fully justified regulative ideal, are educative rather than pragmatic. They illuminate the structures of our social world and encourage us to take responsibility for those portions of that world of which we are the authors. In the area of political theory, this has given rise to considerable interest, most of which has concentrated on that traditional object of political study: the state. Thus, we find Habermasian scholarship addressing questions such as the basis of the legitimacy of liberal institutions, the degree to which political culture supports a post-conventional morality and the connections between morality and constitutional law.

We have also seen that *ex ante* design is ruled out for the theorist, and is instead seen as a task for participants only. For their part, participants also face methodological problems as they attempt to contextualize the universal afforded by the theory. Efforts by participants to use the theory to evaluate institutions *ex post* confront the same discriminative inadequacy as did their theorizing counterparts. Presumably, the problem of comparative evaluation that we explored in the previous chapter would present particular difficulties for participants. Situated in the realm of action, they endlessly confront forking paths, the need to choose one and abandon another, and to select between alternative courses of action that have institutional ramifications. Should we do A or B? What would be the consequences of each? Should we structure our practice in this way or that? This is the form of the problem of comparative evaluation as faced by participants making real decisions.[105] The lack of weighting and lexicographic ordering of the components of ideal speech here results in a difficulty of comparative evaluation amounting to a real incapacity to judge.

The central tension throughout Habermas's work is that between validity and facticity. For the democratic *theorist*, this tension lies at the very heart of Habermasian political interpretation and critique. For the *participant*, it plays itself out in the faculty of judgment. Each, in their attempt to contextualize the theory, seeks to cross from questions of validity to those of facticity, yet they do so from a quite different perspective. The distinction between these two perspectives arises directly out of the limitations Habermas places on his theory. The democratic theorist, oriented primarily to the state, or to society as a whole, seeks normatively grounded social criticism, and perhaps also state-level reforms that would deepen democracy. The participant, situated in an actual group, must maximize democracy on the ground floor: within actual democratic fora.

Both perspectives are clearly important, yet while discourse ethics so carefully preserves a place for the input of participants, it then seems to lose interest in them. We noticed this before when we witnessed the lacuna that arises in those affirmative uses of Habermasian normative theory seeking to deepen democratic practice. Such applications tended to stop at the point of calling for an increase in democratic fora—they did not continue on down, as it were, in order to address the actual functioning of such fora.

So Habermas, himself facing a series of forking paths as he develops his theory, can be seen to have made two important choices. I want to suggest that the combination of these choices is what prevents any further development of a Habermasian political project. First, he chose to concentrate on justificatory and normative matters at the expense of contextual and empirical ones. This important choice was made at the start of his development of a discourse ethics. Second, he has chosen to orient his normative theory, at least in regard to its articulation of democratic legitimacy, to the level of the state and to society as a whole. Again, both these choices are eminently defensible, yet they have an important effect, for they direct our attention away from the one affirmative use of the theory that is not constrained by normative limitation: this being the *ex ante* design of institutions by participants themselves.

Habermas does occasionally make reference to the perspective of the designing participant, and he does so particularly in one intriguing passage where he is exploring the limit to theory. Though he is describing the problem of design for a society as a whole, he makes an offhand remark that perfectly captures the problem of design as it is faced by participants in an actual democratic forum. "I can imagine," he states, "the attempt to arrange a society democratically only as *a self-controlled learning process*."[106] Beyond this, however, Habermas has little to say about such a process.

If, from the participant's perspective, the moment of application entails the taking of a normative ideal by a group and fitting it to a particular context, in other words, in finding arrangements that are as fair as possible, then we seem to be describing a process of moral or political judgment. Habermas himself has referred to this process as one of "mediation,"[107] and it is given a more exact description in an important statement by Benhabib:

> Here we have a model of moral judgment which assumes that in the act of judging, what we do is subsume a particular case under a general rule. We judge this particular X to be an instance of the rule Y. Presumably, communicative ethics is a procedure which enables us to establish the normative rightness of the rule Y.[108]

Yet, she goes on to state:

> this is a very poor model of moral judgment, for moral judgment concerns precisely that mental activity which allows us to identify X as an instance of Y.[109]

Here we confront the significant difficulties incumbent upon construing the moment of application in terms of a mental activity such as moral judgment.[110] For now, application becomes reliant on the attainment of thresholds of mental functioning in such areas as learning processes and experiences,[111] repression, sublimation, and displacement,[112] not to mention the cognitive, temporal, and motivational constraints outlined earlier.

Even if we follow Ingram's clarification[113] and back away from the requirement that ideal speech requires anything more than presently existing truth criteria and informational quality in order to be of normative validity,[114] we still face significant difficulties. First, there are uncertainties as to how a particular situation is to be classified in order that it be subsumed under the correct rule.[115] Second, it may be that in the contingent world of concrete contexts, we might be more in need of justifications for exceptions to generally accepted rules rather than for rules themselves.[116] Third, the general cognitive indeterminacy of moral and political choices may be wider than we care to admit.[117] Subject to problems in the evaluation of local versus global effects,[118] partial versus net effects,[119] short-term versus long-term effects,[120] and transitional versus steady-state effects,[121] Elster suggests that theory may, in fact, be almost wholly useless.[122] We might sum up these concerns by again quoting Benhabib:

> Both moral sagacity and strategic-politic savvy would be involved in the application of communicative ethics to life contexts. And about them [Habermasian] theory has little to say.[123]

Once again we appear to find our route blocked. The difficulties in understanding what precisely is going on when participants deploy an ideal in order to make a moral judgment is causing us to stray close to the Aristotelian notion of prudential judgment, with all the relativistic problems that position entails.[124]

If there is an escape from the iatrogenic dilemma, it can only lie in an understanding of applicatory judgment, for despite all its problems, there is simply no other way across the gap between normative and empirical theory. We clearly know how to make judgments, because we do it everyday.[125] And we clearly know how to communicate, even when we do not thematize the necessary presuppositions of speech-acts. Yet are we entirely sure about the relation between these two activities?

On the one hand, Habermas gives us an argument whereby communication is seen to rest on certain inescapable presuppositions. When these are questioned in argumentation, further presuppositions are called upon that can be formulated as ideal speech. Yet on the other hand, all the problems of application we have been considering suggest that while calling our attention to moral judgment, Habermas's argument pushes us to see such judgment in terms of the application of an ideal. Certainly, all discourses approximate to or anticipate ideal speech, yet it cannot be that we *judge the validity* of those discourses in terms of the degree to which they instantiate the ideal. If this were the case, then just as methodological problems upon application render theorists unable to accurately assess instances of communication with ideal speech, so participants would never succeed in making judgments at all.

In discursive will-formation we deploy the presuppositions of argumentation, and these can certainly be formalized into an ideal of communication that is free from domination. Yet that does not imply, and in fact cannot mean, that participants make judgments solely by way of an act of comparison with that ideal. Using a slightly different language, we might say that while, in regard to instances of communication, the particular is always a negative/regressive instantiation of the universal, our assessment of the particular cannot be characterized in terms of an asymptotic appraisal.[126] It seems more likely that judgment instead resembles a strangely bifurcated process whereby we learn endless cases (and it may be that we are quite unable to grasp any rule at all except by way of its applied instantiations[127]) and only slowly learn to describe general rules.[128] Such rules would then be an expression of some shared predicate of those cases yet would never become the standard by which new cases are evaluated.

The point here is to raise the possibility that Habermas has assumed something substantial and contentious in characterizing judgment along the lines of an asymptotic approach to an ideal,[129] or in terms of an "approximation assumption,"[130] or "in analogy to geometrical idealisations."[131] If the political implications of Habermasian theory *could* be extended into a somewhat different object domain than the state, that is, the functioning of democratic fora themselves, then our understanding of applicatory judgment becomes crucial. From the perspective of participants attempting to arrange their deliberations in a fair manner, and thus engaged in a "self-controlled learning process," we would again be seeking a synthesis of validity and facticity. In such a realm, however, judgment cannot be conceived simply as an act of approximation. For statist democratic theorists, institutional design is restricted by the limit to theory. Yet theorists also tend to ignore questions of institutional design as encountered by participants. When we become interested in such questions we find ourselves severely hampered by a problematic conception of judgment.

The strong universalism of Habermas's project, and its statist orientation, makes for a rigorous justificatory theory and a studiously tentative liberal/deliberative politics. It also distracts attention from the problems of a democratic politics as encountered from the perspective of participants in an actual discourse. As we have seen, like Odysseus when confronted by Scylla and Charybdis, Habermas is a sufficiently gifted captain to have chosen one side of the iatrogenic dilemma. He pays a terrible price for his choice, but it is one he has learned to live with, and afterwards, he is still afloat. There is no Habermasian politics, but there is a normative basis for social criticism, even if all attempts to actually use this basis are subject to chronic methodological problems.

One thing is certain: we should not draw the conclusion, in having articulated the difficulties inherent in asserting that normativity is to be derived in some way from an idealization of rationality, that critical reflection has no role to play in judgment at all. For as Laslett so cogently asserts:

> Rational demonstration may not be the predominant method of getting things done in politics, but it must be the only method which those who analyse society shall use to demonstrate to each other and everybody else what the issues are.[132]

Understanding, in regard to politics, is something that is to be derived from the interplay of normative and empirical concerns. If a gap has opened between them, then we are forced to strain our eyes, for only here can we find knowledge of our interactions with others. It is true that the gap is poorly lit, and that the theoretical beam of light peters out into darkness. But within this gap lies the question of how democratic fora might actually, and rationally, operate. We have referred to this question as the missing tier of theory. In order to begin to address it, we now turn, in the following chapter, to the nature of political judgment.

PART 3

The Nature of Political Judgment

CHAPTER 5

Habermasian Difficulties with Judgment

For Habermas, meaning is internally related to validity. Speech-acts make sense because they raise validity-claims that can be redeemed in rational argumentation. At the same time, argumentation is rational because it anticipates an ideal of communication that is free from domination. Thus, *normative* validity is also internally related to meaning.

In the previous chapter, we looked at the recurrent methodological problems that occur when we try to use the ideal to make interpretative evaluations, and we saw that these problems arise both from the level of abstraction of the normative theory, and the careful limits Habermas places on the practical implications of his theory. In particular, we began to question the assumption that because communication derives its normative validity from the anticipation of ideal speech, we therefore make judgments regarding normative validity by assessing the degree to which a particular act of communication approximates to the ideal. In this chapter, we will look more closely at Habermas's most recent work on the process by which universal knowledge is applied in contexts, and on the various critiques of his position put forward by his commentators.

We begin, therefore, (5.1) with Habermas's and Günther's articulation of the "differentiation thesis," whereby norms generated in discourses of justification are seen to require a second type of discourse, that of application, in order for them to relate to actual contexts. Following this, we will inspect a series of criticisms of this conception of moral judgment (5.2), especially those mounted by Benhabib and Cooke, Wellmer, McCarthy, and Ferrara. Generally, the argument presented is that discourses of application remain tied to what Kant would call a "determinant" model of judgment, whereas the various criticisms of such a model point us rather in the direction of a "reflective" conception of that activity. This will allow us to inspect the various difficulties inherent in a reflective conception of judgment (5.3), and to assess the disagreements among commentators as to the nature of the universal to which reflective judgments appeal. Our concern throughout will be to uphold the internal relation of meaning to normative validity while at the same time to reject Habermas's approximation assumption regarding the nature of judgment.

5.1 JUSTIFICATION AND APPLICATION

In the object domain appropriate to empirico-theoretic knowledge, "facts" are independent of history. That is to say that factual knowledge (even if fallible) is "complete," for the ontology of its object is not contingent, and there is no division between questions of justification and application.[1] The different ontology of the object of moral-practical knowledge, however, admits of historical change, not just in terms of the possibility of subsequent additional knowledge about the object, but also because of variation over time in the object itself. Where objects are intersubjectively constituted, evolution of learning processes produce evolution of objects. In such a realm, attempts to deploy moral-practical knowledge as a guide for action[2] require not only that a claim be justified, but that it be applicable to a historically contingent particularity. Valid practical knowledge claims are, therefore, only complete when "compensated"[3] with a knowledge of how they are to be applied here and now.[4]

As we have seen, Habermas's reformulation of the Kantian basis for normative validity shares with its ancestor an abstraction from contextual concerns. Thus, "the validity of a norm does not depend on the conditions of its application."[5] Indeed, a norm may be valid yet remain inapplicable in a specific situation.[6] The historical dimension of the social world means that, unlike empirical-theoretic knowledge, "no norm contains within itself the rules of its application."[7] According to Habermas then, moral-practical knowledge requires that we carefully distinguish between the justification of a norm and its application to a specific context, a distinction Wellmer has termed the "differentiation thesis."[8]

In a realm where we may confront two (or more) conflicting yet justified norms, how are we to decide which is the most appropriate to our situation?[9] Given that we live in a specific and real world, how is decontextualized knowledge to be contextualized in order that our moral knowledge also be practical?

Once again our problem lies in the space between Kant and Hegel. Buffeted on the one side by the need to abstract from particular situations and individual cases in order to articulate impartiality and consensus as a universalist moral point of view, and on the other by the Hegelian charge that Kant ignored the problem of the application of impartiality,[10] discourse ethics "cannot evade the difficult problem of whether the application of rules to particular cases necessitates a separate and distinct faculty of prudence or judgment."[11] The threat, of course, is that such a faculty "would tend to undercut the universalistic claim of justificatory reason because it is tied to the parochial context of some hermeneutic starting point."[12]

On the one hand then, Habermas accepts the Hegelian charge and makes "a careful distinction between the validity—or justice—of a norm and the correctness of singular judgments that prescribe some particular action on the basis of a valid norm."[13] It is for this reason that a decision to "do the right thing" requires a "two-stage process of argument consisting of justification followed by application of norms."[14] On the other hand, however, Habermas is anxious not to lose the Kantian gain of a context-independent universalist ethics.[15] He thus wants to resist the neo-Aristotelian solution to this problem, which jettisons universalism in favor of a more contextual faculty of judgment.[16] The aporias of this neo-Aristotelian view signal, for Habermas, a degeneration into contextualism that posits the moments of justification and application of a norm as being intertwined,[17] and where moral practical claims are only validated by a particular ethos.[18]

Habermas's attempt to resolve this dilemma has been advanced particularly by the work of Klaus Günther. By showing that the distinction between justification and application emerges as moral consciousness develops,[19] Günther suggests that we now confront *two* problems when we seek to validate a course of action. First, a norm is to be justified *prima facie* by the principle of universalizability (U) pursued in a practical discourse (D) under specified normative conditions (ISS). Second, *prima facie* valid norms are to be appropriately applied to specific situations. Günther understands appropriateness argumentation to include the matching of a norm to a situation, the way in which a situation is described and the coherence of the norm with all the other norms belonging to a given way of life.[20]

Importantly, appropriateness argumentation resists the Hegelian critique of Kantian ethics in that it does not entail an appeal to a separate faculty of judgment. Certainly, the moment of application ushers in a variety of contextual content, such as empathic concern for others, questions of individual and collective identity,[21] new knowledge, new situation descriptions,[22] new understandings of norm coherence,[23] changing circumstances, improved assessments of consequences and side-effects, the particularity of the situation, and so forth.[24] Yet it remains the case that when considering the question of what is appropriate, "the principles of practical reason take effect."[25] We thus delineate a second type of discourse, that of application, where the principle of universalizability is replaced by one of appropriateness, and where hermeneutic insights are incorporated in order to "complete" the initial discourse of justification.

Both types of discourse pursue their respective goals impartially. Thus, "aspects of the good life in a situation can be integrated into practical deliberations without having to surrender the universalistic claim of practical reason."[26] Günther introduces a "time and knowledge index"[27] to (U), producing what he calls the "weaker formulation."[28] This then allows the discourse of application to complete the prima facie claim through an impartial consideration of a specific constellation of knowledge and historical circumstance.

It might be worth pausing here in order to ensure clarity about the precise relation of a norm to a judgment. Our interest in political judgment amounts to an inquiry into "doing the right thing."[29] In other words, we seek to deploy practical reason in such a way as to combine normative validity with a sensitivity to contexts. Discourses of justification concern themselves only with questions of rightness, of normative validity. In such discourses, moral concerns are abstracted from questions of the good life and norms arising from the lifeworld are tested for their universalizability. Norms that pass this test (in a practical discourse conducted under specified normative conditions) are then available for deployment in particular situations. In order to make a decision as to the "right thing to do," participants in discourses of application move beyond the exclusive orientation to the validity-claim of rightness and must consider the claims of truth and sincerity as well. The reason for this is that the appropriate selection and application of a norm to a specific context ushers in questions of needs, of consequences, of side-effects and identities, that range across all three validity-claims. It also raises the question of which validity-claim (or combination thereof) correctly pertains to a particular aspect of the situation being considered.[30] Judgment, here in regard to the right course of action in a specific situation, involves the appropriate application of a norm. *Discourses of application are therefore, in effect, discourses of judgment.*

Because our investigation seeks to derive assistance, from Habermas's theory, for the design and evaluation of democratic institutions, we have described it as an attempt to cross over from normative to empirical theory. Discourses of justification raise purely normative questions; we only confront the question of crossing over when we consider discourses of application (judgment). From here on then, our inspection of collective judgment will concentrate on the analysis of this latter type of discourse. Importantly, both Habermas and Günther are anxious to retain the universalistic and cognitivist core of discourse ethics and have taken great care to preserve this core in the logic whereby norms are applied. In order to further our understanding of collective judgment therefore, we must now consider the way the universal is related to the particular in discourses of application. For this, we must once again return to Kant.

For Kant, practical reason was a cognitive endeavor. His political philosophy was based on a general theory of judgment that saw this faculty as thinking the particular as contained under the universal. In moral questions, Kant largely ignored the problem of application because he viewed the categorical imperative as a law that stipulated how the particular was to be subsumed under the universal.[31] Though application of the rule might require some skill,[32] the kind of judgment involved in moral questions required no deliberation,[33] nor did it admit of rhetoric.[34] There was, therefore, a certain simplicity in the kind of judgment we were seen to deploy in moral questions, for in viewing our duty as essentially obvious to us, we were required merely to be honest with ourselves and consistent in our rationality. Because, in questions of morality, the universal was given in advance, the type of judgment adduced in moral questions was determinant.[35]

As we have suggested, Habermas's dialogic reformulation of Kantian ethics retains a tendency to view judgment as an asymptotic approach to a universal, or in terms of an approximation assumption. This is especially apparent in discourses of justification, for here, discourse ethics supplies us with the universal that we then deploy in order to test the validity of a norm. The type of judgment at work in such discourses is, therefore, clearly determinant. However, when the principle of universalizability is given the weaker formulation by the addition of Günther's time and knowledge index, thus necessitating a second order of discourse in which the norm is appropriately applied, we need to be clear about the effect of such an addition on the characterization of judgment.

Certainly, in discourses of application, where the principle of universalization is replaced by that of appropriateness, we admit a host of contextual concerns that arise in the consideration of a specific situation. Yet the "hermeneutic insight that the appropriate norm gains concrete significance in the light of the salient features of a situation,"[36] which gives rise to the need for discourses of application, does not announce, for Habermas and Günther, the arrival of a type of judgment that is solely hermeneutic.[37] Indeed, we have noted how carefully both Habermas and Günther defend the deployment of both rational discourse and impartiality in their characterization of the logic of discourses of application. Even where the principle of appropriateness replaces that of universalizability, judgment still assumes the form of an *impartial* application of a given universal to the particular.[38] The cognitivist core of the theory, that normative discourses achieve a rational consensus, is preserved in discourses of application, and it is this core that ensures judgment retains its determinant character.

This, of course, is not to say that Habermas's conception of judgment is determinant in the full sense in which Kant understood that term. Unlike Kant, Habermas does not adhere to a universal principle entirely independent of any interpretation and derived solely from some invariant structure of subjectivity. Nor is the relation between the universal principle and the norm to be tested one of strict deduction. Yet nevertheless, as Ferrara points out,

> one essential feature of the model of determinant judgment which they [Rawls, Larmore, Habermas] retain is the conceptual distinction between principle and application, general principles of justice and what is just on a concrete occasion. Even when the perspective suggested is explicitly . . . "reconstructive," we can still observe a substantial difference between the kind of argument developed for grounding the principle of justice and the kind of arguments developed in order to justify any of its applications. . . . Furthermore, both the adequacy of the principle and the inclusion of some intended line of conduct within the scope of the principle are assumed to be possible objects of *demonstration*—where by "demonstration" I mean an argument which, if valid, would thereby make it *unreasonable* for anyone to reject its conclusions.[39]

The determinant character of judgment is thus preserved by the impartial and rational quality of discourses of application. Indeed, such discourses are carefully defended as endeavors with a cognitivist core.

With these considerations in place, we can see why Habermas believes that the studies of moral development undertaken by Kohlberg provide empirical confirmation for his position.[40] Following Piaget, Kohlberg presents an ontogenetic developmental structure through which, he claims, those making moral judgments reach maturity. Importantly, for Habermas, Kohlberg's stages move from an unreflective moral stance to one informed by a hypothetical and disinterested perspective. Moral maturity then appears as an ability to judge actions according to abstract, universal principles.

5.2 CRITIQUES OF THE HABERMASIAN ACCOUNT OF JUDGMENT

We have already noted a number of difficulties with Habermas's conception of judgment, among them the discriminative inadequacy of the universal, the assumption that it proceeds according to an approximation assumption and the lack of attention by Habermas to precisely what it is that enables us "to judge this particular X to be an instance of the rule Y."[41] Now we will consider a further set of criticisms that, when taken together, raise serious questions about the coherence of his project *in toto*. Generally, they turn on issues that are familiar to us, such as his leaning toward Kant rather than Hegel, his distinction between the right and the good and his penchant for abstract normative matters over contextual ones. Our interest here is not so much with the challenge such criticisms pose for the project as a whole. Rather, they are inspected here in order to move us away from a determinant conception of judgment and toward a reflective one, and to assess what is lost and gained in such a move.

The first type of criticism focuses on what is missed out when we conceive of judgment in terms of an impartial yet context-sensitive application of norms. Particularly in the work of Benhabib and Cooke, we find a concern with the principle of universalization that underlies the impartiality of both the justification and the application of norms. As conceived by Habermas, the principle is so strong a presupposition that it has the effect of leveling a whole series of differences that exist between concrete individuals and groups, not least among them, that of gender. Benhabib develops her critique via the work of Gilligan,[42] who draws a distinction between the "generalized other" and the "concrete other" in her analysis of Kohlberg's moral theory.[43] The generalized other describes the form in which we encounter the other in universalist moral theories. In abstracting individuals from their particular life histories and emotional constitutions, it stresses what speaking and acting subjects have in common, and ushers in moral categories such as right, obligation, respect, and duty. Against this, the concrete other is the manner in which we encounter the other in contextualist moral theory. Here, the other appears as an individual with particular experiences and emotional constitutions, and ushers in moral categories such as love, sympathy, care, and responsibility.[44]

This distinction is then used to highlight a series of concerns about moral theories that characterize the encounter between ego and alter as one between self and generalized other. First, such theories rest on a distinction between the right and the good that, at best, leaves unthematized the affective dimension of moral interaction, and at worst, characterizes questions of the good as being essentially beyond rational redemption. Second, it privileges public interaction over the private and thus effectively ignores whole areas of human activity where moral, or often immoral, action in fact takes place. Third, the moral categories ushered in by the standpoint of the generalized other implicitly undervalues an ethics of care, sympathy, and responsibility, in such a way as to elevate what amounts to an ethics of dominant groups (white, male, privileged) to a universal ideal. Generally then, where moral theories rely on strong presuppositions of universalizability, impartiality, and consensus, the effect is to downplay the many real and meaningful differences between people. Feminists have thus very effectively criticized such approaches as being based on poor empirical data and specious reasoning. Accounts of moral judgment that emerge from such distorted approaches then appear to miss out important areas of human activity, and even to degenerate into a kind of formalized rational game. Even if the standpoint of the generalized other *is* extended into areas that it has traditionally missed, such as the private and the affective, it produces further aporetic effects, such as the apparent requirement of complete transparency on the part of individual personalities. Thus, Cooke in particular raises questions about the *desirability* of such strong presuppositions.[45]

The second type of criticism of the Habermasian conception of judgment arises from a concern about the very possibility of achieving consensus in collective deliberation. Whether this threatened impossibility is due to the increasing multiplicity of value-perspectives in modern societies[46] or to the quite extraordinary cognitive capacities seemingly required of participants in order to make valid collective judgments,[47] this kind of criticism accuses Habermasian accounts of judgment of being hopelessly unrealistic. If we seriously follow his conception, so these critiques contend, it becomes impossible to understand how human beings might ever be able to make valid collective judgments at all.[48]

We might collect these growing concerns under the rubric of a threatened "cognitive overload" of participants that appears when we conceive of discourses of application as proceeding according to the strongly cognitive presupposition of impartiality.[49] According to the principle (U), we are called upon to evaluate and reach agreement on the consequences and side-effects of a universal adherence to a norm for each individual concerned. The question is, how could such an evaluation ever be possible,[50] particularly when we confront conflicting norms and the need to justify exceptions?[51]

Wellmer's concern regarding the cognitive impossibility of applying the universalizability principle arises, Habermas suggests, from a misconception of what (U) is intended to achieve. In fact, he states, (U) pertains to the justification of "norms that underlie a general practice" and is to be employed to "test the validity of universal precepts."[52] Thus, the principle of universalizability "belongs properly to justificatory discourses."[53] Its deployment as a principle of application is therefore incorrect.

The problem of cognitive overload leads us to a fourth criticism of Habermasian accounts of judgment, this being, in effect, the denial of the differentiation thesis.[54] To overcome the problem of cognitive over-load, Wellmer restricts (U) to "the correct appraisal of a situation and to the selection of truly relevant circumstances."[55] He thus characterizes the moral principle as itself a principle of application, and in this way denies the distinction between justification and application. In Wellmer's hands, the justification of a norm becomes a marginal prob-lem, and attention shifts to how we generate common and appropriate interpretations of particular situations. In the place of the differentiation thesis, then, he returns to a standard of compatibility, here between a form of action and a common, particular practice. As with the neo-Aris-totelian position, a form of life is to be assessed internally, as it were, and we find the critical power over other conceptual schemes that con-stitutes Habermas's most significant achievement again under threat.[56]

All these criticisms, in their way, are meditations upon the problem of contextualization that follow upon the decontextualization required for the universalist justification of moral norms. If judgment is to have more than context-bound validity; in other words, if it is to partake of an extra-contextual ideal, then the threat is always that our conception of that faculty will wander so far from the contexts in which it is prac-ticed that we find ourselves unable to intelligently discuss something that we clearly know how to do.[57]

It is, I suggest, self-evident that judgment is something more than a context-bound activity. As Benhabib so provocatively states, there *is* a moral difference between liking to abuse children and liking Haägen-Dasz ice cream,[58] and just because a majority of the German electorate voted for Hitler in 1933 does not make their choice morally right. Judg-ment is, therefore, somehow related to a universalist ideal, and it is by virtue of this relation that it can be valid.[59] At the same time, it is self-evident that we make judgments, that we understand those judgments as being redeemable in rational discourse, and that one does not require a mind like a computer to calculate those consequences and side-effects of a judgment in order for it to be valid. These two seemingly incompati-ble insights have, of course, generated two and a half millennia of dis-cussion about how, precisely, an ideal relates to a particular. In its latest manifestation, within that of Habermasian theory, this has given rise to calls for "a phenomenology of moral judgement in order to show how a principled, universalist morality and context-sensitive moral judgment can fit together,"[60] requests for a softened or "context-sensitive univer-salism,"[61] and a resurgence of interest in how judgment succeeds in deploying universals in order to "do the right thing."[62]

Yet, so far, such attempts have not significantly improved our understanding. Habermas's distinction between justification and appli-cation "cannot exempt the discourse theorists from analysing what it is that we do when we supposedly contextualise moral principles and how this activity is related to the work of judging."[63] At the same time, neo-Aristotelians continue to fall back on "the metaphor of the archer hitting the mark,"[64] even though they cannot account for the position of the mark in any way other than as a "dogmatism of the given."[65]

If we are to retain a cognitive conception of judgment, our problem becomes one of somehow delineating the precise manner in which the ideal is related to the particular in the everyday activity of judging. In the literature, this problem has been tackled in two ways. First, there have been moves to soften the strong idealizations that, Habermas claims, operate behind the practice of judgment and render it cognitive. Indeed, a number of commentators are now arguing that consensus is no longer defensible as a strong presupposition of moral discourse,[66] and that it may not even be necessary for discourse ethics to adhere to such a strong idealization. If this is the case, however, it is important that we understand the implications of giving it up.

We should notice that Habermas's cognitivist core in fact provides two criteria for moral validity.[67] The first is that of generalizability and pertains to the *result* of a moral judgment.[68] Generalizability relies on consensus and expresses the grounds of moral truth in terms of a common interest. The second criterion is the manner of argumentation. This assesses the moral validity of the *process* under which the result is generated.[69] Here, the (universal) rules of argumentation embody the moral point of view as impartiality.

To abandon the principle of universalizability is, therefore, to remove the grounds upon which we rely to gain critical power over (whatever) *outcome* was produced in a moral discourse. No longer would we be able to comment upon "the validity of the knowledge embedded by a moral norm or principle;"[70] no longer would we know anything at all about the ideal of moral truth.[71] This loss of critical power is clearly significant, yet no matter how great the discomfort it creates, this could never be sufficient to cause us to overlook the growing indefensibility of positing consensus as a strong presupposition of normative discourse. As Rawls has so cogently argued, we simply do not possess an independent criterion that could adjudicate between competing conceptions of justice. The best we can attain is a "constructivist" and purely procedural conception of practical reason.[72] The question we now face is, therefore, whether or not we retain any critical power once we have given up the notion of moral truth.

If, upon giving up the principle of universalizability, we are now agnostic about the moral truth of an outcome of discourse, then how are we to conceive of an effort to judge an instance of communication in terms of its *procedural* fairness? As we saw in the previous chapter,

Habermas clearly suggests such an evaluation to be a comparative exercise in which we hold up the universal (here the rules of domination-free communication) against the particular instance in order to illustrate how the particular transgresses the components of the ideal. It is thus, according to his view, the "pregiven" universal of ideal speech that enables us to evaluate the procedural fairness of a particular instance of communication.

The various criticisms of such a view, which are particularly apparent when we seek to compare two instances of communication, amount to suggesting that the ideal is simply insufficient to enable it to function as the way in which we evaluate specific instances of communication. The indeterminacy of the ideal, especially regarding the weighting and lexicographic ordering of its components, effectively denies our ability to make such judgments. We have referred to this difficulty in terms of a "problem of comparison." The various criticisms of Habermas's conception of judgment also served to show that the distinction between justification and application does not succeed in avoiding these difficulties.

The second approach to the problem of the role of the universal in judgment, as conceived by Habermas, has concentrated on his assumption that judgment is a determinant activity, in other words, that it proceeds as a subsumption of the particular under the universal. Of Habermas's commentators, Wellmer is the most pellucid in regard to the slippage that has occurred between being able to formalize the ideal and the conception of judgment in terms of the deployment of that ideal.[73] His claim amounts to the assertion that, at least in regard to judgment, too much has been imported from Kant. Habermas, like Kant, articulates a "philosophical architectonics which depends on an ideal as its keystone,"[74] resulting almost in a doctrine of the two realms.[75] Regarding judgment, we then find ourselves attempting to understand the mediation between the particular and the universal in terms of *sub specie aeternitatis* and a "perfection of moral sense."[76] Wellmer attributes this slippage to a "covert scientistic residue,"[77] which he sees at the heart of Habermas's project. Benhabib puts it more bluntly: "The exercise of moral judgment . . . does not proceed according to the model of the subsumption of a particular under a universal."[78]

Wellmer suggests an alternative conception of judgment wherein that faculty relies for its validity on a background of intersubjectively shared understandings within a particular historical and cultural context, or a "collective matrix of interpretation."[79] This conception moves us one step back toward the neo-Aristotelian view of judgment, where it is seen as involving an oscillation between the universal and the particular,[80] in other words, as having a stronger hermeneutic component.[81] Yet a crucial dif-

LIVERPOOL JOHN MOORES UNIVERSITY
LEARNING SERVICES

ference is that Wellmer's conception, while rejecting the principle of universalizability (regarding outcomes), nevertheless retains an attention to the ideal procedures formalized as the presuppositions of argumentation. Indeed, it is precisely this ideal, present in our "collective matrix of understanding," that allows us to communicate to others the reasons for our judgment. With the abandonment of (U), then, we move away from a determinant conception of judgment yet do not, necessarily, entirely dispense with its cognitivism. The inescapable presuppositions of argumentation, by which meaning is related to validity, still represent "a small bit of ideality [which] breaks into our lives."[82] Now, however, the relation of this ideal to the particular as it occurs in judgment is itself problematized, and can no longer be characterized as one of subsumption.

In sum, the first criterion of normative validity within the cognitivist core of the theory, that of generalizability (or appropriateness) is a pre-given universal, and as such, it alone is sufficient to make the type of judgment adduced in both kinds of discourse determinant. If we reject the first criterion of validity, this being the principle of universalizability, the second criterion that remains, albeit a universal criterion (the universal rules of argumentation as set out in the ISS), is not sufficient to render the judgment determinant. We must therefore conclude that the conception of judgment we are exploring can no longer be described as determinant. Upon rejection of (U), there remains some critical bite, and it is for this reason that Wellmer,[83] Benhabib,[84] and Cooke conclude that discourse ethics "does not stand or fall on its reliance on the notion of consensus."[85] It is now possible to see why Ferrara describes the crucial tension to be explored in the search for a context-sensitive universalism as being that between consensus and judgment.[86]

In order to understand a form of judgment that is not determinant yet that somehow relates to a universal for its critical power, it is necessary to inspect Arendt's reading of Kant's theory of judgment.

5.3 THE REFLECTIVE TURN

Though Kant saw judgment as the determinant subsumption of the particular under the universal, he was greatly troubled by the apparent antinomy presented by judgments of taste.[87] In the aesthetic realm, to assert that an object is beautiful seems on the one hand to express an immediate subjective experience,[88] while on the other, a judgment is asserted that claims universal assent, and describes beauty as a demonstrable quality of the object.[89]

The problem occurs because beauty arouses feeling, and this affective response in the observer only occurs in the direct and immediate encounter with the object. Aesthetic judgment is not, therefore, mediated by a concept.[90] For this reason, there is no pregiven universal under which the particular can be subsumed, as is the case with other forms of judgment. Yet to judge an object to be beautiful is to assert that there is something about that object that can be communicated to others.[91] Judgment is therefore a public activity.[92] Explanations for the deployment of the predicate can be given by way of an appeal to a universal,[93] though such appeals allude to the exemplary nature of the object, rather than to a concept. Here then, we encounter a type of judgment for which the universal is not pregiven, and is instead to be found by an inspection of the particular. Kant referred to this form of judgment as reflective, and he subdivided it into two types: aesthetic and teleological.[94]

Though Kant's solution to the antinomy of taste[95] is less than convincing,[96] the difficulty he raises has attracted much attention, particularly since the suggestion by Hannah Arendt that it expresses "Kant's unwritten political philosophy."[97] Arendt's interest in reflective judgment was motivated by a complex array of theoretical concerns,[98] but two are of special relevance to our present enquiry.

First, we are here given an account of judgment whose primary orientation is quite different from its determinant sibling. Instead of beginning our search for validity with a pregiven universal,[99] reflective judgment starts with the direct inspection of the particular. What we reason *about* is the particular, seeking to find its relation to the universal, whereas with determinant judgment, we reason *about* the universal in its relation to the particular.[100] Such a conception of judgment, in treating "particulars in their particularity,"[101] thus shares the strengths of more hermeneutic and contextual approaches wherein concrete practices are seen as being of greater import than rarefied and abstract ideals.

Yet it is important to understand what we are looking for when, according to a reflective conception of judgment, we inspect the particular. With Arendt, reflective judgment offered "the most fruitful solution to the problem of mediating the particular and the universal"[102] because it characterized the end point of judgment in terms of an "exemplary validity." As with beauty, the object embodies the universal; it is an example of it, and it is for this reason that Arendt agrees with Kant when he says that "examples are the go-carts of judgments."[103] Extending this notion beyond the realm of aesthetics, she then sought to show how historical persons and events could serve as examples of good judgment, from which we can learn.[104] Here then, the universal to be looked for in the particular was not a rational construct redeemable in any way analogous to a truth-claim.

The second reason for Arendt's interest in reflective judgment was that, unlike determinant judgment, where the pregiven universal does the real work of judging, the reflective finding of a universal within a particular leaves all the work to the one who attempts the judgment. As is the case with *phronēsis*, crucial to good judgment is the ability of the one who judges.[105]

Seeking to articulate judgment as a noncognitive activity,[106] Arendt saw this ability as a function of two faculties: imagination and common sense.[107] Imagination allows the recollection of objects that have appeared to one's senses, thus "establishing the distance necessary for impartial judgment,"[108] while common sense rises above the particular point of view in order to make appeal to a shared community.[109] These two faculties make it possible for the conditions of judgment to be fulfilled—these being impartiality, disinterestedness, and the development of "enlarged thought."[110] Of course, many of these insights are already incorporated into Habermas's position via his appropriation of Mead's ideal role taking and his articulation of the moral point of view as impartiality. Indeed, Habermas has extended them by suggesting that, as Benhabib puts it, "'enlarged thought' is best realised through a dialogic or discursive ethic."[111]

The notion of a "common sense" links an aesthetic appraisal to the faculty of judgment in general, for here we encounter the centrality of communicability.[112] Judgments are always communicable, for they make appeal to the common sense of others.[113] Indeed, "their validity rests on the consent they elicit from the community"[114] within which they take place. As Kant expressed it:

> The touchstone whereby we decide whether our holding a thing to be true is conviction or mere persuasion is therefore external, namely the possibility of communicating it and of finding it to be valid for all human reason.[115]

Makkreel puts it well when he says,

> It is precisely through common sense . . . that the aesthetic judgment can be intersubjective as well as subjective. According to Kant, common sense makes it possible to represent the "subjective necessity" of the judgment of taste as "objective" in the sense of claiming universal assent.[116]

Such a requirement of "publicity" does not, in the case of reflective judgments, take the form of "demonstrability," as it does for determinant judgments.[117] No one can be compelled to recognise the validity of a reflective judgment. Rather, the availability of a universal that has to be found in the process of reflective judgment allows for a "superiority which ought to be recognised by everybody":[118] it enables the adducement of reasons, offers the grounds for an account or offers plausibility.

A reflective judgment, precisely because it expresses a universal claim, is "graspable by all."[119] It was just this intersubjective component of validity that Arendt found so compelling in Kant, for it allowed her to highlight both the importance of community as the necessary background for a valid judgment and to introduce her theory of argumentation (though not rational argumentation)[120]—here seen in terms of a rhetorical "wooing" of others.[121] Benhabib focuses this point in the following way:

> Arendt intimated that intrinsic to Kant's model of "reflective judgment" may be a conception of rationality and intersubjective validity which would allow us to retain a principled universalist moral standpoint while acknowledging the role of contextual moral judgment in human affairs.[122]

The key word here is 'principled,' for it alludes to the universal that is to be found by inspecting the particular. In effect, Arendt saw judgment as striving for two principles. First, she deployed a notion of being "at home with ourselves."[123] Yet her second principle, that of intersubjective validity, introduces the idea of a common consent that must be won—it is not merely provided by the shared background of understandings that is assumed to constitute a given tradition.

Once again then, we find our attention drawn to the precise nature of the universal that is to be found by reflective judgment. In giving up the strong cognitivism of Habermas's universalization principle, we have clearly admitted a whole host of contextual, ethical, and utopian concerns. Yet reflective judgment does retain some critical power, and it does so because it makes appeal to a universal, albeit one that is to be found (rather than being pregiven). Thus, Arendt's attention to the intersubjective component of validity is seen as meaningful, even without the strong presupposition of consensus. So conceived, judgment involves what we might call a "general competence," which we deploy to inspect particular instances of communication in order to find the embedded universal,[124] and it is the universal that allows for the communicability of the judgment. This general competence operates much like the Aristotelian virtue of *phronēsis*, though as Ferrara has shown,[125] such a competence encompasses more than an appeal to an internal "fit" within an ethos, this being the way the term is deployed by the neo-Aristotelians.

Though a number of recent Arendtian, Kantian, and Habermasian scholars might agree upon a reconception of political judgment in terms of a reflective activity, and even that *phronēsis* might be taken to be the general competence to discern the universal exemplified in a given particular, there is less agreement in regard to the nature of the universal that is to be found within the particular. Of these various positions, Ferrara's has perhaps received the fullest articulation. His claim is that the "soft" universal[126] for which reflective judgment searches is the construction, maintenance, and development of identity.[127] Such an explicit expression of the universal for which we search has many advantages, perhaps the most important being that it explicates the prioritisation of values and needs in terms of their implications for identities, both individual and collective. It also serves to focus the relation, in judgment, between questions of justice and of the good life. Yet such an approach also raises a number of intriguing difficulties.

First is a concern about the "level" upon which a category such as identity operates in the activity of judgment. It would certainly seem to be the case that one of the prime teleological orientations of judgment, and indeed of all human activity, is the maintenance of individual and collective identities. Similarly, human activity displays an orientation to such issues as the preservation of the mechanisms for sociation, socialization, and solidarity, for the fabric of the lifeworld, of forms of life, and indeed of life itself. Issues at this level operate as a background against which activity is evaluated and undertaken. This concern therefore centers on the difficulty of moving from the level of a highly generalized *telos* operating in the background of human activity to the level of a formalizable concept (to use Kant's terminology) that allows for the communicative redemption of a judgment. A parallel move, within the confines of Kant's conception of aesthetic judgment, would be to equate the level of the concept of beauty with the more general *telos* evinced by all human attempts to be in "perceptual contact" with the world. Certainly, the concern with accurate perception is an issue against which all aesthetic evaluation takes place, but it is the formalizable concept of beauty, operating on a "different level," that allows for the intersubjective consensus on validity.

Another concept that operates at the background level for a theory of judgment, rather than as a formalizable universal, is that of a "life plan" in Rawls's theory of justice.[128] As Walzer and others (including Rawls) have acknowledged, such a concept is not something that can be confirmed in the original position, for it operates on the level of a background assumption.[129] No matter how bound up questions of identity and authenticity are with matters of judgment, and with ethical and moral judgments where "strong preferences" are being adduced they might be bound up very tightly indeed, this is not sufficient to say that the category of identity constitutes the universal sought for in reflective judgment.

Second, notions such as fulfilled identity, integrity, authenticity,[130] or the complete satisfaction of psychological needs,[131] cause us to stray dangerously close to the pathologizing discourse of psychoanalytic interpretation, a cul-de-sac already explored by Habermas[132] and subsequently rejected in the face of resounding criticism. The concern with such a move therefore amounts to the claim that, where subjective identities are being evaluated, demands for complete transparency and publicity might be excessive, oppressive, or indeed impossible to redeem.

Third, Ferrara's argument confronts a theoretical lacuna regarding a language with which to describe the notion of collective identity. He is, therefore, forced to rely upon a language that was developed to describe the components of *individual* identity: this being object relations theory, and then to apply this to identity on the level of the collective.[133] The result is an ongoing difficulty in his work regarding the precise relation of identity on the two levels. Sometimes he describes this relation in terms of a "link" or "bridge," sometimes as an "analogy,"[134] as being "derivative" of,[135] sometimes as applicable "*mutatis mutandis*,"[136] as a "tentative comparison,"[137] as requiring "careful translation,"[138] and, finally, in terms of a "parallel."[139]

The apparent difficulty he has in stipulating the relation between individual and collective identity does not imply that there is no relation, simply that the move is a problematic one. This concern is exacerbated by his reliance on the conceptual framework of object relations theory and other forms of neo-Freudianism, which even at the level of individual identity, raise significant and well-charted problems of conceptual consistency, empirical confirmation,[140] and ideological distortion.[141] For these various reason, Ferrara's attempt to stipulate the universal sought for in reflective judgment is problematic.

The precise nature of the "concept" or universal to be found in reflective judgment, especially in regard to the evaluation of instances of communication in terms of their relative fairness, is given a different formulation by Benhabib, and again by Wellmer and Warnke. All have articulated positions that attempt to fruitfully retain the cognitivism remaining in Habermas's position following upon the abandonment of (U). These commentators continue to suggest that the universal to be found in some way pertains to the validity of the procedure whereby discourses are undertaken.

Because Wellmer believes that discourse ethics is unable to guide our judgments or to offer any moral grounds for particular actions, he does not articulate a universal with the clarity of that offered by Ferrara. What he does offer, however, is perhaps the most sophisticated interpretation of discourse ethics as a principle of legitimacy.[142] His account of the procedural validity of judgments proceeds negatively. Instead of seeking to articulate the nature of political judgment, a task Wellmer believes to be beyond the scope of theory, he seeks to deploy discourse ethics to rule out certain judgments as invalid. In rejecting Habermas's conception of "moral sense" in terms of a perfect ideal, he turns his attention instead to the "elimination of nonsense."[143] Such a process is conceivable, he argues, even without the ideal of perfection, because what is involved is a series of "specific negations rather than advances towards some ideal."[144] Instead of grounding the legitimacy of a moral norm on the possibility of its generalizability, he seeks to ground the exceptions to moral norms[145] that so frequently occur in morally complex situations[146] upon the specific negation of "non-generalizability."[147] "Ways of acting are . . . legitimate . . ." he states, "if they are not non-generalizable."[148]

Such an orientation has a number of interesting effects. First, the difficulties we encountered when we tried to follow Habermas in basing legitimacy on consensus alone seem to disappear. Now, our concern would be whether or not there is a single person who cannot accept the norm, (or the outcome of a judgment) for if there is, it is nongeneralizable and therefore illegitimate. Second, the "cognitive overload" that occurred when we tried to factor in all the consequences and side-effects of a proposed norm (or judgment) is reduced, for if we can anticipate a single situation in which it would be wrong for the norm to be acted upon, the norm would fail the test.[149] Wellmer's concern here is to increase the context-sensitivity of our conception of moral validity and to move away from the idea that the legitimacy of an action is only to be gained by recourse to a grounded norm.[150] As we saw earlier, he rejects the "differentiation thesis" advanced by Habermas whereby the grounding of a norm is to be distinguished from its application. Instead, he asserts that "the process of moral grounding is a problem of application."[151] In regard to judgment, we are here offered an account that rejects the strong presupposition of generalizability, yet retains a cognitivist component, albeit in a negative form. This cognitivist component still pertains to the outcome of the discourse, however. If we are to better understand how judgment relates a particular to the ideal of fair procedure, we must turn to the work of Benhabib.

Unlike Wellmer, Benhabib does present us with a universal for which reflective judgment searches, but she does so in a somewhat different way to Ferrara. Seeking to argue for an "interactive universalism,"[152] she begins by outlining two metanorms that she sees as contextual expressions of the normative content of the presuppositions of argumentation.[153] These metanorms—universal moral respect and egalitarian reciprocity—are "our philosophical clarification of the constituents of the moral point of view from within the normative horizon of modernity."[154] She then seeks to deploy these metanorms to ground certain "procedural constraints"[155] upon the participants of a discourse. Benhabib, contra Wellmer, believes that discourse ethics gives us something more than merely a model of legitimacy,[156] yet she stipulates the universal for which we search in reflective judgment in a different way to Ferrara; here in terms of the contextually specific presuppositions of argumentation. Her "interactive universalism" is, therefore, a qualified procedural universalism. According to such a view, (U) is abandoned, yet judgments remain cognitive by virtue of their reflective appeal to a context-specific ideal of fair procedure.

We notice a similar approach in the work of Warnke.[157] While agreeing that the rejection of (U) leads us to consider the validity of moral judgment in terms of the presupposition of fairness, she is never able to offer us a formalization of such a presupposition (as does Habermas) or even an account of its actual role in judgment (as do Ferrara and Benhabib). For this reason, her (Hegelian) context-sensitivity is insufficiently buttressed with the Kantian requirement for an idealization.[158] The result is both a loss of clarity regarding the concept of fairness, and an inattention to the problem of how normative validity is exemplified in actual discourses.

In this chapter we have explored a number of difficulties with the Habermasian conception of judgment. In particular we have seen that the tension between a universalist and a contextual understanding of that faculty cannot be adequately resolved by a determinant conception, even where a distinction is drawn between justification and application. In addition, the reflective turn among Habermas's commentators, while offering significant gains in our understanding, often endangers the universalist element in judgment. If we are to follow these commentators in their abandonment of (U) and in their characterization of judgment as reflective, we must hold to the second aspect according to which judgments are cognitivist in Habermas's work, which he expresses as the inescapable presuppositions of argumentation. These presuppositions pertain solely to the procedure of the discourse, and describe the sense in which discourses can be described as being fair. It is by virtue of this cognitivist aspect of judgment that validity can be communicatively defended. We therefore arrive at a conception of judgment whereby the ideal of communicative fairness is sought for reflectively. Particular judgments are inspected for their exemplary validity, in other words, for the ways in which they embody the ideal of communicative fairness.

Communicative fairness, formalizable as the inescapable presuppositions of argumentation, is the universal sought for in reflective judgments in all modern cultures, that is, where reasons are adduced for judgments. This is a cognitivist claim still made by a discourse ethics that has rejected (U). Yet in different cultures, communicative fairness is interpreted and even perceived in different ways. Reflective judgments inspect particulars, yet judgments themselves are always particular, undertaken by real people in real contexts. To question the validity of a judgment is to inspect its procedure for communicative fairness and this can only ever take place from within a particular "collective matrix of interpretation" (Wellmer), or "normative horizon of modernity" (Benhabib). In different cultures, people therefore experience the "ideal in the real" in different ways. Habermas puts this admirably when he says that "the moral point of view remains identical: but neither our understanding of this fundamental intuition, nor the interpretations we give morally valid rules in applying them to unforseeable cases, remain invariant."[159]

We might focus this idea by borrowing from Taylor[160] and stating that the way in which communicative fairness is perceived or experienced is ethically patterned in different ways in different contexts. This is not to suggest anything other than what is currently being asserted by Habermas in his recent attempts to reconstruct the normative core of modern constitutional law and parliamentary democracy.[161] In specific cultures and historical contexts, validity has a particular and ethically patterned facticity. Thus, Habermas states that every legal system is an expression of a particular form of life, and that post-traditional moral norms represent a form of cultural knowledge. While the internal structure of a situationally specific ethical patterning has occupied many theorists,[162] Habermas's dogged adherence to the possibility of a universalist ethics retains the possibility of valid adjudication between judgments in different conceptual schemes. Where such "cross-cultural" judgments are attempted, their validity turns on the transparency and consistency of the ethical patterning itself.

Yet have these considerations really advanced our understanding of judgment? Or have we merely become transfixed with the problem of how it is that a judgment can claim validity? Participants in a discourse, confronting problems of institutional design and evaluation, must judge and decide between alternative courses of action. They must, as we have seen, "establish, not that some position is correct absolutely, but rather that some position is superior to some other."[163] Even when we understand such a comparative judgment in terms of a reflective inspection of the two particulars for their relative exemplary validity, do we not remain tied to an evaluative strategy wherein we seek to ascertain the relative *degree* to which each embodies the ideal of communicative fairness? Once again, we find an approximation assumption lurking behind our conception of judgment.

The reason we have not, so far, escaped this assumption, is that we continue to conflate questions as to the *grounds* of normative validity with those pertaining to the manner in which validity is *evaluated*. This conflation amounts to an ongoing confusion regarding the role of the ideal of communicative fairness in the actual process of evaluative judgment. Certainly, the *sense* in which a judgment is valid is a function of its exemplification of the ideal. But this does not necessarily mean that it is *by virtue* of this ideal, or its preponderance in one particular over another, that we make judgments.

Time and again, Habermas's commentators imagine that their reflective turn overcomes the problem of the precise role of the universal in contextual judgments, thus moving them closer to understanding the actual phenomenology of that practical faculty. In fact, what the reflective turn achieves is to focus the role of the universal in the abstract question of grounding. A particular instance of communication can legitimately claim to be fair because it can be said to exemplify the ideal. Judgment, proceeding reflectively, is then the process by which participants inspect that instance of communication in order to evaluate the quality with which it exemplifies the ideal.

But what does this tell us about the actual process by which participants make evaluative judgments between particulars? Surely, this process cannot be characterized simply as two asymptotic assessments that are then compared. If this was how judgments took place, we would be at a loss as to how to judge in those many situations where approximations were multidimensional and incommensurable. As Wellmer puts it, "a consensus under ideal conditions does not give us a criterion for the truth/rightness of a consensus under factual conditions."[164]

What is precisely so fascinating about judgment is that it is so much more complex and sophisticated than this, that it seems to leap beyond rule governed measurement, and that, while it somehow relies upon an ideal for its validity, it does not proceed via an assessment of the degree to which a particular exemplifies an ideal. Somehow we must characterize judgment as an everyday activity, as a "spontaneous coping,"[165] that can, at the same time, generate and appeal to validity. Yet we must also break apart the sense in which judgments can achieve validity from the manner in which they proceed in everyday life. The concrete question of how we actually evaluate communication must not, *methodologically,* be conflated with the abstract question of validity. And it is this conflation that, preserving as it does the approximation assumption, continues to constrain accounts of judgment by those who have taken the reflective turn.[166]

If we want to retain a cognitivist conception of judgment, how are we to understand the role of the universal in the actual manner by which participants evaluate instances of communication? It is to this question, and its implications, that we turn in the next chapter.

CHAPTER 6

Discursive Phronēsis
with a Cognitivist Core

We began our inquiry into the question of what assistance Habermas's theory might afford, in the design and evaluation of democratic institutions, with an account of his theoretical position, and we then looked at the various attempts to apply his theory to practice. This initial tour of the problem generated a series of difficulties. We noticed first that attempts to apply the theory to practical questions generated recurrent methodological problems, particularly when we sought to compare instances of communication in order to assess their relative fairness.

While some of these problems were seen to derive from confusion around the negative limit Habermas places upon his theory, others were a result of his conception of judgment. In the previous chapter, we focused on this conception and on the various criticisms mounted against it by his commentators. In doing so, we began to reformulate judgment in terms of a reflective discourse of application whereby the presuppositions of argumentation, or communicative fairness, were sought for in ethically patterned ways. Yet even when we conceived of judgment as a reflective activity, we found ourselves constrained by an approximation assumption, whereby evaluation of the fairness of an instance of communication was assumed to proceed methodologically in such a way as to mirror the sense in which a judgment could be said to be valid. This constraint continued to render our understanding of expertise, in respect of judgments, somewhat abstract. The actual phenomenology of everyday judgment continued to elude us, even having made the reflective turn. Certainly, the reflective account of judgment helped us to see the sense in which a judgment can claim validity. But once again, we found that holding to a cognitivist view of judgment, no matter how softened, generated confusion regarding the actual role of the universal, this time in the everyday practice of judgment.

The question to which we now must turn, then, is this: How do reflective judgments actually proceed, given a methodological distinction between grounding and evaluating the fairness of a particular instance of communication? In order to answer this question, we will first inspect (6.1) Wittgenstein's work on the "problem of universals." This will allow us to focus on the role of the ideal of fairness in the actual evaluation of particular instances of communication. The attempt here will be to complete our reformulation of political judgment along the lines of a discursive *phronēsis* with a cognitivist core. With this in place, we will proceed to offer a derivation for a particular conceptual tool that will enable a more meaningful instantiation of the normative theory into empirical practice, this being a normative and discriminative principle of preservation. Thus, in the second section (6.2), we will focus on judgments that preserve fairness. Having completed our reformulation of the nature of judgment, we will, in the following chapter, be ready to direct our various insights at a somewhat different object domain from that usually entertained by democratic theorists, this being the actual functioning of deliberative fora themselves.

6.1 HOW DO WE EVALUATE FAIRNESS?

Habermas's imputation, that we deploy the ideal in order to distinguish more from less domination in particular practices, is best scrutinized by considering a comparative judgment, not between two instances of communication, but between two different games. At an anthropological conference, let's say, two rather similar native practices, each involving beads and bowls, are described in detail by a researcher who has recently returned from studying an island culture never before encountered. The researcher shows a film of these practices, and suggests that even though the two appear very similar, practice A is in fact an economic transaction, whereas B is a kind of game. In the ensuing discussion, the question arises as to how we might decide which of the two practices has the most "gamelike" qualities. One discussant therefore suggests a list of elements common to all games, and subsequent contributions attempt to compare the preponderance of these elements within the two practices.

Of course, this example of comparative judgment has been selected because it borrows heavily from Wittgenstein's discussion of "the problem of universals."[1] In *The Blue and Brown Books*, Wittgenstein refers to what he sees as "our craving for generality."[2] First, he highlights our tendency to subsume under a common name all those properties that are shared by a group of practices. The general concept is thus seen as a common property, appearing in each practice as a kind of ingredient. Second, we often imagine that to understand a common term, such as "leaf," means that we possess a "kind of general picture of a leaf, as opposed to pictures of particular leaves."[3] Such a general image, wrung from the inspection of many particular leaves, constitutes a "thing" that somehow contains all the common properties whereby particular leaves are leaves. In the *Philosophical Investigations,* Wittgenstein develops this discussion by asking what various kinds of games have in common.[4]

> Don't say: "there must be something common, or they would not be called 'games'"—but look and see whether there is anything common to all.—For if you look at them you will not see something that is common to all, but similarities, relationships, and a whole series of them at that.

He then considers a series of games and identifies their various similarities and differences. This allows him to assert that

> we see a complicated network of similarities overlapping and crisscrossing: sometimes overall similarities, sometimes similarities of detail. I can think of no better expression to characterise these similarities than "family resemblances." . . . And I shall say: "games" form a family.

Seeking to redress our "contemptuous attitude towards the particular case," Wittgenstein shows us that it is not by virtue of some common ingredient that a game is a game, but rather, it is by virtue of its membership of a family.[5]

Returning to our anthropological conference, it now becomes clear that the discussion has taken an erroneous turn in its analysis of the two practices. By identifying the elements common to all games, and then comparing these with the two practices under consideration, no meaningful assessment of their comparative "gamelikeness" is going to be achieved. Far more revealing than having experts review the film would have been to have asked the participants what *they* thought was going on in each practice. In this way, their intersubjective understanding of each practice could have been exposed whereby each practice was perceived by participants to be a member of a particular family of practices. It might thus have been revealed that practice A was a decision-making procedure that went wrong, and that, when repeated (practice B), arrived at the decision not to eat the anthropologist and to let him return to his home.

If not according to a process of approximation to an ideal, how, then, do we evaluate communication? How do we compare two instances of communication in order to discover which is the least distorted by power? If we accept Wittgenstein's "solution"[6] to the problem of universals, it is not by virtue of their respective partaking of the ideal that they are judged to be more or less distorted. Rather, instances of communication that are distorted bear family resemblances to each other, and nothing short of our individual and collective exposure to a great array of instances of distortion will allow us to make such judgments. As Wittgenstein says, "Don't think, but look!"[7] In effect, we are here counseled to immerse ourselves in a particular labyrinth of words and signs, where rules of language usage and matted threads of family resemblances make up a way of life.

If we seek, within our own language game, to justify or interpret, or to evaluate an instance of communication in terms of its degree of distortion, we are, according to this view, similarly engaged in unpacking the labyrinth of mutual understanding that constitutes our way of life.[8] What therefore concerns us is whether any attempt at such critical reflection could be anything other than a mere misunderstanding. In other words, can we make any sense of a cognitivist ethics that conceives of judgment in terms of the recognition of family resemblances?

First, to reject a conception of judgment that characterizes the faculty in terms of the accurate perception[9] of a preponderance of a common ingredient does not preclude the ability to imagine, and even to formalize, an ideal of undistorted communication. Certainly, one can identify common elements in instances of undistorted communication, just as one can identify common elements in various games. Habermas's argument, wherein he reconstructs and formalizes the ideal of undistorted communication from the inescapable presuppositions of argumentation, remains compatible with the insight that it is not by virtue of this idealization that we make judgments. Indeed, Habermas's reluctance of late to express these presuppositions in terms of a "situation"[10] seems to indicate a growing awareness on his part that such an idealization invites just the kind of philosophical confusion that Wittgenstein described as being bound up with our "craving for generality."[11] Certainly, no other aspect of Habermas's theory has been subjected to such systematic misunderstanding.

Wittgenstein's solution to the problem of universals allows us to separate, methodologically, the sense in which a judgment is valid from the way in which participants in a discourse make actual judgments regarding comparative validity. Judgments are thus cognitive because they exemplify the ideal of validity that can be reconstructed from argumentation as such. There is such a thing as fairness, there is such a thing as legitimacy, precisely because there is an internal relation between meaning and validity. Yet at the same time, this does not translate directly into an understanding about how we make evaluative judgments. Such judgments, rather than assessing the preponderance of an ideal in particulars, in fact involve the recognition of family resemblances between them.

To recognize the family resemblances between fair procedures requires practice.[12] It requires that one learns how to see.[13] In such a learning process, it may well be that Habermas's regulative ideal can help us to "train our eyes," but it can never be a substitute for direct experience,[14] for making mistakes, for seeing others do it well. Individuals and groups must learn to recognize family resemblances between fair and unfair procedures. The way in which these resemblances appear, become thematized, and are described, forms an important component in a common "horizon of understanding," and can be quite different in different ethical contexts. Yet in all contexts where reasons are adduced for judgments, a legitimate judgment involves the inspection of institutional arrangements and decision-making methods for their relative fairness. Decision procedures are to be as fair as we can make them, which is the same thing as saying they should be as fair as we are here and now able to see. Such judgments are reflective, for they inspect particulars for their exemplification of the ideal of communicative fairness. But the perception of that exemplification is here understood to mean the recognition of family resemblances.

We might label this reformulation of political judgment as a "discursive *phronēsis* with a cognitivist core." It entails *phronēsis*, here conceived as a general competence[15] to see family resemblances and differences and to make a good decision between alternatives. It is deployed in situations where "it is not possible to deduce the correct choice from *a priori* principles and yet there is a definite sense in which one choice is better than another,"[16] and where "two alternatives seem both right in their own terms . . . and both sides have some claim to validity."[17] It is used, also, wherever the type of rationality proper to the object of choice is in contention,[18] where the way a problem is to be described is both crucial and contentious and where we confront what appear to be exceptions to moral norms.[19]

If political judgment is fair deliberation, where "fairness" is assessed reflectively and according to family resemblances, then we can follow Wellmer when he asserts that "a well developed faculty of judgment is . . . an expression of what we might call the 'faculty' of discursive rationality."[20] According to such a view, ethical expertise no longer appears as an advanced ability for rational, detached judgments based on universalist principles, as it does in Habermas's and Kohlberg's work. Instead, ethical expertise appears to be directly related to intuition, where intuition is an ability, born of experience, to perceive family resemblances. Dreyfus and Dreyfus point out that "it seems that beginners make judgments using strict rules and features, but that with talent and a great deal of involved experience the beginner develops into an expert who sees intuitively what to do without applying rules."[21]

Such a conception of expertise in judging, which they unpack in five stages,[22] has a number of advantages. First, it remains firmly fixed on the everyday ability to judge that seemed so hard to reach when we approached it from a more overtly normative standpoint. Second, it incorporates the advances afforded by Gilligan, privileging involvement rather than detachment and paying a greater attention to ethical concerns. And third, it finally breaks free from the approximation assumption that operates behind so much of the contemporary discussion of judgment. Yet according to the reformulation of judgment that we are here pursuing, the notion of "intuitive expertise"[23] does not signal a degeneration into ethical relativism, for judgment remains capable of cognitive redemption, and thus communication, by virtue of its exemplifying the ideal of communicative fairness.[24]

6.2 JUDGMENTS THAT PRESERVE FAIRNESS

Having reconceived of judgment in terms of discursive *phronēsis* with a cognitivist core, we are now in a position to return to questions regarding the design and evaluation of democratic institutions. Such questions are clearly matters for collective judgment; they form a class of collective judgments in which participants, in a practical discourse, seek designs and evaluations that exemplify the ideal of fairness. We have seen that such judgments are to be conceived reflectively, and that the actual everyday process in which their exemplary validity is assessed proceeds in terms of the recognition of family resemblances. In this section, we pursue a series of issues relating to collective judgments regarding the design and evaluation of democratic institutions, particularly those arising from the inherent fallibility of judgments. In this way, we begin to unpack the practical implications of our various theoretical adjustments to Habermas's position.

Judgments do not arrive at the truth, but are, instead, inherently fallible.[25] As Habermas puts it, within the inevitable "existential provinciality"[26] of our knowledge-claims, all instances of empirical consensus should remain open to revision in the light of new knowledge, the development of "unforeseeable learning processes" and "historical transformations in the objects themselves."[27]

Learning processes that render judgments and the methods of judgment subject to revision might be of two types. First, new and relevant knowledge might arise. Second, there may be developments in the ethical patterning within which communicative fairness is recognized. Whichever takes place, and the likelihood is that both will occur, it is clear that no decision-making procedure ever achieves a level of adequacy after which it would be immune to improvement.

In addition, we confront not only an irreducible plurality of values, but also a tremendous range of possible interpretations of communicative fairness. Ethical patterning varies between cultures, between groups, and even between individuals. At the same time, judgment is a faculty that must be practiced and learned, introducing further variation, even between groups and individuals who share matrices of ethical patterning.

When we take these considerations together, it is clear that judgments are only, ever, provisional, and that we can never dispense with the possible requirement that, at some point in the future, a discourse will need to be reopened. Yet at the same time, living in the world requires that we make decisions, that we close discourses. Judgment is therefore something that does not end. Wellmer inspects this problem in an intriguing way:

> The rationalization of the lifeworld is after all not a process at the end of which it would even be possible to conceive of a perfectly rational lifeworld . . . it is much rather a process in which the consciousness that there are no secure foundations for potential validity is put into effect socially.[28]

This way of stating the issue highlights the absence of a "vanishing point"[29] of rationalization of the lifeworld, and also the importance of seeing discourses of judgment in terms of an ongoing process. This accords well with our reformulation of judgment as a discursive and reflective process of searching, and we find a number of commentators being drawn to the view that communicative ethics in fact expresses the "ideal of an ongoing moral conversation."[30] Bohman deploys such a notion in his discussion of ideology critique, which he sees as being insufficiently treated in Habermas's work, and which is best conceived as an ongoing communicative process.[31] Similarly, Warnke proposes a hermeneutic conversation aimed at an "ongoing dialogue."[32] Warnke is explicit that the need to have the dialogue be ongoing is due to the inevitability of interpretative pluralism,[33] and it is interesting to note a point of contact here with liberal/skeptical democratic theory. Such a notion is also redolent of more avowedly deliberative theories that stress the importance of participation by appealing to its ability to proceduralize the search for moral consensus, and yet where, because of the fact of pluralism, such consensus can never be reached.[34]

A further implication of the inherent fallibility of judgment is that it suggests that all we can hope to achieve in evaluating a practice for its communicative fairness is that we "do our best." We encountered this issue previously when we were looking at the possibility that there was no apparent cut-off point where we could state a practice to have adequately approximated to the ISS. The comparative nature of the word 'best' is important, because it highlights the fact that an interpretation is involved in predicating it to one practice rather than another. For the predication of the word 'best' to have any normative meaning, it must have a cognitive core. If we were to follow Habermas in his assertion of a "strong cognitivism," that is, to adopt a model of generalizable interests or the principle of universalization, then the notion of doing one's "best" in a discourse can be unpacked either in terms of an achieved rational consensus, or in terms of a rational consensus that we have in fact done our "best." It is precisely his firm adherence to the possibility of locating a common interest that allows him to claim normative priority for consensus,[35] and thus to state that anything less is not just second best, but of a fundamentally different nature.[36]

This distinction gained clarity in Habermas's debate with Tugendhat,[37] which showed that while, for Habermas, compromise has its place, it can nevertheless only attain normative validity in situations where a common interest cannot be found. Even in such situations, compromises are only capable of being "indirectly justifiable,"[38] for there remains a fundamental distinction in the *kinds* of activity being undertaken in each case:

> Participants in a practical discourse strive to clarify a common interest, whereas in negotiating a compromise they try to strike a balance between conflicting particular interests.[39]

The danger here is that while consensus involves the bracketing of particular interests, compromise entails nothing more than a "balance of power"[40] between them. If we fail to make this Rousseauesque distinction, and limit ourselves to compromise alone by denying the possibility of consensus, we are inches away from being guilty of the charge Habermas so convincingly levels at Tugendhat—that we are "conflating validity claims and power claims."[41] Our problem then, in following those who have shown that consensus is both cognitively and morally beyond our reach in a pluralist society, is to locate any criteria by which we could, with normative validity, predicate the word 'best' to a communicative procedure. Consensus may, where achieved, still indicate validity, yet it is no longer a necessary condition of it.[42]

In our discussion of judgment, we noted that the abandonment of (U) did not in fact remove the entire cognitive core from discourse ethics. By reformulating judgment in terms of a reflective discourse of application, we described that faculty as a general competence whereby the universal of communicative fairness, expressed by the presuppositions of argumentation, was sought for in ethically patterned ways. It was the reflective nature of judgment, and its ethical patterning, which captured the context-sensitivity of the faculty and also its horizons of intersubjective validity. Political judgment was therefore conceived along the lines of a discursive *phronēsis* with a cognitivist core.

To say of point X, in a practical discourse, that it is the "best" that was possible, is therefore to assert that X is the most communicatively fair solution attainable in the circumstances. Predication of the word 'best' is therefore a judgment, once again to be made reflectively and in a practical discourse, which occurs of necessity within a particular horizon of ethical patterning. This is no more than to say that there must be reasons for the provisional closure of a discourse, and that these reasons must themselves be discursively redeemable.[43]

Forester's treatment of this issue is instructive. He uses the phrase "socially necessary distortion" in order to capture the fact that in real discourses, constraints are such that X is often a compromise rather than an achieved consensus.[44] Yet his adherence to the strong cognitivism of Habermas's principle of universalizability means that he sees the discursive redemption of what constitutes a "socially necessary distortion" as itself requiring an actual consensus. The problem with this view is that in acknowledging that consensus might not be reached in a given discourse, and that circumstances require a compromise, we must also face the possibility that consensus might not be reached upon the question of whether a compromise was required. We would then require a further discourse to reach consensus upon this secondary question, whereupon we face an infinite regress of compromised validations of compromises. If, instead of this, we seek to redeem the reasons for predicating the word 'best' to a point X reflectively, and in terms of a judgment of communicative fairness, we begin to conceive of the notion of "best" in a cognitivist fashion, though in a weaker sense. To say of X that it was the best attainable is therefore to reach a sort of "discursive reflective equilibrium,"[45] instead of involving ourselves in an infinitely regressive chase for a consensus that might never emerge.

One possible objection to this approach is to claim that the idea of a discursive reflective equilibrium in fact masks a regress of its own, for now we seek reflective equilibrium for a compromise via a further attainment of reflective equilibrium, and so on, ad infinitum. This objection amounts to saying that *at no point* in the regress is there any contact with the notion of a common interest or universalized consensus, and therefore, at no point is normative validity ever reached. In order to understand why this objection fails, it is necessary to recall the distinction between the types of interest that constitute consensus and compromise respectively. While, according to Habermas, the first concerns a common interest, the second concerns particular interests. Normative validity is, claims Habermas, only to be deduced from the former.

Yet our reformulation of judgment in terms of a reflective activity involving the search for communicative fairness in ethically patterned ways effectively replaces the notion of consensus with that of "reaching an understanding."[46] It is simply not possible to claim that such an understanding, particularly when reached discursively and in a manner judged to be fair by the participants, excludes any orientation to a common interest, or restricts participants to an orientation to particular interests alone. Reaching an understanding entails finding common ground, where locatable, and listening to the particular interests of others. It involves enlarged thinking, an attention to solidarity, and an appraisal of the unavoidable constraints on practical discourses. For this reason, reaching an understanding or a discursive equilibrium is both attainable, in other words, not infinitely regressive, and also of normative validity; not because it reached consensus or a generalizable interest, but because it was attained under the "best" or most communicatively fair procedure that the participants could find.

Compromises requiring normative validity have two dimensions along which they transgress the ideal. The first involves compromises that are necessitated by the fact of value pluralism, and this is the type most often discussed in the literature. The second involves a particular source of transgression that we confront in real discourses, this being the inevitability of trade-offs with efficiency.[47] Such trade-offs are responses to externally imposed pressures on a discourse, and they procure a necessary gain in efficiency, or more accurately, effectiveness,[48] by limiting participation in some way. Here, in attempting to effectively procure such gains as survival, stability, and rapid, high-quality decisions, we encounter the pragmatic requirement for certain kinds of strategic action, oriented to success, that themselves require legitimation.

Trade-offs between effectiveness and participation can take a number of forms. Temporal pressures often require a limit on participation by drawing a discourse to a close in order for a decision to be made. Similarly, trade-offs can involve responses to cognitive constraints that require the limitation of participation by recourse to some centralization of decision-making power. This takes the form of a hierarchy or a concentration of the necessary functions of leadership in a single person or group. Such trade-offs can also be necessitated by the usurpation of some portion of the decision "zone" by the media of the functionally integrated subsystems of the economy and the administrative state. These serve to limit participation by taking away decisions from participants, either by handing them decisions already made by no one (by the system), or by issuing functional imperatives which must be honored and over which the participants have no control.

The idea of a rational compromise therefore entails not just normatively valid compromises between value perspectives, but also compromises between participation and the demands for effectiveness emanating from the real world and from a functionally integrated system. All these types of compromise require discursive redemption if they are to receive the valid predication of the word 'best.' While in the case of value pluralism, reaching an understanding might take the form of "agreeing to disagree," in regard to real pressures from the world and from the system, reaching an understanding takes the form of the discursive redemption of trade-offs between efficiency and participation.

We might now collect the various issues that have arisen from the fallibility of judgment and combine them with the reformulation of the nature of that faculty attempted in the previous chapter. Political judgment is cognitive, for it involves the reflective search for the universal of communicative fairness, formalized in the presuppositions of argumentation. Such a search is a process without end, and it takes place in ethically patterned ways that reflect both the intersubjective background that allows for the communication of judgments and also the forms in which family resemblances are recognized. In a multicultural society, compromises are inevitable, though they cannot be characterized as excluding all forms of enlarged thinking or of the common good. Sometimes they take the form of a trade-off between participation and effectiveness. There is a cognitivist sense in which the word 'best' can be predicated of a practice, of a compromise, and of a trade-off. The act of predication is a discursive judgment that proceeds via the recognition of family resemblances and whose validity is due to its reflective exemplification of the ideal of communicative fairness.

These insights begin to make the theoretical adjustments that are required if we are to more fruitfully address the design and evaluation of democratic institutions, and to shed some light on how those institutions might actually function. As regards the design of institutions, our investigation of the negative limit to theory showed that it is simply beyond the remit of the normative theorist to prescribe such designs *ex ante*. To attempt to do so is to commit the fallacy of the "shortcut." Thus, the act of designing was seen to have meaning only in terms of self-determination by participants, and while normative theory might rule out certain designs, it cannot stipulate an *a priori* choice among the quite different types of institutional arrangements. For this reason, we cannot simply take our reformulations of theory and do what so many commentators do: we cannot say "these normative considerations are best institutionalized in the following ways," or "for judgments to be pursued in the manner here outlined, we require the following institutions." For while it may well be the case that normative theory seems to call for certain institutional arrangements, we can never be sure that such arrangements are the only or even the best instantiations.

Nor can we dispense with the issue of *ex ante* design altogether. Habermas has certainly taken this approach, particularly in his later writings, where he concerns himself increasingly with the *ex post* evaluation of the normative validity of existing institutions. The result of such a move is to make further gains in normative theory, and to offer sophisticated grounds for the critique of existing institutions, but it moves us ever further away from a radical "Habermasian politics." More and more sophisticated normative theory, particularly with its almost exclusive orientation to the level of the state, does not further our understanding of "what we should do." There is a real danger also, particularly with *Between Facts and Norms*,[49] that he is providing normative grounds that can as well be adduced to defend existing practices as they can to criticize them. While it is still early for the interpretation of this rich and important work, Habermas seems to be sailing dangerously close to an apologist position. I would suggest here, in a provisional manner, for I intend to return to the issue of the growing "statism" of recent developments in critical theory, that Western states require only *de facto* legitimacy to function, and perhaps not even that.[50] Having already enjoyed a plethora of theoretical attempts to offer them *de jure* legitimacy after the fact, ranging from Hobbes to Rawls, it would be sad to see Habermas's project go the same way.

Of course, his position retains significant critical bite, and this is still in evidence in the many fruitful uses of his theory in *ex post* evaluations of democratic institutions. This traditional strength of critical theory is underlined by those who value Habermas's work not so much for its account of moral validity, as for its theory of democratic legitimacy. Indeed, there is a tension running throughout Habermas's project between these two ways of seeing communicative ethics.[51] While some commentators have suggested that it can only function as the latter,[52] others claim it provides insight into both.[53] This tension has also produced claims that Habermas is hopelessly confused as to the relation between the two issues,[54] that he is "generally attentive" to it,[55] and finally, that his confusion in fact opens the door for an understanding, not of the conditions of legitimacy, but of the conditions of the illegitimacy of moral norms.[56]

Without getting into the complexities of these various evaluations of Habermas's understanding of this relation, we should notice that there is something rather compelling about the possibility of deploying discourse ethics in a negative form, and that this relates directly to our inquiry into the kinds of judgments that preserve fairness. While the notion of a consensus theory of legitimacy as conceived by Habermas is a continuation of modern social contract theory, the idea of a lack of consensus as marking what was illegitimate can claim a similar ancestry. A thinker like Rousseau, for example, could be said to have been a good deal more pellucid in regard to the forms of government that were illegitimate, than he was in regard to ones that might be legitimate.[57] If illegitimacy is an easier concept to identify in the world, this might just be due to our having so frequent an experience of it. Or it might be that there is an *entropic* quality to legitimacy, whereby it is constantly in danger of slipping away, thus revealing its negative counterpart.[58]

It is precisely this entropic quality to legitimacy that accounts for the negative orientation of a theory of legitimacy such as that advanced by Scanlon.[59] We notice this same orientation in the example of institutionalized discourse proposed by White[60] and in many of the discursive designs presented by Dryzek.[61] Heller defines this orientation in the following way:

> We can recommend that everyone should check his or her norms on the basis of universal maxims. But if a set of norms does not contradict universal maxims, then the choice of one set of norms over another cannot be rationally grounded, nor need it be. Even if we push moral rationalism to the extreme, we can only go so far as to claim that the rejection of moral norms should be rationally grounded, but never so far as to claim that their acceptance should be rationally grounded.[62]

Applying this orientation to Habermas, she states

> we cannot obtain any positive guidance from the Habermasian reformulation of the categorical imperative. Rather, what we could get is a *substantive limitation* placed on our intellectual intuition: we, as individuals, should only claim universal validity for those moral norms which we can assume would be accepted by everyone as valid in an ideal situation of symmetric reciprocity.[63]

The idea of a "substantive limitation" on our intellectual intuition sees the appropriate task of a communicative ethics as providing a moral test that the various norms thrown up by the lifeworld must pass. Such a notion has greatly interested Benhabib,[64] and she carefully inspects the operation of such a limit in regard to the norm "do not inflict unnecessary suffering."[65] In the previous chapter, we saw a somewhat similar notion given an original twist by Wellmer when he sought to use discourse ethics in the "elimination of nonsense."[66] By articulating the conditions of illegitimacy through his notion of "nongeneralizability," Wellmer draws our attention to the importance of a negative orientation to the question of justification. Such a negative orientation clearly captures the entropic nature of political legitimacy. Applying this to moral norms, he investigates how such a negative principle might operate in regard to a norm of prima facie validity such as *neminem laede*.[67] Both he and Benhabib are here asserting a kind of "relativism with a caveat."

If relativism can be summed up with the phrase "anything goes," then their positions might be described as "anything goes but these things."

In chapter 3, we listed a series of objections to a move being made by a growing number of Habermas's commentators; this being the attempt to unpack discourse ethics into a series of communicative rights. There we saw that such a "shortcut" tends to place the burden of proof upon the wrong object. If, instead of following such a move, we were to deploy discourse ethics with a negative orientation, thus capturing the entropic quality of legitimacy in the realm of politics and setting out the conditions of illegitimacy, then we can see why "saying it with rights" involves aiming our critique at the wrong target.

Those who espouse such a position, such as Cohen, Arato, and Ingram,[68] are keen to point out—and in this they follow Hegel—that rights are underpinned by, or are an expression of, normative learning within civil society.[69] Habermas puts this point thus:

> the social basis for the realization for the system of rights is made up of . . . the communication flows and mediatized influences which emerge from civil society and the political public sphere and are transformed, via democratic processes, into communicative power.[70]

While it is certainly true that legal rights express a configuration of ethical patterning and may even be a "high-water mark" of the collective reflective perception of communicative fairness, there is a sense in which "saying it with rights" tempts us into a distorted conception of democratic legitimacy. This temptation is evident in the development of rights-based discourse generally. Proceeding, as we have historically, from a position in which the power of the state is extant, flagrant examples of the oppression of individuals and minority groups raise suspicions about the legitimacy of the state. This gives rise to the normative dimension of rights, wherein they guarantee individual freedoms,[71] and express the limits of state power. The instantiations of normative learning in civil society therefore takes the form of an incremental "winning back" of power for individuals to resist the power of the state. It is for this reason that Marshall[72] advances the thesis that "the status of the citizen in modern societies has been expanded and buttressed step by step."[73] This is a similar idea to the one we earlier saw advanced by Wellmer with his "specific negations of inequality."[74] Such normative development must, of course, also be seen to be working in tandem with a functionalist view of rights that "institutionalize a market-steered economy,"[75] and that crystallize around private ownership.

On the one hand then, such an incremental construction of the structure of rights, proceeding as it does from the fact of extant state power, represents a genuine gain for the freedom of individuals. This is the liberal discourse of protective rights we inherit from Locke. What we are inspecting here, however, is the tendency of this discourse to occlude and displace what is *in fact* a question regarding the legitimacy of the state. Suspicions, on the part of individuals, as to the legitimacy of the state are stimulated by the experience of oppression, yet these suspicions are, then, in liberalism siphoned off into an argument over rights.

Because no modern state has ever been normatively supported by a discursive infrastructure that might serve to constantly thematize, scrutinize, and affirm its claim to legitimacy, the entropic quality of legitimacy has never been a serious concern. Rather, the state, being a construct of purely strategic and functional origin, need only address the issue of its legitimacy in terms of *ex post* rationalizations and the management of appearances. When the moral outrage of individuals and minority groups expose the legitimation deficit, the state is only too happy to engage in a legalistic argument over rights. States thus functionally encourage the process of displacement of questions regarding their legitimacy into arguments over rights. The resulting displacement serves to occlude their legitimation deficit, and to channel the utopian energies of the lifeworld away from the search for institutional structures that, by enabling collective discursive will-formation, might more genuinely treat the legitimacy of the state as an inherently entropic affair. Rights are, therefore, *just the place* a state would wish to fight its (now highly distorted) battle for legitimacy. Such a tendency for displacement has often, historically, come to the aid of the state, presenting radical collectives with a bloody constitutional wall upon which they dash themselves and expend their utopian energies.[76] This displacement has thus, in part, compensated for the palpable inability on the part of political theory to provide the state with an adequate *ex post* legitimation.

In terms of the question of justification, the burden of proof falls not upon the legitimation of individual rights, but upon the entropic legitimacy of the state. It is not, therefore, the task of a discourse ethics to ground political rights such as participation or freedom of speech—no matter to what extent the pressure to participate grows out of the individual pain engendered by exclusion. Rather, it is up to the state to include individuals in its decision-making processes *if it wishes to remain legitimate*. Such a view can be read back into history, suggesting the possibility that we did not win participatory rights after the French Revolution because individuals appealed to natural law to criticize their exclusion. Instead, and this is more in keeping with Hume's damning attack on natural rights and Habermas's account of the development of the public sphere, normative learning advanced to the point that the legitimacy of the state could no longer survive the mass exclusion of individuals. Subsequent enlargements of the franchise, particularly in regard to the Reform Bills and the Suffrage Movement, could be said to have been motivated in the same way.

The advance offered us by discourse ethics is that it points us at the correct object: it calls into question the legitimation of power. As Benhabib puts it:

> The shoe is really on the other foot. It is up to the critic of . . . egalitarian universalism to show, with good grounds, why some individuals on account of certain characteristics should be effectively excluded from the moral conversation.[77]

As is always the case with a theory of legitimacy, significant problems arise when one tries to cash it in for a theory of institutions.[78] This was precisely the problem we encountered in Habermas's discussion of Rousseau when we saw that the principles that legitimate authority do not pick out particular institutional arrangements in which that authority might be embodied. Such difficulties will certainly be shared by a theory that points instead at the conditions of illegitimacy, or that conceives of legitimacy as entropic. Before we can apply ourselves to the problem of institutional design, however, we need to bring together our reformulated account of judgment with our understanding of its proper object: entropic legitimacy.

Instead of seeing a structure of institutionalized rights as being in need of a justification, we have sought to shift the burden of proof onto the question of the legitimacy of decision-making practices themselves, be they at the level of the state or within civil society. We have also seen the importance of taking a negative orientation toward the question of legitimacy, and it was this orientation that allowed us to highlight the inherently entropic quality of the legitimacy of decision-making practices.

Taking discourse ethics as a theory of moral validity, we were able to see how it might operate as a substantive limit on our intuitions. Taking it as a theory of legitimacy allowed us to focus on the entropic nature of legitimacy. One important way in which these two approaches within discourse ethics might be brought together is to begin to delineate those judgments that must be ruled out in order for legitimation (as an ongoing discursive practice) to be preserved. Thus, Benhabib's "interactive universalism"[79] has the "interesting consequence"[80] of shifting the emphasis of the moral test to the question of whether or not the application of a norm would serve to undermine the procedure of moral argumentation itself. As she puts it:

> we begin to ask not what all would or could agree to as a result of practical discourses to be morally permissible or impermissible, but what

would be allowed and perhaps even necessary from the standpoint of continuing and sustaining the practice of the moral conversation among us. The emphasis now is less on rational agreement, but more on sustaining those normative practices and moral relationships within which reasoned agreement as a way of life can flourish and continue.[81]

She then goes on to use this shift in emphasis in order to advocate a post-conventional *Sittlichkeit* in which questions of justice are seen to involve the evaluation of particular conceptions of the good. In this way, she seeks a utopian crossing from normative to empirical theory, here in a substantive yet minimal sense. Instead of generating another example of "moral monism,"[82] discourse ethics is here deployed to justify those practices that sustain the moral relationships allowing for rational agreement. Such an approach serves to bring together questions of the good life with those of justice,[83] and at the same time to highlight the importance of the role of caring in any conception of morality, a dimension so inadequately treated by Kohlberg.[84]

We should notice that Habermas himself has become increasingly cognisant of such a deployment of his theory. Indeed, there is a sense in which his various discussions of the relation between identity formation and "the vital fabric of ties of mutual recognition through which individuals reciprocally stabilise their fragile identities,"[85] leads him beyond Kant and into an elaboration of "certain structural aspects of the good life."[86] What both Habermas and Benhabib are suggesting, then, is that no matter how communicative fairness is ethically patterned, there is clearly a minimal requirement to protect practices wherein discursive will-formation takes place. Such an assertion amounts to saying, as did Hobbes, that while there may be no *summum bonum*, there is clearly a *summum malum*. For Hobbes, you have to be alive to contract with others. For Benhabib and Habermas, you have to be able to discourse morally if you want to have a moral life.

A similar notion operates behind many of the efforts to apply discourse ethics to a theory of institutions. So, for example, Keane follows Dewey and states that "Whatever obstructs and restricts communication also limits and distorts the formation of a democratic and many-sided public."[87] Forester, in seeking a critical theory of public policy, asserts that:

Any particular policy proposal, then, may promise to influence . . . institutions so that they may either enable or disable, empower or disempower, specific possibilities of popular political debate and mobilization, of popular challenge or traditional class struggle.[88]

Again, some writers express similar ideas in regard to the protection, in law, of the institutional prerequisites of democratic argumentation,[89] or stress the sociopolitical conditions necessary for the institutionalization of a genuine normative plurality.[90] Other examples of such an idea are contained in approaches that seek to outline a series of conditions of human agency, such as those of Gewirth,[91] Fishkin's "essential benefits" for membership of a reflective democratic society,[92] Doyal and Gough's "basic human needs,"[93] and Ferrara's conditions for the development of *phronēsis*.[94] Habermas himself has recently discussed the "basic rights to conditions of life which are socially, technically and ecologically secure to the degree necessary for equal ability to make use of [other] rights."[95]

One might sum up these positions by quoting Cohen's discussion of the issue in Rousseau: "the *preservation* of a general will," he states, "needs to be addressed institutionally."[96] In regard to questions of moral validity, then, it is suggested that discourse ethics operates as a substantive limit on our intuitions. It rules out the application of norms in situations where that application would serve to damage the capacity of agents to engage in practices of moral argumentation. In regard to the justification of political power, therefore, legitimacy is called into question wherever there is inadequate provision for, or institutionalization of, the essential requirements for political actors to participate meaningfully. Central to both is the *preservation of the moral discourse*.

We can now bring our characterization of political judgment as discursive *phronēsis* with a cognitivist core to bear directly on the question of political legitimacy. To do so, we should recall that political legitimacy is itself a matter of judgment; that it is, again, a judgment regarding the degree of power distortion evinced by a discursive procedure.

Our concern throughout this inquiry can now be restated as an attempt to make sense of two kinds of political judgment: the *ex ante* design and the *ex post* evaluation of democratic institutions. The former, if it is not to violate the negative limit to theory, can only be undertaken by participants; it makes sense only in terms of a reflective and discursive act of self-determination. The latter, because it encounters inescapable problems of comparison, can, similarly, only be undertaken by participants themselves, for only within a particular situation and a particular collective matrix of interpretation can the relative weighting of the components of ideal speech be assigned. Both kinds of judgment are to be conceived in reflective terms: as the discursive, ongoing, and fallibilistic search for communicative fairness, this being an ethically patterned structure of family resemblances expressing the normative content of the presuppositions of argumentation.

If these two kinds of political judgments are to be normatively valid, if they are themselves to retain their legitimacy, they must not detract from, or fail to sustain, the ability to make such judgments in the future. We can formalize this procedural constraint in terms of a *Principle of Preservation*:

> (P) Outcomes of, arrangements for, and interventions in political judgments, must not, if they are to be normatively valid, have the effect of damaging the general capacity to make political judgments.

Such a principle operates as a substantive limit on institutional designs for, and outcomes of, decision-making processes. In either case, the principle does not affect the vast majority of possible outcomes, procedures, and interventions, but it provides significant critical power in regard to a minority of each. As a "caveat on relativism," it is advanced as a strong cognitivist claim, though it is, of course, only applicable reflectively. Any decision as to what constitutes "damage" is itself a matter of discursive judgment, though it should be immediately apparent that such practices as the systematic exclusion of citizens from meaningful input into the decision-making apparatus of the state, and the creation of an underclass, are strong candidates for violation of (P). The legitimacy of such practices are thus to be seriously called into question.

In some senses, (P) can be seen as merely a restatement of (D) together with the presuppositions of argumentation, both of which are already available as normative tools for those engaging in reflective judgment. As such, it articulates the normative core of democracy. However, unlike the presuppositions of argumentation, it admits of no ambiguity in regard to whether it pertains to individual communicative rights or to the conditions of legitimacy: (P) is squarely pointed at the latter. It captures the entropic nature of legitimacy, and is not susceptible to the displacement of a legitimation deficit into an attempt to justify individual rights.

We have already noted that reflective judgments that search for communicative fairness necessarily involve trade-offs with efficiency. Such trade-offs, whether they be the result of an inability to reach consensus or due to external pressures, are themselves to be discursively and reflectively redeemed. Perhaps the most important effect of (P) is that it draws a line under these trade-offs. It says, in effect, that any trade-off can be agreed upon by participants, but where these trade-offs are in violation of (P), they cannot be rationally defended.

Such a deployment of (P) might seem to have counter-intuitive effects, particularly as regards a polity's ability to trade-off with efficiency in order to survive. But in fact this is not the case. If, say, the Romans decide, in a reflective political judgment, to choose a dictator in order to resist an invasion, and thus to trade-off some participation for efficiency, it is certainly valid for them to do so. If, however, that dictator begins to engage in practices that effectively impair the ability of the populace to make such judgments; in other words, if he seeks to insulate himself from the discursive process from which his legitimate power is derived, then he is in violation of (P). Another way of saying this might be to say that at the point where (P) is violated, the internal threat (to the legitimacy of the democratic process) equates with the external one. At such a point, the issue becomes the very ability of the populace to generate the (legitimate) power that is necessary to live in a hostile world, and one in which they will have to make judgments even where consensus may not be possible.

This example suggests that, though we abandoned (U), we have, with the introduction of (P), resurrected a quite specific generalizable interest. (P) lends weight to O'Neill's assertion that:

> In the case of reasonable yet conflicting particular interests, it seems plausible to argue that a fair compromise would constitute a generalisable interest, in protecting the conditions for a democratic way of life, for example.[97]

In fact, looking at an example from ancient history where trade-offs with efficiency are obviously required alerts us to a quite specific efficiency problem we encounter in modernity. In addition to the obvious "we must survive," a generalizable interest that has greatly interested environmentalists, we encounter another, this being: "we must survive as democrats." For it seems increasingly obvious that if we continue to be unable to effect any democratic control over the economy, our survival as a species may be in jeopardy. If the choice is indeed between "democracy and barbarism," then not violating the principle of preservation becomes a matter of physical survival.

A further characteristic of (P) is that it pertains not just to outcomes and procedural arrangements, but also to *interventions* in discourses of judgment. This is of particular interest because it enables us to address the question of what individuals *actually do* in democratic assemblies. It therefore gives us a tool that is firmly situated in an area normative theories have so often failed to address; this being what we have referred to as the "missing tier of theory."

The recurrent methodological problems we encountered when we tried to use Habermas's theory affirmatively were seen to arise from a number of sources, and we have been working through these sources systematically. First, some were due to the limits of normative theory, which we showed have caused significant confusion among Habermas's commentators. Second, those difficulties were caused by his conception of judgment, and this led us to reformulate our account of that faculty in terms of discursive *phronēsis* with a cognitivist core. When taken together, the problems encountered upon application of his theory were seen to effectively block the development of a Habermasian politics. We turn now to the final source of methodological problems, this being the object domain to which his theory has been applied.

We have noted this latter problem variously as "lacuna," the "statism" of the theory, and as a "missing tier." Now we must take our various normative tools into the very heart of the question of a democratic politics: to the actual functioning of deliberative fora themselves. In doing so, we will show that that there *is* a political difference between Habermas and Rawls,[98] that there *is* a Habermasian politics, but, because it does not follow his recent liberal turn, such a politics is one that Habermas himself would not countenance. Throughout our inquiry, we have used him as a guide, and have adopted his orientation to approaching the empirical problem of oppression from a normative standpoint. Now we must step out into the cold and immerse ourselves in the real problems of a democratic politics, while at the same time holding hard to what we have learned.

If we forget what he has taught us, we will achieve nothing, for the world is full of theories of deliberative democracy that, in lacking normative sophistication, amount to little more than heart-warming remonstrances, fantasies of positivistic control, or mere semantic incantation.[99] But no matter how great the value of his contribution, it cannot hide the fact that the time has come to part company with our guide.

PART 4

Real Participation

CHAPTER 7

Changing the Object Domain of Application

Throughout our inquiry, we have noted a number of ways in which Habermas and his commentators seem to have shied away from questions concerning the actual functioning of democratic fora. We have seen how many of their discussions seem to end, as it were, in midair, and to use the concept of the public sphere as a kind of placeholder wherein domination-free discourse is intended to take place. In our discussion of the methodological problems that occurred when we sought to use the theory affirmatively, we detected a lacuna, or a missing tier of theory, and in Habermas's latest work, with its increasing orientation to the normative basis of law and constitutional procedure, all hope of this tier's being addressed seemed to finally disappear.

In many ways, this lack of attention to actual discourses is shared by all democratic theory, which has always maintained, as its primary object, the legitimacy and efficiency of the nation-state. Indeed, Eder suggests that there has been, within social science generally, a lack of interest in the functioning of groups.[1] Such a lack is particularly troubling in deliberative democratic theory, however, precisely because such fora are appealed to in order to provide the fair discursive input required for the state to be legitimate. A plethora of new work in deliberative democracy has stressed the importance of deliberative fora, describing them in a variety of ways. Whether they be in the form of secondary associations,[2] autonomous public spheres operating at the periphery of the state,[3] functional demarchies,[4] deliberative opinion polls,[5] New Social Movements,[6] discursive fora,[7] or subaltern counterpublics,[8] few theorists give adequate attention to what actually takes place within such fora. Empirical work on such fora has therefore been thin on the ground,[9] and there remains an implicit distinction between "constitutional" politics, seen as the proper domain of political science, and "ordinary" politics, which is not.[10] It is precisely this distinction that has so much troubled feminist theorists in their attempts to draw attention to the importance of power relations in what have all too often been written off as "private" spheres.[11]

In order to understand why deliberative fora have traditionally fallen outside the concerns of theorists, it is necessary, first (7.1), to understand that the theorist confronts the problems of democracy from a certain perspective. When we have focused this perspective, we will be able to distinguish it from that of participants in a practical discourse (7.2), who, as we shall see, encounter quite different problems. From the perspective of such participants, the problems presented by trying to make democracy real result in the need to make judgments that design and evaluate decision-making procedures, and that preserve the capacity to make decisions that are both legitimate and efficient.

7.1 DEMOCRACY FROM THE THEORIST'S PERSPECTIVE

The lack of attention to deliberative fora can be seen partly as an excessive and seemingly blinding attention to democracy as a problem for nation-states, and partly as an avoidance. Historically, theorists have plied their trade against a background of extant states that claim legitimacy, and have been concerned for all the individuals who live within them. Against such a background, the possibility of deepening democracy, or equality, or fairness, must enter a strategic game where one player is far more powerful than the others. In regard to the efficiency of a democratic order, therefore, the presence of the state raises practical problems that cannot be avoided. For those theorists who seek to deepen democracy, it has meant doing battle with the state, with all the problems of vanguardism and dirty hands that are so entailed. For those who seek to legitimate the status quo, it has meant retaining a careful attention to what is actually possible and practical within a political order of such size and complexity. These, of course, are very good reasons to conceive of democracy as properly pertaining to the level of the nation-state, and such a conception has, historically, resulted in significant gains in freedom and efficiency.

It has also resulted in the traditional accusation against a deliberative politics: that it is utopian, unrealistic, and impractical. This accusation has been so accepted that, as we noted at the outset of our inquiry, it has become intuitively obvious to almost everyone in modernity. Whether due to there being simply too many of us, to the excessive complexity and interdependence of the problems we face, to the apparent inefficiency of deliberation, or to a perceived lack of ability and motivation on the part of the *demos*, democratic theorists since Plato have taught us that the people, while being sovereign, require structures that limit their participation in order for the operation of the nation-state to be possible.

The impracticality of a deliberative politics, or the charge that it is inefficient, refers us also to a second and related accusation: that such a politics is dangerous. Unchecked participation is to be feared, not just because it threatens inefficiency, but also because it can result in terror. The French and Russian Revolutions are the historical examples most often adduced to support this claim, but the treatment this issue received at the hands of those who framed the American Constitution shows that democratic theory has always had a profound distrust for the people.[12]

This distrust, based on accusations of ignorance, volatility, and partial judgment on the part of the *demos*, begins to suggest some of the reasons why the interactions that occur between ordinary people in their political debates have been passed over by democratic theorists. For the world of deliberative fora is one of seemingly petty concerns, of emotional outburst, of unschooled argumentation and unstructured decision-making. It reveals the full spectrum of human affect and the distasteful and faintly embarrassing world of private interaction. If this were not reason enough to avoid looking closely at deliberative fora, there is also the fact that the emotional component of actual discourses renders the processes that go on within them extremely hard to thematize. Thus, having been left to inspect such interactions by an uninterested and disdainful political science, social psychologists have not, themselves, been able to shed much light on the process of decision-making within small groups.[13]

This combination of concerns has had the result of moving democratic theory away from the inspection of everyday interactions between ordinary people and toward those that constitute the administration of the nation-state. Theorists thus take up a position high above the earth, from which they gaze out upon the entire institutional landscape.[14] In most deliberative theories of democracy, this perspective operates as an unexamined assumption. Beginning with a diagnosis of the political order *as a whole,* and now oriented to a totalized conception of society, suggestions for reform inevitably share that totalized and elevated view. No matter how limited the suggested reforms, no matter how restricted to a mere portion of society, theorists seldom escape this ubiquitous perspective. Thus, to take an example, the many recent developments in civil society theory, though not primarily oriented to democracy at the level of the state, retain an orientation to the problem of democracy as properly pertaining to the entire political order. Similarly, communitarians "advance their proposals as a contribution to the politics of the nation-state,"[15] and even Habermas's carefully limited suggestion for "peripheral" public spheres remains oriented to the meaning of legitimacy in the polity as a whole. Lest we imagine that this perspective is somehow a product of an excessive attention to normative concerns, and a "passé" interest in questions of legitimacy, we should note the following from a theorist who, as a postmodernist, eschews all normative questions:

> What we need is a hegemony of democratic values, and this requires a multiplication of democratic practices, institutionalizing them into ever more diverse social relations, so that a multiplicity of subject-positions can be formed through a democratic matrix. It is in this way—and not by trying to provide it with a rational foundation—that we will be able not only to defend democracy but also to deepen it. . . . A project of radical and plural democracy . . . requires the existence of multiplicity, of plurality, and of conflict, and sees in them the *raison d'être* of politics.[16]

All these examples serve to illustrate what we might call the perspective of the theorist. From such a perspective, democracy appears as a problem requiring institutional forms, conduits whereby the people feed informed consent into the nation-state and restraints on participation in order to preserve efficiency and stability. Such institutional forms raise problems regarding the location of democracy,[17] and of legitimate and efficient design: and all on a massive scale. Situated *outside* the realm of action, the theorist gazes in upon it as a spectator. As with the doctor who possesses knowledge about health and sickness, the attempt is to apply this knowledge to problems encountered by *someone else*.

Now, of course, democracy *is* a very large wood, and forestry legitimately studies it as such. But it is also made up of trees. There is, therefore, a quite different perspective from which to inspect the problems of democracy. From this second perspective, democracy presents quite different problems, for which democratic theorists, and most glaringly deliberative theorists, have not provided any meaningful assistance. Clearly, theories of deliberative democracy are of value if they can reveal illegitimacy at the level of the nation-state, and where they can provide motivation and guidance for future institutional reform. As such, they offer much to political theorists and perhaps also to politicians. They might even be of some use to ordinary people, particularly those who are concerned with understanding what is wrong with our society and whether or not to offer support to a political cause or leader. But they do not address the ordinary question: "How could there ever be fair deliberation in, say, my place of work?"

If deliberative theory is to be of real use, if it is to be a pragmatic and earthbound practice, it will need to address democracy not just as it appears in the elevated view of the political theorist, but also as it is actually encountered in the everyday world of ordinary people. Most of us do not practice statecraft. We do not face the problem of reforming an entire social order, or of ridding *all* discourses of exclusionary practices. We live firmly upon the earth, grubbing around in our work, our civic involvements, our religious affiliations, our familial and social groups and in our intermittent political activism. For the most part, it is in face-to-face discussions that ordinary people actually confront the problems of democracy. Here, more democracy means greater fairness and participation *in the decision-making process of an actual group*. All the work put in by the theorist to make democracy real by giving it an institutional location[18] is a matter of little interest to us as participants in an actual discourse. This is because, in a real situation, the dimension of "where" simply does not arise. What we want is more democracy right here, right now. The democratization of society is certainly an intriguing thought, but as a meeting drags on, as it is once again taken over by the same people and the same interests prevail, such a notion seems very distant indeed.

Democracy presents different problems when considered from the perspective of the participant rather than from that of the theorist. From the perspective of the participant *inside* the realm of action, the problem is to make decisions as fairly as possible and at the same time to preserve efficiency. Yet any attempt to use discourse ethics for procedural guidance in such matters reveals the theory to be profoundly utopian in a quite specific sense, for it does not reach down to their real concerns.[19] While theorists busy themselves with cultural criticism and seek institutional forms that maximally instantiate the ideal of fairness, participants instead seek normatively valid ways of improving the fairness of their decision-making process. Thus, while the theorist faces the problem of making the ideal real, participants must make something real more ideal. Here, to continue our metaphor of the doctor, sickness is not an abstract concern. It is a cause of immediate and personal pain.

It is for this reason that Wolin suggests, "Democracy is not about where the political is located but how it is experienced."[20] He goes on to show that democracy, as something that *happens to participants* in a discourse, is characterized by the loss of form, by immediacy and by the breach of design.[21] Thus, participants confront occasional revolutionary moments in their everyday lives that either recede naturally, are repressed, or are "tamed" by an institution. Wolin cites the constitutional arrangements of liberal democratic states as being the ultimate "domestication of politics."[22]

We might extend these insights and assert that, from the participant's point of view, democracy, or discursive fairness that is nevertheless efficient, is something that occasionally *breaks out* among particular people in particular situations. Suddenly, we find we have risen above the power-saturated ways in which we normally interact and that something quite different is taking place between us. From the perspective of the participant, democracy involves not a form for participation, but a breach of form.

Political theory's inattention to *this* kind of democracy was criticized by Pizzorno in 1970, especially for its inability to provide a historical reconstruction[23] and since then, perhaps only feminist theory has seriously inspected it.[24] Yet if we combine the conceptual gains developed by the various new theories of deliberative democracy with the scant literature that has considered it as an empirical phenomenon, we can begin to delineate the characteristics of a democratic breakout, to inspect the kind of theoretical assistance its participants might require and to sketch its history.

7.2 DEMOCRACY FROM THE PARTICIPANT'S PERSPECTIVE

A breakout of democracy has identifiable characteristics, confronts recurrent problems, and may even have a discernible life cycle. Once we broaden our vision away from the state to include civil society and everyday life, history provides us with numerous examples of democratic breakouts.[25] A somewhat arbitrary list might highlight occurrences in the political clubs of revolutionary France,[26] in workers' societies of the nineteenth century,[27] and in anarchist patrols in the Spanish Civil War. More recently, breakouts have taken place in the women's movement, in user groups challenging Community Care provisions, among miner's wives during the 1985 strike, and in sections of the anti–poll tax movement.[28] There are many more examples that are so short-lived as to never attract the attention of the media. Indeed, it seems reasonable to suggest that almost *all* of us have had *some* experience of a breakout of democracy.[29]

What then, are the characteristics of *this* kind of democracy? The primary characteristic must be that of noise.[30] All accounts note that speech becomes animated, and debate heated. This sudden increase in discussion follows upon the discovery of a common preoccupation. Now, people are keen to be heard, they listen to others with interest, and concern is expressed to elicit all views.[31] Exclusionary tactics are directly challenged, as are attempts to distort the needs and interests of others.[32] Whatever the common interest under discussion, all salient facts are actively explored, and the group, now pooling its cognitive resources, confronts the matter at hand in its full complexity.[33]

Another early indication is that people become highly suspicious of all forms of existing authority.[34] The women's movement in particular found that one of the effects of this suspicion was that people identified new ways in which they were oppressed.[35] In effect, during open discussion, people become politicized. As republican theory has always pointed out, participants in deliberation broaden their tight focus on individual interests, first to seeing things from the point of view of others, and then to those interests the group has in common. As the group continues to meet, friendship, vitality, and rapid learning all draw people in.[36] Now, to use Rousseau's phrase, they "fly to the assemblies."[37] In a democratic breakout, the cost of participation is completely swamped by the benefits.[38]

Social psychologists have found that what seems to drive these processes, and to give them their extraordinary energy, is that, in a breakout of democracy, conflict *works*.[39] It generates cohesion, it causes people to re-evaluate their preferences and needs, and it brings about consensus.[40] There *are* disagreements, and these are acted out—often in highly dramatic ways. Livy's history of early Rome has many good examples of such political drama, and it was precisely this energizing conflict to which Machiavelli attributed the vitality of that republic.

A further characteristic of a breakout of democracy is that participants seek ways to deliberate that are seen to be right and fair.[41] Was that decision made fairly? Could it have been more so? Accounts of democratic breakouts would indicate that argumentation around such issues includes not only reason, but also a variety of rhetorical devices, such as irony, ridicule, and *ad hominem*.[42] In Athenian debates, for example, it is noticeable that verbal abuse of a speaker's ancestry often took the place of substantive criticism of the speaker's views.[43] And no matter how ingeniously egalitarian the procedure being used, it is the subject of almost constant assessment and complaint.[44]

As the women's movement found, in a democratic breakout, leadership is no longer based on social roles, but becomes more fluid: its functions divided and shared.[45] Where it does accrue to particular individuals, it is because the *group* benefits from that individual's abilities.[46] Whether the benefits of leadership outweigh its dangers is a constant topic of discussion for the group. On those rare yet inevitable occasions where ostracism is necessary, it tends to be practiced against those more powerful members of the group who are widely seen to be actively working against the collective interest.[47] Thus, the ejection of a leader is often the first act of an eruption of democracy.

As the forum continues to meet, networks of alliance and disagreement emerge, group boundaries harden, and adversarial postures are adopted toward the institutions of power.[48] The group develops in-jokes,[49] stereotypical images of opponents, and symbolic representations of its cohesion.[50] Nevertheless, a characteristic of fairness is openness of membership, and informal and unbureaucratic procedures to include new arrivals.

Generally, activity remains frenetic,[51] people make extraordinary sacrifices and act in uncharacteristic ways. A great deal of emotion continues to be expressed, both positive and negative: people can't sleep, they fall in love, and what they are able to achieve surprises both others and themselves. Now, the group's deliberations result in innovative and even extreme decisions, rather than in ones that tend toward the mean of their individual preferences.[52]

With a breakout of democracy we have Sartre's "group in fusion," Pizzorno's "mobilization" type of political participation, Mansbridge's "fragile bubbles" of "unitary democracy," Phillip's "internal democracy," Moscovici's "consensual" participation, Arendt's "oases in the desert" or "elementary republics," Charter 77's "parallel poleis," and the opening of a Habermasian "public sphere."[53]

Such moments of fairness enjoy some successes: power is challenged, its ways revealed, and efficient and creative decisions are made.[54] If breakouts become extended and networked together, new rights can be won, and sometimes even governments fall. But usually there is failure. The demise has multiple causes, both external and internal. Externally, one of the most significant difficulties to be faced by any genuinely democratic forum is the unbridled hostility of the state and other institutions of power. Usually, breakouts can be safely ignored, ridiculed, denied resources, and allowed to peter out. Should they manage to survive and network together so as to present a threat to existing structures of power and property distribution, other strategies, such as informants, payoffs, and dirty tricks will be used. Finally, if these prove ineffective, the state will deploy direct and violent repression in order to restrict the growth of democracy.[55]

A further source of difficulties is that, as the scale of their activities increase, contacts with the institutions of power become more frequent, and the group finds it needs delegates, representatives, and spokespersons.[56] Gradually, this begins to erode the face-to-face quality of the initial breakout. Now, what was once done discursively, is taken over by particularly able individuals, or even by bureaucratic procedure. As the group comes to increasingly rely on such methods of organizing its activity, the texture of its interactions becomes profoundly changed. It is, to use Habermas's phrase, gradually "colonized" by instrumental forms. At last, if it has not fizzled out or been repressed, the breakout is co-opted and fully institutionalized.[57] Participants now find themselves mere spectators of a process that was once their own. So domesticated, discourse returns to its more common power-saturated and "normalized"[58] form. If the breakout was widespread and prolonged, its slogans will be adopted hypocritically, aped by politicians, and used to advertise clothing to teenagers.

Internal causes of failure are not hard to identify. Stress and exhaustion,[59] fear of repression, frustration, resignation, repeated narcissistic injuries,[60] and withdrawal are among them. Often, these take the form of group divisions that serve to constrict deliberation, or the emergence of a faction or leader whose methods undermine fair communication. Old power differentials reappear, so that once again men dominate the discussion, experts automatically take on tasks that become increasingly invisible to the group, and the more confident members, now doing almost all the talking, complain about the level of participation of the less active.[61]

Riven by conflict that is now destructive,[62] the noise at last begins to abate. As the cost of participation rises, people no longer attend with the same frequency. When the democratic moment is over, apathy returns, as does the exclusive concern with self-interests. Instead of agreeing to disagree, as they might have done during the democratic breakout, conflict goes underground,[63] and consensus becomes, once more, a sham. As the recriminations begin, people tend to pathologize those who hold views different from their own.[64] Difference is now seen as sabotage, and ostracism tends both to be used against the less powerful members, and to be increasingly divisive. The ideology of the group hardens further still, and in a kind of micro Thermidor, "group think" dominates.[65] Now, in a parody of self-rule, the group takes on the task of oppressing itself.

With the eclipse of fairness, leaders and subgroups begin to *force* cohesion and agreement, and the negative side of direct "democracy," characterized by the pressure to conform and the loss of individual freedom, raises its head.[66] As it does so, it is greeted with gleeful shouts of "I told you so!" by all those who felt threatened by the breakout. But those who experienced the breakout know that something of importance occurred there. Though bruised and confused by its demise, they have tasted fairness, and they will not forget. What they learned: that humans are capable of compassion and autonomy, meanness and subservience, that the "democratic" state is profoundly antipathetic to democracy, that fair deliberation can be efficient, cannot be easily unlearned. Their disappointment is therefore acute, as is their need to search for reasons for their failure.

Whatever the combination of causes, genuinely democratic fora seem to have a discernible life cycle: they burn brightly, then either fizzle, are repressed, become profoundly unfair, or are co-opted and institutionalized. They can last for moments, or for months, but eventually, they come to an end.[67] In a breakout of democracy, the entropic nature of legitimacy is an unavoidable fact of life.[68] Whether something so transitory has any value is a difficult question. But it is one that might also be asked of an individual human life. Whether our lives are worth living, given that they will one day end, is not only a difficult question, but perhaps also, a pretheoretical one. Certainly, some combination of the denial of death and the seemingly irrational affirmation of the present gets most of us through, and this may also be so for participants in a breakout of democracy.

If, from the participant's perspective, democracy is something that breaks out in specific situations, then what kind of help does the theoretical inquiry we have been undertaking provide those who find themselves embroiled in such moments? We have already noted that the dimension of location, so thoroughly investigated by democratic theorists, is of little consequence for participants. What then, of the first and second dimensions of democracy, the "who" and the "how"?

Certainly, participants in actual discourses face questions like, Who should be included in this decision? How should we decide? How do we maximize participation and yet remain efficient? Are we doing things right? What about this leader, this power imbalance, this nondecision, their apathy, and her complaint about his coercion? To ask for assistance with such questions is not to turn like sheep to theory. Participants do not require instruction on *what* their judgment should be. The need is rather for procedural guidance, for empirical ways of managing their interactions that are normatively valid. In attempting to address such questions, participants have received little assistance from democratic theory generally and none at all from Habermas and his commentators.

Judgments, we have argued, are normatively valid because they exemplify the ideal of communicative fairness. Participants make such judgments by recognizing the complex similarities and differences that exist between various fair and unfair procedures. The family resemblances between these procedures are an integral part of their "matrix of understanding." What they recognize here is, therefore, ethically patterned, for it is a manifestation of their way of life. At the same time, participants must balance the need for legitimacy with that of efficiency if they are to survive as a democratic entity. Somehow, they must make judgments that preserve the fairness of their decision-making process in the face of the entropic nature of legitimacy.

The question to which we now turn, therefore, is this: How can participants make judgments that preserve, nurture, network, and extend those moments when fairness breaks out between them? In approaching this question, we are attempting to deploy the various tools and insights derived from discourse ethics in a distinct object domain: that of the actual functioning of democratic fora. Effectively, we are moving away from considering the ever elusive addressee for critical theory to be, as Habermas suggests, the whole of humanity. Instead, we are conceiving that addressee to be *those who are currently trying to be democrats*; in other words, participants in a breakout of democracy.

CHAPTER 8

Toward a Democratic Politics

From the first moment a breakout of democracy occurs, participants are involved in a struggle for survival as a democratic entity. Engaged in an activity whose legitimacy is entropic, they now face significant pressures and constraints, many of which will, if improperly managed, serve to return them to a power-saturated form of discourse. Whenever they select a procedure, they must do their "best" to make it as fair as is possible under the circumstances. From now on, their ability to survive as a legitimate democratic entity will be directly related to their collective expertise in making judgments that preserve the fairness and efficiency of their decision-making process.

A decision-making process can be described as having five elements.[1] First, there is the moment of problem recognition, in which some difficulty or issue becomes figural[2] for the group, and which seems to demand their attention. Second, there is the moment of deliberation, during which information is collected, opinions exchanged, and argumentation takes place. At some point, deliberation must be brought to a provisional closure in order to move to the third moment in the process, this being the actual making of the decision. The decision is then, in the fourth moment, implemented. Finally, there is a moment of evaluation, whereby the entire process is examined retrospectively.

If the process of decision-making as a whole is to be legitimate, all these moments must be as fair as is possible under the circumstances. Only in this way can the group, upon completion of the process, be validly described as having done its "best." Each moment of the process raises cognitive issues around the ability of the group to perceive and recognize what they are dealing with. At the same time, each moment requires procedural arrangements by which they are to be undertaken and resolved. In any of these moments, a failure in perception, or a failure to find ways to do things that are fair, constitutes a threat to the legitimacy of the decision-making process as a whole.

As table 2 shows, there are a number of issues that arise with frequency across the five moments that constitute the decision-making process. One cluster of issues arises from the pressures and constraints that fall upon participants in a breakout of democracy. These result in par-

TABLE 2
The Decision-Making Process

Moments in the Decision-Making Process	Perceptual Issues	Procedural Issues
1. Problem Recognition	Noticing a decision is required. Seeing the need for a gain in effectiveness. Seeing, in a problem, a threat to deliberative capacities.	How are problems brought to group's attention? How to prioritize problems? How to set agenda?
2. Deliberation	Having the necessary information. Seeing relevance of information. Recognizing fair deliberation. Seeing threat, in chosen procedures, to deliberative capacities. Seeing need for trade-off.	Can all join in debate? How is debate arranged? Is debate fair? Is debate efficient? Is there a place for raising emotional issues? Is damage to deliberative capacities minimized? Trade-offs fairly redeemed?
3. Decision	Recognizing when to close deliberation. Seeing how to best make a decision.	Method for making fair yet efficient decision. Minimizing threat to deliberative capacities.
4. Implementation	Understanding the decision. Seeing how and when to implement. Seeing inappropriate implementation.	Procedures for implementation. Procedures for handling difficulties in implementation.
5. Evaluation.	Seeing fairness of process. Seeing effectiveness of process. Seeing need for trade-off. Recognizing damage to deliberative capacities.	Procedures for evaluation. Procedures for changing elements in process. Re-assessing damage. Re-assessing trade-offs.

ticipants having to constantly make trade-offs between participation and efficiency. Their procedure must be fair, yet if they are to survive, it must also be efficient. The set of procedures and actions from which they can select are therefore *all* repressive in some way.[3] The problem they face is to somehow become aware of, to understand the need for, and to give informed consent to, the fairest *unfair* practices. These questions, as we have already noted, constitute a class of judgments that the participants must make. In so doing, participants must remain cognisant of the effects of such trade-offs upon their capacity to deliberate fairly in the future. We will consider the problem of judgments regarding trade-offs and their effects upon the deliberative capacities of the group below (8.1).

In addition, there is a further cluster of issues which arise when democratic break-outs try to increase the scale and scope of their activities. The problems of networking and democratic-movement building will be inspected in section 8.2. Here also, we will focus on a recurrent difficulty that confronts both participants in deliberative fora and those who attempt to thematize the actual functioning of those fora, this being the problem of managing emotion.

8.1 JUDGMENTS REGARDING THE REDEMPTION OF TRADE-OFFS

Habermas has formalized the ideal of communicative fairness in terms of a series of pragmatic rules.[4] These rules articulate the cognitive core of a judgment regarding the fairness of a deliberative procedure. In table 2, they would thus pertain to the second moment of the decision-making process (item 2) in column 2 (under procedural issues). When participants design, or select, or evaluate a deliberative procedure for its fairness, they are making a discursive and collective judgment that is cognitive. The method by which they make such judgments, however, proceeds not by the intellectual appraisal of approximation to this ideal, but via the schooled intuition that recognizes family resemblances.

Decision-making in the real world requires effectiveness as well as fairness, and gains in the former often entail a loss in the latter. It is for this reason that the relation between them can, on occasion, be expressed in a trade-off function. For example, temporal pressures might mean that the process of deliberation needs to be speeded up or brought to a close. Similarly, cognitive and motivational pressures might require the selection of hierarchical arrangements and, for a moment at least, communication might need to proceed in a quite unfair manner. In such situations, the legitimacy of the decision-making process turns on the legitimacy of the process by which that trade-off was made. Thus, legitimate trade-offs themselves require fair deliberation, agreement, and review. One of the characteristics of "good" decision-making procedures is, therefore, the provision of opportunities for the discursive redemption of trade-offs.

The discursive redemption of a trade-off is also a discursive and collective judgment with a cognitivist core. Just as deliberation must be as fair as is possible under the circumstances, so too, the deliberation of trade-offs must be pursued fairly. Often, a group is confronted with the need to make a gain in effectiveness that would involve a loss of fairness. Now, as their attention shifts to the discursive redemption of that trade-off, they often find that this level of deliberation is itself under pressure. If, for example, they must quickly make a decision about a trade-off for effectiveness, they once again confront the need to trade-off participation, here at a deeper level still. In such situations, a group must, if it is to avoid the paralysis of an infinite regress, "reach an understanding," or some degree of "discursive equilibrium," as to the legitimacy of the trade-off. Such an "understanding" then becomes an important issue to prepare for pro-actively, and to evaluate retrospectively. This would suggest that one design question a democratic group must address pertains to "good" arrangements for the discursive redemption of trade-offs before they occur, and for their subsequent evaluation.

In regard to limiting participation in order to gain effectiveness, the question for participants centres on whether they have really done their "best" with a particular trade-off. Have we been as fair as circumstances allowed? Clearly, there are levels of trade-off beyond which the process is no longer democratic. Indeed, one of the signs that a democratic breakout is over is that such trade-offs are no longer made by participants themselves, but are forced upon them, and do not receive adequate discursive redemption.

At some level then, in the struggle against the entropic nature of legitimacy, we encounter a cut-off point, beyond which we can no longer validly describe a decision-making process as legitimate. In our reformulation of judgment, we attempted to give some clarification to this cut-off point by deriving a principle of preservation (P). This principle was seen to operate as a procedural constraint that served to highlight the importance of preserving the capacities of the group to continue to deliberate fairly in the future. Where we conceive of democracy as an ongoing decision-making process in which good judgments will continue to be required of participants, care must be taken to avoid those practices that *damage* the capacities of participants to make good judgments, in other words, those practices that violate (P).

In regard to judgments pertaining to trade-offs between participation and efficiency, (P) serves to alert us to the dangers inherent in such trade-offs. Often, a gain in effectiveness comes at such a cost to the discursive capacities of the group that it is irreversible. An example might be a politics of vanguardism, for here, the gain in effectiveness is seen as requiring only a short-term loss in participation, yet this, due to the damage wrought on the deliberative capacities of the populace, clearly constitutes a violation of (P), and thus leads to a failure of democracy to survive. Other examples are afforded by styles of leadership and expertise that masquerade as assistance yet that stimulate dependency, and by the common use of procedures within small groups that were developed to maximize effectiveness at the level of parliamentary decision-making. Thus, the principle would rule out those inappropriate structures of voting and representation that so debilitate fair debate in voluntary associations, local party and government committees, and public-sector teams meetings.

Survival of the democratic moment depends upon the preservation of the deliberative capacities of the group. As to what constitutes "damage" to these capacities, only participants in an actual discourse can decide. Yet the principle of preservation would urge them to carefully consider the meaning of the word 'damage,' and to focus on the various components of those capacities that they must preserve.

First, alternative procedures will require discursive examination as to their impact on the quality of information available to participants. Deliberative capacity is clearly dependent on good information, on its accessibility and on its continued provision.

Second, the capacity to deliberate well seems to be something that is habitual, and that therefore requires practice if it is to be preserved. This would indicate that opportunities for deliberation should be frequent and substantive. Long gaps between deliberative sessions, or the reduction of importance of those sessions, even though they may be the result of trade-offs that have procured significant gains in effectiveness and that have themselves been discursively redeemed, pose significant dangers. Once broken, the habit of deliberation may be hard to regain.

The fact that deliberation requires regular practice leads us to a third component of deliberative capacity, that of motivation. As our inspection of democratic breakouts showed, the energy level of a group is its most significant resource. Upon it relies the ability of individuals to stay oriented to their tasks, to reap the benefits of conflict, and to search diligently for ways of doing things that are fair. Damage would here take the form of reducing the energy available to the group by failing to preserve their morale, and thus endangering their motivation. There are, for example, many practices undertaken by organizations that do not seem especially unfair, or even particularly significant in the substantive power issues that they raise, yet that nevertheless undermine morale. Such practices, though not directly exclusionary, damage the deliberative capacity of participants by, instead, alienating them, and thus reducing their motivation to do what is required of them to make the organization function effectively.

The capacity to deliberate effectively is, as we have noted, intimately related to expertise in the making of judgments. As such, it requires practice, learning, and may even develop through identifiable stages. In considering what damages the capacity to deliberate, then, and this is our fourth component, participants must understand that it takes time to learn to do it well. Immediate expectations of expertise, the devaluation of individuals due to their lesser ability and the failure to provide opportunities for learning, would all constitute damage to deliberative capacity.

At the outset of a democratic breakout, it is likely that many members of the group will not evince the "intuitive expertise"[5] required to recognize family resemblances between instances of fair communication. They may not see the need for trade-offs for effectiveness, or may make them too readily. They may not realize that a trade-off is damaging their deliberative capacities in such a way as to make it irreversible. This is, of course, precisely the problem that has always bedeviled democracy, for without a perfectly informed and wise populace, the devolution of power appears a very dangerous undertaking. It is for this reason that Goodwyn states that "the stages of development, both in numbers of recruits and the level of political consciousness the recruits attain, unfold slowly, which is why the building of democratic movements requires patience above all."[6]

While mistrust of the political consciousness of the populace has served to ground the need for elitism in democracy, participation itself is just as frequently appealed to as the supreme educator.[7] If practiced regularly, perhaps at first on tasks appropriate to the level of learning, participants can make significant gains in proficiency.

If we adapt Dreyfus and Dreyfus's account of the development of ethical expertise[8] to describe the stages of learning involved in the recognition of family resemblances between instances of communication, we can see how different the individual capacities of group members might be. While the judgment of the "novice" proceeds according to context-free features and rules, the "advanced beginner," upon seeing a sufficient number of examples, begins to see situational aspects and to be able to use maxims rather than rules. Now that more and more situational aspects become visible, there is an information explosion. As this is organized and reduced to categories, it becomes possible for one with "competence" to make plans for action and to assess a variety of possibly applicable rules for their appropriateness. At some point, such a feedback loop is no longer required, and with the attainment of "proficiency," the individual stops looking for guiding principles and becomes able to "see" or "be struck by" ways forward. As this ability advances, the "expert . . . seems gradually to decompose this class of situations into subclasses, each of which share the same decision, single action, or tactic."[9] With the attainment of intuitive expertise, individuals can recognize the necessity of trade-offs for effectiveness and family resemblances between instances of fair communication. Now, "what must be done, simply is done."[10]

If learning to deliberate well can be described as moving through stages such as these, then we can see why Wittgenstein said "Don't think. But look!" Here, learning to recognize becomes more important than learning to apply rules, and as participants improve their ability to make judgments, they would increase their perceptual ability without necessarily increasing their ability to theorize, or even to rationally account for, their judgments. For this reason, the wide range of expertise in the making of judgments that would occur within a group can never give rise to a quantification of such expertise, let alone the labeling of some participants as "advanced beginners," and others as "competent." At the same time, groups do come to value the judgments of certain individuals more highly than others, precisely because when their judgment is expressed, people *come to see things they did not see before.* It is in this form that sapiential power remains a differentiation between individuals in a fair interaction.

The degree to which the selection of fair procedures is reliant on the perceptual and cognitive capacities of the participants is a direct outcome of our reformulated understanding of the faculty of judgment. By stressing, in our account of judgment, the recognition of family resemblances over the approximation to an ideal, we have come to raise extraordinarily high expectations on individual capacities,[11] even to the extent of claiming that the preservation of those capacities constitutes a crucial component of democratic legitimacy. It is therefore reasonable for participants to ask themselves whether or not they might wish to relieve, and even to replace, such expectations by institutionalizing certain procedures in such a way as to make them available without constant deliberation. Our fifth concern regarding the preservation of deliberative capacities therefore pertains to the degree to which participants can legitimately commit their procedures to settled written "law."

This question has, of course, been well aired in political theory, notably in discussions of the value of "precommitment" and under the rubric of constitutional design.[12] First, it has been cogently argued that institutions that refine or "launder" preferences can help to preserve certain valuable higher-order preferences (or preferences for preferences), and that these institutions can be legitimate when they are the product of "self-binding," or "auto- or self-paternalism."[13] Here, the advantages of insulating the decision-making process from the volatility of actual preferences are stressed, for it makes possible the reflection of more complex preference structures and better political decisions.[14] Second, some theorists have concentrated on collective forms of self-binding that serve to restrict the kinds of arguments and issues for political deliberation, and that are thus seen to provide for more democratic outcomes.[15] It may, therefore, be the case that certain kinds of institutional buttressing of the moral capacities of participants can offer significant gains in effectiveness, lessen the constant need for participants to deliberate, and more adequately preserve the legitimacy of the decision-making process. For these very good reasons, participants might choose to adopt a constitution that fixes certain procedures and that even insulates those procedures from constant change.

Certainly, such institutions can be legitimately agreed to in fair deliberation, for there is nothing about *self*-binding per se that precludes its discursive redemption. If, however, a group does choose to adopt a constitution that fixes procedures, the principle of preservation would counsel them to see it not as a one-off founding event, but as subject to regular discursive review. Whether this review takes the form of an informed recommitment, in other words, as a reaffirmation of the contract by which such institutions were brought into being, or merely as a celebration, as advocated by Machiavelli,[16] the regularity of review cannot be avoided. This is no more than to say that genuinely *democratic* constitutions should not replace the ongoing discursive capacity of the group with untouchable written law.[17] Significant damage is inflicted upon participants by (semi-)permanent ossification of procedures, no matter how great the gains in effectiveness they make available, for the simple reason that deliberative expertise is so easily forgotten. The principle of preservation here underscores the word "self" as it appears in the notion of "self-binding." There can be no binding of alter, for to do so is to damage the deliberative capacity of alter. We cannot, therefore, avoid the charge that our account of democratic legitimacy rests too heavily on the deliberative capacities of individuals, or that our expectations of individuals are excessive. Inescapably, democrats rule themselves. They cannot be ruled by the words of the dead.

Finally, participants must take care with the interventions they make in deliberations. Here, the principle of preservation has the effect of limiting what one might call free speech. While "anything goes" in terms of interventions in deliberation, some things are ruled out, precisely because of the damage they do to the deliberative capacities of other individuals. The current debate in the United States around the First Amendment is paying increasing attention to the conditions of deliberation. Thus, Sunstein has suggested that the right to free speech be withheld when an intervention is not a genuine contribution to the discursive search for solutions.[18] (P) would offer something rather different here, for it would rule out interventions such as racist propaganda that serve to intimidate others, and thus to constrain their capacity to deliberate. For this reason, we could not follow Chomsky in his defense of the right of the fascist to free speech. The prevention of flag burning, however, which seems the issue most likely to galvanize public opinion for an amendment to the U.S. Constitution limiting free speech, cannot be described as harming the deliberative capacities of any individuals, and for this reason would not be ruled out by (P).

8.2 MORE PROBLEMS FOR PARTICIPANTS

In the previous section, we sought to apply a series of normative tools derived from Habermas's theory to the new object domain of the functioning of deliberative fora. These applications focused on the legitimation of the decision-making process of a small group under empirical conditions that demanded some trade-off between participation and effectiveness. In effect, we have been posing the age-old problem of how a deliberative democratic politics can be realistic.[19] Having acknowledged the need for some unfairness in decision-making practices within a group, we concentrated on the conditions under which those practices can be legitimate. Our normative tools were here used to indicate ways in which participants might seek to nurture and preserve the legitimacy of their decision-making process, and to extend the life of the breakout of democracy.

In the unlikely event of participants' success in this regard, a further set of problems ensues for the democratic group. Now it must confront the difficulties of networking its activities with other fora in which democracy has broken out, of coordination, of democratic movement building, and perhaps even of challenging the state for power. In considering these problems, we move closer to the traditional accusation against a deliberative politics, particularly as leveled by theorists who have concentrated on legitimacy at the level of the state, this being the charge that a deliberative politics is utopian in its expectation that it could ever constitute a political order on a larger scale.

Eder's conceptual categories are helpful here.[20] Society, he claims, involves human interaction on three levels. The micro level consists of personal relationships between friends, neighbors, and coworkers, and

LIVERPOOL JOHN MOORES UNIVERSITY
LEARNING SERVICES

within families and groups. Interactions on this level are face-to-face and involve small numbers of people. Largely oriented to mutual understanding, social intercourse, cooperative action and socialisation, they also involve the strategic interactions that constitute micro-economic activity and the power-saturated discourses observable in private spaces such as the family.[21]

At the meso level, we see an increase in group size and a broadening of loyalties. Here we encounter civil associations, social movements, ethnic and religious groups, firms, and the institutions of civil society. The move from the micro to the meso level introduces a new order of difficulties for efficient coordination and consensual action, for the increase in size begins to necessitate methods of information exchange that are no longer face-to-face. Interaction at this level therefore starts to change its texture.[22]

Finally, the macro level brings us to the structures of the state, the economy, and to decision-making fora at the suprastate level. Here, efficiency imperatives arising from the complexity of issues and the number of people involved results in a complete change in the texture of political interaction. At the macro level, face-to-face interactions occur only within the elite "village" of elected representatives and corporate directors.

The problem of size and democracy is well aired in the literature of democratic theory.[23] In particular, Dahl's argument on the inevitability of nondemocratic decision-making structures above the micro level is a compelling articulation of our widely held intuitive belief that, at the level of the state, direct democracy would be hopelessly ineffective.[24] Yet, as we have seen in our analysis of procedures within the small group, it is not the presence of unfair or nondemocratic practices that signals illegitimacy so much as the process by which those unfair practices have been selected. It is, therefore, at least conceivable that the trade-offs for effectiveness that are necessary at the macro level could be discursively redeemed at the micro level in such a way as to ensure their legitimacy.

What is immediately apparent here is that the conception of legitimacy we have been developing in our inquiry, turning as it does on fair deliberation and on the fair discursive redemption of unfair practices that offer gains in effectiveness, highlights the absence of legitimacy within the liberal democratic state. If our understanding of legitimacy is correct, nothing short of the most extraordinary theoretical gymnastics could mount a defense of the present structures of parliamentary decision-making, constitutional law, and the operation of the market. The reason for this is, again, *not* that these practices are unfair, but that the trade-offs between participation and effectiveness that they represent have not been, and never are, redeemed in fair deliberation. Indeed, not only do liberal democratic states make no effort to discursively redeem such trade-offs, but they also show a consistent inability, and even refusal, to increase the deliberative input into the making of collective decisions, to experiment with discursive designs, or even to promote grassroots party organisation. In addition, states can be relied upon to stamp out democratic breakouts wherever they occur. How, then, could this state, or *any* state, ever enjoy democratic legitimacy? While many theorists work tirelessly to answer this question,[25] others have suggested that the state is simply *not the kind of thing* that ever could be legitimate.[26]

But *if* it could, it would need to be built up from a base of deliberative fora. Such fora would need to find ways of networking their activities at the meso and then macro levels that preserved their fairness. They would need to manage their increasing contacts with the institutions of power in such a way as to resist the bureaucratic, institutionalizing, and colonizing tendencies of such contacts. They would need to somehow retain that quality of the democratic breakout wherein it appeared as a loss of form in the face of a democratic tradition that has always sought to "domesticate" participation,[27] to manage it with comfortable designs, to reduce it to a tame and institutionalized form.

In the building of democratic movements, as Goodwyn has shown in his discussion of "democratic patience," to move too quickly is fraught with danger.[28] Only as groups learn to operate their own procedures with fairness and effectiveness, only as they find ways to network with other such groups while retaining their democratic core, can they begin to challenge existing structures of power. Each stage through which a genuinely democratic movement must evolve requires additional learning, and as the history of the socialist movement shows, the closer such a movement comes to power, the greater the danger that it take on the characteristics of their oppressors.

When we begin to consider the possibility of such a movement seriously challenging the power of the state, we reveal the extraordinary lack of knowledge we have accumulated over our history regarding what it actually means to rule ourselves. The flight into liberal democracy evinced by those countries who have recently joined the "democratic" club shows both the collective paucity of our understanding of such a process and also the dangers in imagining that one "revolutionary" push, one legitimating social contract, one constitutional founding, can relieve us of the need to preserve genuine democracy. Where we conceive of a social contract as an ongoing procedure requiring constant work and attention, so do we understand that deliberative capacities must be learned, practiced, preserved, and patiently extended.

Perhaps the most significant questions an emerging democratic movement would have to confront are those pertaining to the operation of the market. Historically, liberal democracies have spared no violence in preventing the subordination of market forces to justice and democratic control. Indeed, Marxism retains its coherence as a critique of liberal capitalism precisely because it remains the most cogent critic of a political order predicated upon the protection of economic inequality. At the same time, the obvious gains in effectiveness afforded by capitalism,[29] as well as the bloody history and subsequent demise of state socialism, have so frightened even those who are aware of the oppression that capitalism engenders, that they too refrain from advocating democratic control of the market. Attention therefore shifts to ways of regulating market activity rather than directly controlling it.

Such a shift is clearly articulated by Habermas. With his concept of a "self-limiting" public sphere, he draws our attention to an area in which a democratic movement should, as it were, hold its fire. Habermas forcefully shows that politics is a discursively coordinated activity and that the legitimacy of authority derives from fair deliberation. Yet he also understands that the market is coordinated by steering mechanisms that are strategic rather than discursive. Thus, for a polity to attempt democratic control over a market is to use the wrong kind of coordinating activity, the result of which can only be a grotesque loss of efficiency and the growth of bureaucratic power. His position thus amounts to a call to regulate the market, here in the form of democratic countersteering, while also warning against the overextention of that regulation. Indeed, at times, Habermas seems more concerned to describe the dangers of too much democratic countersteering than those of the inadequately regulated market.

The distinction between system and lifeworld, and between their appropriate action coordinating mechanisms, raises the question of how a strategically coordinated activity such as the market can be legitimate, where legitimacy is conceived as a discursive judgment. Yet, once again, deliberation *can* legitimately result in agreement to practices that are unfair yet that offer gains in effectiveness. There is, therefore, no *reason* why areas of economic activity could not be allowed to function according to quite different methods of action coordination, provided they are scrutinized and agreed to by a genuinely democratic political order. The gains in effectiveness available from market forces are not *themselves* illegitimate trade-offs with participation. They only become so when they are made immune to democratic scrutiny and deliberative redemption, as of course they are in liberal democratic regimes.

Habermas's concern with the overextension of countersteering does not, therefore, preclude significant freedom for market-driven activity, nor does it rule out substantive regulation of such activity. But it does serve to highlight the almost unimaginable deliberative sophistication required of a populace in order for it to subject a vibrant economy to democratic regulation.

Were a democratic movement to reach a point in its development where it had to consider questions on this scale, then what began as democracy from the perspective of participants in a deliberative forum takes on the perspective of the theorist. Now standing beside their theoretical counterparts, they too must gaze out over the entire institutional landscape and seek designs that allow participants to be citizens in a genuinely democratic state. At such a point, participants could derive significant assistance from democratic theory. If breakouts of democracy became widespread and extended in time, if they begin to seriously challenge the institutions of power at the macro level, the question of institutional design emerges as a problem in *the realm of action*. In times of revolution, participants must become theorists and try to design democratic institutions themselves.

The final type of difficulty faced by participants in a democratic forum concerns the question of emotion. When people engage in agonistic debate, there is a tremendous outpouring of emotion, and while this can be both enjoyable and empowering, it also presents the group with a significant management problem. By the word 'management,' I do not mean control, but rather, coping. For when a group fails to manage the emotional content of its interactions, this can, and often does, constitute a threat to its ability to survive as a democratic entity.

Human beings do not hold preferences without interest. Often, preferences are an expression of deeply felt concerns and are manifestations of identities, both collective and individual. Such "strong evaluations"[30] thus carry tremendous emotional energy, which they derive in a process described by Freud as one of cathexis.[31] Recent investigations into this process, particularly as undertaken by object relations theorists and self-psychologists, have stressed the importance of emotional investment in deeply held beliefs as being constitutive of identity. In agonistic debate, then, what is often at stake is not just questions of what to do, but also, of the survival of the individual self.

The conflation of preference and identity means that, "each person takes criticism of his ideas as criticism of himself and evaluates others' ideas as extensions of themselves."[32] This results in individuals frequently having their feelings hurt by other members of the group,[33] a phenomenon described by Kohut in terms of a narcissistic injury.[34]

Deliberative fora are thus dangerous places, and if they become too dangerous, they will, quite rationally, be avoided by participants.[35] Some people are, of course, more comfortable with interpersonal conflict than others, and so are more likely to remain able to express themselves and to continue with the debate. Those who are less comfortable with such conflict can become effectively excluded from the group's deliberations. Though this exclusion is not intended, and is not caused by procedural practices that are unfair, it can nevertheless have the result of rendering the decision-making process illegitimate. For this reason, the question of how to manage emotional issues is an important one, and it will certainly require the pro-active attention of the group.

Individuals differ significantly in how they approach the management of emotion in groups.[36] While some see this issue as irrelevant, and as being little more than a way of deflecting attention from the real concerns of the group, others wish to spend a great deal of time discussing emotional matters in order to render the forum a safe environment, and thus one in which substantive issues can be dealt with in an amicable and efficient way. Still others seek to use decision-making groups almost solely to process their own emotional concerns and find it very difficult to move beyond such an orientation in order to make decisions about substantive issues.

A crucial and early decision a group must make is, therefore, how much, and when, they are to deal with emotional questions. Regarding the quantity of attention to such questions, it is clear that there must be opportunities for the processing of emotion. People need to speak of such matters, to receive support, and to feel safe, if they are to remain as members of the group. Also, some attention to emotional matters is required if the decision-making process is not to become hopelessly clogged by such concerns. For this reason, groups who avoid emotional questions find, ironically, that they must deal with them more and more, even to the point of having those issues erupt in such a way as to cause the demise of the deliberative breakout.[37] There must, therefore, be a method and a time for the processing of emotion, and it cannot be seen as simply a waste of time.

Yet deliberative fora that form around common concerns, that seek to make decisions, and that try to act in the world, do not exist primarily as therapeutic groups. If they expend all their energy in dealing with emotional issues, they are effectively prevented from being political actors in any meaningful sense, and will certainly be unable to cope with the pressures they encounter from the world in which they attempt to operate. Individuals cannot expect all their emotional needs to be met by such a group, nor can they expect to receive any *guarantee* of emotional safety.

The question of the management of emotion thus shifts to one of when such concerns are to be processed. Should it occur as part of the moment of deliberation, as part of the moment of evaluation, or both?

While therapeutic models tend to stress the primacy of emotional issues and thus, when considering decision-making processes, to suggest that emotion be processed first,[38] political groups, where they do recognize the need for such a process, tend to build it into the evaluative moment. Perhaps the most sophisticated combinations of the political and the therapeutic models are contained in recent work coming from a Gestalt orientation, which seeks ways to integrate emotional and substantive issues (of process and content) into both deliberation and subsequent evaluation.[39]

8.3 CONCLUSION

We began our inquiry by reaching for Habermas's theory in order to address questions of the design and evaluation of democratic institutions. When we attempted to apply his theory to these questions, however, we encountered a series of recurrent methodological problems that served to prevent the development of the political implications of his theory. In inspecting the source of these problems, we focused, first, on the theory's level of abstraction, then on the limits Habermas places upon the application of his theory, and then on his conception of judgment. Following this, we sought to reconceive the faculty of judgment in terms of a discursive *phronēsis* with a cognitivist core. With this in place, we returned to the final source of methodological problems in his theory, this being his increasingly macro-orientation to the normative basis of political and legal authority. In declining to follow this orientation, we found that a quite different object domain for application became visible: this being the actual functioning of democratic fora.

Our attempted application of our reformulated theory of judgment to the problems encountered by participants upon a breakout of democracy explores what amounts to a radical proceduralization of the social contract. Here, questions pertaining to the design and evaluation of institutions take the form of judgments by participants to select and rule out various decision-making procedures. When we inquired as to how participants might extend their democratic procedures to levels above the micro, we encountered again the traditional accusation against a deliberative politics: that it is unrealistic and utopian.

In regard to questions pertaining to the design and evaluation of democratic institutions, we must therefore follow Rousseau and conclude that "Once you have citizens, you have all you need." The problem is that where we conceive of citizenship in terms of a highly developed "intuitive expertise" in the making of political judgments, deliberative democracy becomes utopian in a more profound sense. It is utopian because we are so poor at face-to-face interactions that are both fair and efficient. We know so little about how we make judgments, how we might behave better in groups, how we might nurture and network democratic fora without destroying their fairness. When suitably humbled by this lack of knowledge, the question of how we might have more democracy escapes from the hands of the designing theorist and becomes one that participants can only ask themselves. Do we want to be autonomous citizens? Or do we want merely to watch as those forces that work against democracy increasingly take over our lives and perhaps even destroy us completely?

Learning to make judgments well enough to become citizens may be so difficult as to be almost impossible. Certainly, this problem is not given sufficient attention in the literature of democratic theory. Such theorists tend either to offer us ever-increasing sophistication in normative questions, or endless empirical designs for the political order as a whole that have little normative understanding behind them. Perhaps if theory could look again at the language developed during the Italian Renaissance in order to describe the realm of action, it might more adequately bridge the gap between normative and empirical democratic theory. Though realistic in its appraisal of the threats to democracy,[40] this conceptual scheme was by no means only empirical. The political actor sought, for the city, ways of operating that insured survival and at the same time exemplified the normative ideal of civic humanism. Machiavelli used this language when he set out his political theory. The result was a series of suggestions and cautionary tales for political actors regarding the *kinds of things they should think about as they act*. Narrative, historical example, and case-based knowledge were used to evoke and exemplify the methods of "good" collective judgment. Effectively, he tells hard-nosed stories intended to help participants recognize and evaluate trade-offs with efficiency and to understand what constitutes damage to their deliberative capacities.

That we could ever learn to be citizens on such a scale as to be able to rule ourselves must be considered very close to impossible. At the same time, the possibility of our present political order ever becoming legitimate confronts a similar chance of success. As Benhabib puts it, "the question is not whether discursive democracy can become the practice of complex societies but whether complex societies are still capable of democratic rule."[41]

Our attempt to probe the possibility of a deliberative politics has, in effect, sought to take Habermasian theory somewhere it does not usually go: into the arena of deliberative fora themselves. "I can imagine the attempt to arrange a society democratically," he remarks in whimsical mood, "only as a self-controlled learning process."[42] Our inquiry has been an extended meditation on this remark. For participants in a break-out of democracy, who must make real what Habermas himself can only imagine, such a learning process seems, almost inevitably, doomed to failure. Yet his use of the word "only" alludes to a hope that is more than none.

NOTES

INTRODUCTION

1. J. Dunn, *Western Political Theory in the Face of the Future* (Cambridge: Cambridge University Press, 1979), p. 1.

2. These two intuitions are apparent in the work of a theorist such as Robert Dahl. For a normative principle of affected interests, see *After the Revolution* (New Haven: Yale University Press, 1970), pp. 49–51; for the impracticalities of participation, see R. Dahl and E. Tufte, *Size and Democracy* (Stanford: Stanford University Press, 1974), pp. 68–69.

3. See B. Holden, "New Directions in Democratic Theory," *Political Studies*, vol. 36, 1988, pp. 324–333.

4. See Q. Skinner, "The Empirical Theorists of Democracy and Their Critics: A Plague on Both Their Houses," *Political Theory*, vol. 1, no. 3, 1973, pp. 287–306.

5. See R. Beiner, "On the Disunity of Theory and Practice," *Praxis International*, vol. 7, no. 1, 1987, p. 25, for an argument against this fashion.

6. Beiner calls this "bad conscience," and suggests it tempts theorists into faulty thinking. Ibid., p. 33.

7. Thucydides, *The Peloponnesian War* (Harmondsworth, U.K.: Penguin, 1982), p. 245.

8. J. Locke, *The Second Treatise of Government* (Indianapolis: Bobbs-Merrill, 1952), p. 52.

9. Q. Skinner states in "Habermas's Reformation," *New York Review of Books*, October 1982, p. 38, that "Reading Habermas is extraordinarily like reading Luther, except that the latter wrote such wonderful prose." Dunn suggests that Habermas has some trouble making himself "lucidly intelligible," in *Western Political Theory in the Face of the Future*, p. 76.

10. J. Habermas, *Between Facts and Norms: Contributions to a Discourse Theory of Law and Democracy* (Cambridge: Polity Press, 1996).

1. THEORY OF DISCOURSE ETHICS

1. J.-F. Lyotard, *The Postmodern Condition: A Report on Knowledge* (Minneapolis: University of Minnesota Press, 1984), p. xxiv.

2. S. K. White, *Political Theory and Postmodernism* (Cambridge: Cambridge University Press, 1991), p. 72.

3. J. Habermas, *Communication and the Evolution of Society* (Boston: Beacon Press, 1979), pp. 202–203.

4. Ibid.

5. J. G. A. Pocock, *The Machiavellian Moment* (Princeton: Princeton University Press, 1975), p. 38ff.

6. H. Albert, *Treatise on Critical Reason* (Princeton: Princeton University Press, 1985).

7. See F. Dallmayr, "Introduction," in *The Communicative Ethics Controversy*, ed. S. Benhabib and F. Dallmayr (Cambridge, Mass.: MIT Press, 1990), p. 5; J. Habermas, *Moral Consciousness and Communicative Action* (Cambridge: Polity Press, 1990), pp. 7, 79.

8. J. Rawls, *A Theory of Justice*, (Cambridge Mass.: Harvard University Press, 1971); K. Baier, *The Moral Point of View* (New York: Random House, 1965); R. Dworkin, *Taking Rights Seriously* (Cambridge, Mass.: Harvard University Press, 1977); A. Gewirth, *Reason and Morality* (Chicago: Chicago University Press, 1978).

9. K. Baynes, *The Normative Grounds of Social Criticism: Kant, Rawls, and Habermas* (Albany: State University of New York Press, 1992), p. 11ff.

10. I. Kant, *Groundwork of the Metaphysic of Morals* (New York: Harper & Row, 1964), p. 61.

11. Ibid., p. 67.

12. Ibid., p. 69.

13. See Habermas, *Moral Consciousness and Communicative Action*, p. 56.

14. Ibid., p. 63.

15. I. Kant, "Perpetual Peace," in *Kant's Political Writings*, ed. H. Reiss (Cambridge: Cambridge University Press, 1983), p. 99.

16. Baynes, *The Normative Grounds of Social Criticism*, p. 44.

17. Ibid., p. 42.

18. Kant, "Perpetual Peace," p. 74.

19. Ibid., p. 126.

20. Baynes, *The Normative Grounds of Social Criticism*, p. 41. As Baynes points out, this interpretation is that put forward by Rawls in "Kantian Constructivism in Moral Theory. The John Dewey Lectures," *Journal of Philosophy*, vol. 77, September 1980, pp. 515–572.

21. Habermas describes his project in just these terms in *Moral Consciousness and Communicative Action*, p. 116.

22. J. Habermas, *The Theory of Communicative Action*, vol. 1 (Boston: Beacon Press, 1984), p. 392.

23. Habermas, *Moral Consciousness and Communicative Action*, p. 207.

24. S. Benhabib, *Critique, Norm, and Utopia* (New York: Columbia University Press, 1986), p. 282.

25. Habermas, *Communication and the Evolution of Society*, p. 1.

26. J. L. Austin, *How to Do Things with Words* (Cambridge, Mass.: Harvard University Press, 1962); J. Searle, *Speech Acts: An Essay in the Philosophy of Language* (New York: Cambridge University Press, 1969).

27. J. Habermas, *The Philosophical Discourse of Modernity* (Cambridge: Polity Press, 1987), p. 312, emphasis in original.

28. J. B. Thompson, "Universal Pragmatics," in *Habermas: Critical Debates*,

ed. J. B. Thompson and D. Held (Cambridge, Mass.: MIT Press, 1982), p. 119.

29. Habermas, *Communication and the Evolution of Society*, p. 8.

30. He is here closely following the work of Apel. See K. O. Apel, *Towards a Transformation of Philosophy* (London: Routledge and Kegan Paul, 1980).

31. Habermas, *Communication and the Evolution of Society*, p. 68.

32. Ibid., p. 58; see also Habermas, *The Theory of Communicative Action*, vol. 1, p. 99; Thompson, "Universal Pragmatics," p. 123.

33. Benhabib, *Critique, Norm, and Utopia*, p. 294.

34. Habermas, *Communication and the Evolution of Society*, p. 97.

35. Benhabib, *Critique, Norm, and Utopia*, p. 279.

36. Ibid.

37. Apel, *Towards a Transformation of Philosophy*, p. 225ff.

38. See Habermas, *Moral Consciousness and Communicative Action*, pp. 79–82.

39. Apel in fact uses Descartes' *cogito* as an example of an argument that can be reconstructed in terms of a performative contradiction in K. O. Apel, "The Problem of Philosophical Foundations in Light of a Transcendental Pragmatics of Language," in *After Philosophy: End or Transformation?* ed. K. Baynes, J. Bohman, and T. McCarthy (Cambridge, Mass.: MIT Press, 1987), pp. 250–290.

40. A. J. Watt, "Transcendental Arguments and Moral Principles," *Philosophical Quarterly*, vol. 25, 1975, p. 40.

41. M. Jay, "The Debate over Performative Contradiction: Habermas versus the Poststructuralists," in *Philosophical Interventions in the Unfinished Project of Enlightenment*, ed. A. Honneth, M. McCarthy, and A. Wellmer (Cambridge, Mass.: MIT Press, 1992), pp. 261–279.

42. Habermas, *Moral Consciousness and Communicative Action*, pp. 33–35.

43. See Benhabib, *Critique, Norm, and Utopia*, p. 284 and p. 400 n. 10.

44. Habermas, *Moral Consciousness and Communicative Action*, p. 201.

45. Habermas, *Legitimation Crisis*, p. 107.

46. Habermas, *Moral Consciousness and Communicative Action*, p. 201.

47. S. Toulmin, *An Examination of the Place of Reason in Ethics* (Cambridge: Cambridge University Press, 1970), p. 64.

48. Habermas here breaks down argumentation along the Aristotelian lines of product, procedure, and process. See Habermas, *The Theory of Communicative Action*, pp. 22–42, and *Moral Consciousness and Communicative Action*, pp. 87–88.

49. Habermas, *Moral Consciousness and Communicative Action*, p. 86; see also Habermas, *The Philosophical Discourse of Modernity*, p. 314.

50. G. H. Mead, *Mind, Self, and Society* (Chicago: University of Chicago Press, 1934), p. 379ff.; see also Habermas, *The Theory of Communicative Action*, vol. 2 (Cambridge: Polity Press, 1987), p. 92ff.

51. Baier, *The Moral Point of View*.

52. Habermas, *Moral Consciousness and Communicative Action*, p. 65.

53. Habermas, *Legitimation Crisis* (Cambridge: Polity Press, 1976), p. 108.

54. Habermas, *Moral Consciousness and Communicative Action*, p. 197.

55. Ibid., p. 66.

56. Ibid.

57. Ibid., p. 67.

58. Ibid., pp. 67–68.

59. Baynes, *The Normative Grounds of Social Criticism*, pp. 146–150.

60. R. P. Wolff, *Understanding Rawls* (Princeton: Princeton University Press), 1977, p. 133ff.

61. For an overview of the communitarian critique of Rawls's "unencumbered self," see, for example, M. J. Sandel, "The Procedural Republic and the Unencumbered Self," *Political Theory*, vol. 12, no. 1, 1984, pp. 81–96.

62. S. K. White, *The Recent Work of Jürgen Habermas* (Cambridge: Cambridge University Press, 1988), pp. 70–71.

63. Benhabib, *Critique, Norm, and Utopia*, p. 288.

64. S. Lukes, "Of Gods and Demons: Habermas and Practical Reason," in *Habermas: Critical Debates*, p. 141.

65. S. Benhabib, "The Utopian Dimension in Communicative Ethics," *New German Critique*, vol. 35, 1985, p. 87.

66. Habermas, *Moral Consciousness and Communicative Action*, p. 93.

67. Ibid., pp. 86–94, and R. Alexy, "A Theory of Practical Discourse," in *The Communicative Ethics Controversy*, ed. S. Benhabib and F. Dallmayr (Cambridge, Mass.: MIT Press, 1990), pp. 51–192 .

68. Benhabib, *Critique, Norm, and Utopia*, p. 285.

69. Ibid.

70. Ibid. Benhabib is here quoting Habermas's *Wahrheitstheorien*, p. 256, in her own translation. The emphasis is hers.

71. Habermas, *The Philosophical Discourse of Modernity*, p. 323; also Habermas, *Legitimation Crisis*, p. 110.

72. Habermas, *The Theory of Communicative Action*, vol. 1, p. 42.

73. R. Beiner all but asserts that this is the only kind of knowledge Habermas is interested in, "Do We Need a Philosophical Ethics? Theory, Prudence, and the Primacy of Ethos," *The Philosophical Forum*, vol. 20, no. 3, 1989, pp. 230–243.

74. Habermas, *Moral Consciousness and Communicative Action*, p. 93.

75. Habermas, *The Philosophical Discourse of Modernity*, p. 322.

76. Habermas, *Moral Consciousness and Communicative Action*, p. 68.

77. Apel, *Towards a Transformation of Philosophy*, p. 225ff.

78. Habermas, *The Philosophical Discourse of Modernity*, p. 322, emphasis in original.

79. J. Habermas, "A Philosophico-Political Profile," *New Left Review*, no. 151, 1985, p. 84.

80. Benhabib, *Critique, Norm, and Utopia*, p. 279.

81. A. Ferrara, "Postmodern Eudaimonia," *Praxis International*, vol. 11, no. 4, 1992, p. 387.

82. J. Habermas, "Questions and Counterquestions," in *Habermas and Modernity*, ed. R. J. Bernstein (Cambridge: Polity Press, 1985), pp. 192–216, here at p. 214.

83. P. Stern, in "On the Relation between Autonomy and Ethical Community: Hegel's Critique of Kantian Morality," *Praxis International*, vol. 9, no. 3, 1989, pp. 234–248, describes Hegel's critique of Kant as being an "episode in the history of philosophy that has special relevance" to the problem of a normative ethics, here at p. 234.

84. See G. W. F. Hegel, *Philosophy of Right* (New York: Oxford University Press, 1967), pp. 75–104; Benhabib, *Critique, Norm, and Utopia*, pp. 70–84.

85. G. W. F. Hegel, *The Phenomenology of Spirit* (Oxford: Oxford University Press, 1977), pp. 252–261.

86. Stern refers to this as a "paucity of content" in "On the Relation between Autonomy and Ethical Community," p. 238; There have been attempts to reformulate the categorical imperative in order to overcome this inadequacy, and to match it more closely with liberal morality. See, for example, J. L. Mackie, *Ethics—Inventing Right and Wrong* (Harmondsworth, U.K.: Penguin, 1977), pp. 90–97.

87. Günther suggests that the moment of application can also be implemented argumentatively, that is, as a form of discourse in *The Sense of Appropriateness: Application Discourses in Morality and Law* (Albany: State University of New York Press, 1993), passim.

88. Benhabib, *Critique, Norm, and Utopia*, p. 76.

89. Ibid., p. 309.

90. Stern, "On the Relation between Autonomy and Ethical Community," p. 239.

91. Ibid.

92. M. Passerin d'Entrèves, *Modernity, Justice and Community* (Milan: Franco Angeli, 1990), pp. 20–23; Benhabib, "The Utopian Dimension in Communicative Ethics," pp. 83–96. See also M. J. Matuštík, *Postnational Identity: Critical Theory and Existential Philosophy in Habermas, Kierkegarrd, and Havel* (New York: Guildford Press, 1993).

93. Stern, "On the Relation between Autonomy and Ethical Community," p. 239.

94. See C. Gilligan, *In a Different Voice: Psychological Theory and Women's Development* (Cambridge, Mass.: Harvard University Press, 1982).

95. Stern, "On the Relation between Autonomy and Ethical Community," p. 239.

96. Ibid., p. 240.

97. See S. Benhabib's discussion of the "consequentialist confusion" in (U), in *Situating the Self* (Cambridge: Polity Press, 1992), p. 37.

98. Habermas, *Moral Consciousness and Communicative Action*, p. 211.

99. Ibid., p. 207; emphasis in original.

100. Stern points out that Hegel held no such limit to his own theory, which effectively defined an ethical world *in toto*. See "On the Relation between Autonomy and Ethical Community," p. 243.

101. Ferrara describes this as the really original part of Habermas's procedural universalism in "Universalisms: Procedural, Contextual and Prudential," *Philosophy and Social Criticism*, vol. 14, no. 3/4, pp. 243–269, at p. 251.

102. Habermas, *Moral Consciousness and Communicative Action*, p. 204.

103. Habermas, "A Philosophico-Political Profile," p. 84.

104. See, for example, B. Williams, *Ethics and the Limits of Philosophy* (London: Fontana, 1985).

105. For an introduction to the players of each team, see C. Taylor, "Cross-Purposes: The Liberal-Communitarian Debate," in *Liberalism and the Moral Life*, ed. N. L. Rosenblum (Cambridge, Mass.: Harvard University Press, 1989), pp. 159–182; for an overview of the arguments, see A. Gutmann, "Communitarian Critics of Liberalism," *Philosophy and Public Affairs*, vol. 14, no. 3, 1985, pp. 308–322. The work of both teams can viewed as the continued unpacking of the implications of the five Hegelian criticisms of Kantian ethics outlined above.

106. See, by way of example, R. Beiner. "Do We Need a Philosophical Ethics?" pp. 230–243.

107. See Benhabib, *Situating the Self*, p. 71; Habermas, *Moral Consciousness and Communicative Action*, p. 213 n. 15.

108. M. Walzer, "Liberalism and the Art of Separation," *Political Theory*, vol. 12, no. 3, 1984, pp. 315–330.

109. Habermas, *Moral Consciousness and Communicative Action*, p. 94.

110. J. Habermas, "Questions and Counterquestions," p. 214.

111. S. Benhabib, "Afterword: Communicative Ethics and Current Controversies in Practical Philosophy," in *The Communicative Ethics Controversy*, pp. 331–334, especially p. 333; Stern, "On the Relation between Autonomy and Ethical Community," p. 247 n. 4.

112. Benhabib, "Afterword," p. 333.

113. Stern, "On the Relation between Autonomy and Ethical Community," p. 235.

114. See Günther, "Impartial Application of Moral and Legal Norms: A Contribution to Discourse Ethics," *Philosophy and Social Criticism*, vol. 14, no. 3/4, pp. 425–432, here at p. 425.

115. Habermas, *Moral Consciousness and Communicative Action*, p. 206.

116. Baynes, *The Normative Grounds of Social Criticism*, p. 119.

117. As such, the problem is similar to that found within the Catholic tradition, where the distinction is between general and special ethics. See T. L. Beauchamp, "On Eliminating the Distinction between Applied Ethics and Ethical Theory," *The Monist*, vol. 67, 1984, pp. 514–531, here at p. 517.

118. Habermas, *Moral Consciousness and Communicative Action*, pp. 206–207; see also Günther, "Impartial Application of Moral and Legal Norms," p. 426.

119. As does Günther in *The Sense of Appropriateness*.

120. Habermas, *Moral Consciousness and Communicative Action*, p. 106; the same point is made in A. MacIntyre, "Does Applied Ethics Rest on a Mistake?" *The Monist*, vol. 67, 1984, pp. 498–513, here at p. 501, though MacIntyre uses it to illustrate the absurdity of a contentless ethics.

121. Such a dilemma is described particularly well in Stern, "On the Relation between Autonomy and Ethical Community," p. 237; MacIntyre alludes to a similar notion in "Does Applied Ethics Rest on a Mistake?" p. 508; as does I.

Young, "Towards a Critical Theory of Justice," *Social Theory and Practice*, vol. 7, no. 3, 1981, pp. 279–302, here at p. 294.

2. THEORY WITH A PRACTICAL INTENT

1. R. Beiner, "On the Disunity of Theory and Practice," *Praxis International*, vol. 7, no. 1, 1987, pp. 25–34.

2. G. Lukács, *History and Class Consciousness* (London: Merlin Press, 1971), pp. 1–26.

3. N. Lobkowicz claims that in Hegel's thought, all questions of the relation of theory to practice are considered under the is/ought distinction. See *Theory and Practice: History of a Concept from Aristotle to Marx* (Notre Dame, Ind.: University of Notre Dame Press, 1967), p. 143.

4. Beiner, "On the Disunity of Theory and Practice," p. 26.

5. K. Marx, "The Critique of Hegel's Philosophy of Right," in *Marx's Early Writings*, ed. T. B. Bottomore (Harmondsworth, U.K.: Penguin, 1963), p. 52.

6. Beiner, "On the Disunity of Theory and Practice," p. 25.

7. Ibid., p. 27.

8. Ibid., p. 28.

9. Fay points out that there already exists within the essays of *History and Class Consciousness* a drift toward an instrumentalist and elitist notion of Marxist theory. See B. Fay, *Social Theory and Political Practice* (London: Unwin Hyman, 1988), p. 102 n. 10.

10. Beiner, "On the Disunity of Theory and Practice," 31.

11. Ibid.

12. Ibid., p. 29.

13. J. Dunn, *Western Political Theory in the Face of the Future* (Cambridge: Cambridge University Press, 1979), pp. 32, 41.

14. Beiner, "On the Disunity of Theory and Practice," p. 28.

15. Ibid., p. 33.

16. Fay, *Social Theory and Political Practice*, p. 12.

17. Ibid., p. 68.

18. Ibid., p. 12.

19. Ibid., p. 14; MacIntyre, under the heading of ethics and applied ethics, objects to a similar distinction. See "Does Applied Ethics Rest on a Mistake?" *The Monist*, vol. 67, 1984, pp. 498–513.

20. Fay, *Social Theory and Political Practice*, p. 110.

21. On positivistic social science, see ibid., pp. 18–69; on interpretative, see ibid., pp. 70–91; on those of the critical model, see ibid., pp. 92–110.

22. Beiner, "On the Disunity of Theory and Practice," p. 29.

23. Fay, *Social Theory and Political Practice*, p. 68.

24. Beiner, "On the Disunity of Theory and Practice," p. 32.

25. See for example R. Rorty, "A Discussion," *Review of Metaphysics*, vol. 34, no. 1, 1980, pp. 51–52.

26. For an overview of those who criticize Habermas for authoritarianism, see S. K. White, "Reason and Authority in Habermas: A Critique of the Critics,"

American Political Science Review, vol. 74, 1980, pp. 1007–17; Spaemann and Maurer base their critique on Habermas's adherence to a universalist ethics. See also Q. Skinner, "Habermas's Reformation," *New York Review of Books*, October 1982, pp. 35–38.

27. J.-F. Lyotard, *The Postmodern Condition: A Report on Knowledge* (Minneapolis: University of Minnesota Press, 1984), p. 60.

28. White states Habermas has "elicited a chorus of criticism from many who think that he cannot close the gap he has opened between theory and practice." In S. K White, "The Normative Basis of Critical Theory," *Polity*, vol. 16, Fall 1983, p. 160.

29. Misgeld has noted the almost exclusive concentration on foundational, metatheoretical, and methodological questions in Habermas's critical theory. See D. Misgeld, "Critical Theory and Sociological Theory," *Philosophy of the Social Sciences*, vol. 14, 1984, p. 104. More recent reviews of secondary work, such as A. Parkin, "Rethinking the Subject: Habermas, Critical Theory, and the Challenges of Postmodernism" (Ph.D. dissertation, University of Bradford, 1993), pp. 4–5, draw the same conclusion. Descriptions of the drift away from questions of application toward those of justification can be found in H. Schnädelbach, "The Transformation of Critical Theory," in *Communicative Action: Essays on Jürgen Habermas's The Theory of Communicative Action*, ed. A. Honneth and H. Joas (Cambridge: Polity Press, 1991), pp. 19, 22, and D. Ingram, *Habermas and the Dialectic of Reason* (New Haven: Yale University Press, 1987), pp. 172–188. Habermas himself states in "A Philosophico-Political Profile," *New Left Review*, no. 151, 1985, p. 89, that he finds it "unfortunate that for the last two decades (if one disregards some shorter political writings) my interest has been taken up exclusively with problems which can be characterized in a broad sense as problems of theory construction. I must accept the criticism which, most recently, Tom Bottomore has directed at me in this respect."

30. This was being claimed quite early on by writers such as D. Howard, "A Politics in Search of the Political," *Theory and Society*, vol. 1, 1974, pp. 271–306, here at p. 300, where the concern was that Habermas's work was becoming apolitical, and by J. O'Neill, "Critique and Remembrance," in *On Critical Theory*, ed. J. O'Neill (New York: Seabury Press, 1976), p. 3. More recently, D. Held has criticized Habermas for leaving the political implications of his work undeveloped. See "Crisis Tendencies, Legitimation and the State," in *Habermas: Critical Debates*, ed. J. B. Thompson and D. Held (Cambridge, Mass.: MIT Press, 1982), pp. 181–195, here at p. 195. Keane suggests Habermas has become lost in metatheoretical concerns, in J. Keane, *Public Life and Late Capitalism: Towards a Socialist Theory of Democracy* (Cambridge: Cambridge University Press, 1984), p. 187. Benhabib has argued that his normative theory must be more strongly related to practice if it is to preserve its utopian moment, in S. Benhabib, "The Utopian Dimension in Communicative Ethics," *New German Critique*, no. 35, 1985, pp. 83–96.

31. Beiner, "On the Disunity of Theory and Practice," p. 29.

32. R. M. Unger, *Knowledge and Politics* (New York: Free Press, 1975).

33. Beiner, "On the Disunity of Theory and Practice," p. 29.

34. Ibid. See also R. Beiner, "Do We Need a Philosophical Ethics? Theory, Prudence, and the Primacy of Ethos," *The Philosophical Forum*, vol. 20, no. 3, 1989, pp. 230–243, here at p. 239.

35. Beiner, "On the Disunity of Theory and Practice," p. 32.

36. Aristotle, *Nicomachean Ethics* (New York: Bobbs-Merrill, 1962), p. 156.

37. Ibid., p. 152 .

38. Beiner, "On the Disunity of Theory and Practice," p. 30.

39. Ibid., p. 33.

40. Aristotle, *Nicomachean Ethics*, p. 153; A. MacIntyre, *A Short History of Ethics* (New York: Macmillan, 1966), p. 74.

41. See T. A. McCarthy, *The Critical Theory of Jürgen Habermas* (Cambridge, Mass.: MIT Press, 1978), p. 126; and especially A. MacIntyre, *After Virtue* (Notre Dame, Ind.: University of Notre Dame Press, 1981), pp. 58, 191.

42. M. Passerin d'Entrèves, "Aristotle or Burke? Some Comments on H. Shnädelbach's 'What Is Neo-Aristotelianism?'," *Praxis International*, vol. 7, no. 3/4, 1988, pp. 238–245, here at p. 243.

43. Beiner, "Do We Need a Philosophical Ethics?" p. 234.

44. Ibid., p. 236.

45. Beiner, "On the Disunity of Theory and Practice," p. 33.

46. J. Habermas, *Communication and the Evolution of Society* (Boston: Beacon Press, 1979), pp. 202–203.

47. For a defense of contextual universalism, see M. Walzer, *Spheres of Justice* (New York: Basic Books, 1983). As P. Stern points out, in "On the Relation between Autonomy and Ethical Community: Hegel's Critique of Kantian Morality," *Praxis International*, vol. 9, no. 3, 1989, pp. 234–248, here at p. 244, Hegel's mode of justification suffers from just such a constraint, and we see it again in Walzer when he suggests, in *Spheres of Justice*, pp. 312–315, that the Indian Brahmin's superior position is justified by the shared understandings of what constitutes legitimate entitlements within the caste system. See Stern, "On the Relation between Autonomy and Ethical Community," p. 248 n. 30. For discussions of the weaknesses of contextual universalism, see A. Ferrara, "Universalisms: Procedural, Contextual and Prudential," *Philosophy and Social Criticism*, vol. 14, no. 3/4, 1989, pp. 254–257; and J. F. Bohman, "Communication, Ideology, and Democratic Theory," *American Political Science Review*, vol. 84, no. 1, 1990, p. 99.

48. J. Habermas, "Modernity versus Postmodernity," *New German Critique*, no. 22, 1981, pp. 3–14; Passerin d'Entrèves, "Aristotle or Burke?"

49. Fay, *Social Theory and Political Practice*, p. 91.

50. Beiner, "On the Disunity of Theory and Practice," p. 28.

51. J. Habermas, *Theory and Practice*, London: Heinemann, 1974, p. 3.

52. J. Habermas, *Knowledge and Human Interests* (Boston: Beacon Press, 1968).

53. Keane, *Public Life and Late Capitalism*, p. 118. It is hard to know quite what Keane means by this claim as the distinction is so prominent in *Theory and Practice*; see, for example, pp. 2–3, 41–81, 255; also the historical demise of the distinction was a central theme of Habermas's inaugural lecture at

Marburg in December 1961. One discussion of Habermas's early thought, and probably the most widely read, certainly did not miss the importance of this distinction; see McCarthy, *The Critical Theory of Jürgen Habermas*, esp. pp. 2–4.

54. Habermas, *Theory and Practice*, p. 286 n. 4; see also J. Habermas, "On the German-Jewish Heritage," *Telos*, nol. 44, Summer 1980, pp. 127–131; H. Arendt, *The Human Condition* (Chicago: University of Chicago Press, 1958).

55. Habermas, *Theory and Practice*, pp. 50–54, 59–60.

56. Ibid., pp. 168–169.

57. J. Habermas, *The Theory of Communicative Action*, vol. 2 (Cambridge, Mass.: MIT Press, 1987), p. 358.

58. Habermas, *Theory and Practice*, p. 3.

59. See J. J. Rodger, "On the Degeneration of the Public Sphere," *Political Studies*, vol. 33, 1985, pp. 203–217. Habermas outlines a historical/sociological account of the emergence and degeneration of the public sphere in J. Habermas, *The Structural Transformation of the Public Sphere* (Cambridge: Polity Press, 1989). For an overview of Habermas's work on the public sphere, see J. Cohen, "Why More Political Theory?" *Telos*, no. 40, 1979, pp. 70–94.

60. See Habermas, *Knowledge and Human Interests*, pp. 17–18. Also Keane, *Public Life and Late Capitalism*, p. 119.

61. MacIntyre, *After Virtue*, p. 123.

62. Ibid., p. 84.

63. Such a position is often attributed to Weber, though this is contentious. For Weber's position, see *The Methodology of the Social Sciences* (New York, 1949), and "Science as a Vocation" in *From Max Weber*, ed. H. H. Gerth and C. W. Mills (Oxford: Oxford University Press, 1946); McCarthy's discussion in section 3.2 of *The Critical Theory of Jürgen Habermas* highlights the contention; Habermas discusses Weber in this regard in *The Theory of Communicative Action*, vol. 1, p. 247.

64. Habermas, *Theory and Practice*, p. 208.

65. M. Horkheimer and T. Adorno, *The Dialectic of Enlightenment* (New York: Seabury Press, 1972); M. Horkheimer, *The Eclipse of Reason* (New York: Continuum, 1947).

66. J. Habermas, "The Dialectic of Rationalization: An Interview with Jürgen Habermas," *Telos*, no. 49, Fall 1981, pp. 1–12.

67. Habermas, *Theory and Practice*, pp. 32–37.

68. Ibid., p. 3.

69. McCarthy, *The Critical Theory of Jürgen Habermas*, p. 6.

70. Fay, *Social Theory and Political Practice*, p. 15.

71. McCarthy, *The Critical Theory of Jürgen Habermas*, p. 7.

72. Ibid., p. 12.

73. J. Habermas, *Towards a Rational Society: Student Protest, Science, and Politics* (London: Heinemann, 1971), p. 67.

74. McCarthy, *The Critical Theory of Jürgen Habermas*, p. 12.

75. Ibid., p. 13.

76. Habermas, Towards a Rational Society, p. 60.

77. Ibid., p. 74.

78. A. Wellmer, "Reason, Utopia, and the Dialectic of Enlightenment," in

Habermas and Modernity, ed. R. J. Bernstein (Cambridge: Polity Press, 1985), pp. 35–66, here at p. 56.

79. Ibid., p. 56.

80. See J. Habermas, *The Theory of Communicative Action*, vol. 2 (Cambridge, Mass.: Beacon Press, 1987), p. 355ff.; S. K. White, *The Recent Work of Jürgen Habermas* (Cambridge: Cambridge University Press, 1988), pp. 107–115.

81. Habermas derives his concept of the "lifeworld" from Schutz and Parsons. He uses the word to indicate the canopy of meaning, symbolization, and implicit knowledge that forms the background of everyday communication. See J. Habermas, *The Theory of Communicative Action*, vol. 1 (Cambridge, Mass.: Beacon Press, 1984), pp. 13, 70–71, 335–337; vol. 2, 121–126, 130–135, 140–148. It thus stands for "the whole ensemble of human relations which is coordinated and reproduced via communicative action, and thus via the medium of language." A. Brand, *The Force of Reason*, London: Allen & Unwin, 1990, p. xii. The lifeworld is thus to be distinguished from the "system," which designates those areas of human activity geared toward material reproduction. Habermas sees the system, in modern society, as being differentiated into two primary subsystems, those of the market and the state, wherein activity is coordinated via the media of money and power respectively. See Habermas, *The Theory of Communicative Action*, vol. 2, pp. 153–155, 185–186, 225–231, 249–250.

82. For the Frankfurt School, see D. Held, *An Introduction to Critical Theory* (Berkeley: University of California Press, 1980). Earlier writings and commentaries are contained in A. Arato and E. Gebhart (eds.), *The Essential Frankfurt School Reader* (New York: Urizen Books, 1978). For a historical treatment of critical theory, see M. Jay, *The Dialectical Imagination* (Boston: Little, Brown, 1973).

83. See R. Geuss, *The Idea of a Critical Theory* (Cambridge: Cambridge University Press, 1981), p. 55.

84. As Habermas points out in *A Philosophico-Political Profile*, p. 89, "Theories, especially of Marxist inspiration, ultimately only prove their worth by making a contribution to the explanation of concrete historical processes." Marx himself was ambivalent as to whether his theory was critical or positivistic. A. Wellmer's *Critical Theory of Society* looks closely at this question in chapter 2; S. Avineri's *The Social and Political Thought of Karl Marx* comes down firmly on the critical theory side, see chapter 5. For the sociological implications of such an interpretation, see H. Lefebvre, *The Sociology of Marx* (Harmondsworth, U.K.: Penguin, 1968).

85. Fay, *Social Theory and Political Practice*, p. 92.

86. Ibid., p. 97.

87. Ibid., p. 92.

88. Ibid., p. 94.

89. Ibid., p. 91.

90. Ibid., p. 94.

91. Ibid., p. 95.

92. Ibid., p. 97.

93. Habermas, *A Philosophico-Political Profile*, p. 92.

94. We are here passing over a major contention in Habermas's early work, this being the precise nature of the "emancipatory self-reflection" that is afforded by a critical theory. In *Knowledge and Human Interests*, op. cit., Habermas conflates the Kantian and Hegelian/Marxist senses of the term "self-reflection." See R. J. Bernstein, "Introduction," in *Habermas and Modernity*, pp. 12–14. This conflation lead Habermas to use Freudian psychoanalysis as an example of a critical science and as an analogy for political enlightenment. See also *Theory and Practice*, pp. 9, 22ff., and *Knowledge and Human Interests*, chaps. 10–12. In *Public Life and Late Capitalism*, pp. 165–172, Keane shows the many problems this analogy leads Habermas into. The issue is fully discussed in McCarthy, *The Critical Theory of Jürgen Habermas*, pp. 193–213. The historical interplay between psychoanalysis and critical theory is explored in J. Whitebook, "Reason and Happiness: Some Psychoanalytic Themes in Critical Theory," in *Habermas and Modernity*, pp. 140–160.

95. Parkin, *Rethinking the Subject*, p. 7.

96. Habermas, *Theory and Practice*, pp. 3–4.

97. Ibid., p. 34; see also *A Philosophico-Political Profile*, p. 92.

98. Habermas, *Theory and Practice*, p. 40.

99. Ibid., pp. 38–39.

100. A. Ferrara, "Universalisms: Procedural, Contextual and Prudential," *Philosophy and Social Criticism*, vol. 14, no. 3/4, 1989, pp. 247–251.

101. J. Habermas, *Communication and the Evolution of Society* (Boston: Beacon Press, 1979), p. 184.

102. Habermas, *A Philosophico-Political Profile*, p. 91.

103. Beiner, "On the Disunity of Theory and Practice," pp. 25–34, and p. 33, where he quotes H. Gadamer, *Reason in the Age of Science* (Cambridge, Mass.: MIT Press, 1981), pp. 133–134.

104. White, "Reason and Authority in Habermas," p. 1007. White is here following Isaiah Berlin, who states that authoritarianism is based on a "dogmatic certainty" that is precluded by effective participation. Participation generates a "general" (rather than a "real") will; see p. 1012.

105. McCarthy, *The Critical Theory of Jürgen Habermas*, p.14.

106. Aristotle, *Nicomachean Ethics*, p. 160.

107. J. Habermas, "The Scientization of Politics and Public Opinion," in *Towards a Rational Society: Student Protest, Science, and Politics* (London: Heinemann, 1971), p. 75, emphasis in original.

108. Habermas, *Theory and Practice*, p. 38.

109. Early critical theory named its addressee in no uncertain terms. Habermas does not stipulate an addressee and this has caused some confusion among his commentators. See, for example, Geuss, *The Idea of a Critical Theory*, p. 65ff.; McCarthy discusses this issue in *The Critical Theory of Jürgen Habermas*, p. 385; as does Benhabib in *Critique, Norm, and Utopia*, p. 315.

110. See McCarthy, *The Critical Theory of Jürgen Habermas*, pp. 16–39, regarding Habermas's encounter with this aspect of Marx's thought.

111. Habermas, *Theory and Practice*, p. 3–4.

112. See White, *The Recent Work of Jürgen Habermas*, chap. 5 for a dis-

cussion of how this view has been used to describe the activities of New Social Movements.

113. R. J. Bernstein, *The Restructuring of Social and Political Theory* (London: Methuen, 1979), p. 219.

114. Habermas, *Towards a Rational Society*, p. 33.

115. See Habermas, *Theory and Practice*, p. 2, for his distaste for vanguardism, and also Habermas, *Moral Consciousness and Communicative Action*, p. 208.

116. Keane, *Public Life and Late Capitalism*, p. 156.

117. Ibid., p. xliv.

118. See White, *The Recent Work of Jürgen Habermas*, p. 7.

3. THE AFFIRMATIVE USES OF THEORY

1. Such a survey is, of necessity, selective. Habermas's influence has now become so pervasive that it escapes exhaustive documentation.

2. This formulation simplifies, hopefully without reducing the sense of, that advanced in P. Strydom, "Metacritical Observations on a Reductive Approach to Critical Theory: Ruane and Todd's 'The Application of Critical Theory'," *Political Studies*, vol. 38, 1990, pp. 534–542, here at fig. 1, p. 541.

3. Ibid., p. 540.

4. Ibid., p. 542.

5. Ibid.

6. In the final section of J. Habermas, *The Theory of Communicative Action*, vol. 2 (Boston: Beacon Press, 1987).

7. J. Ruane and J. Todd, "The Application of Critical Theory," *Political Studies*, vol. 36, 1988, pp. 533–538, and A. Parkin, "Rethinking the Subject: Habermas, Critical Theory, and the Challenges of Postmodernism" (Ph.D. dissertation, University of Bradford, 1993), chap. 6.

8. R. J. Bernstein, "Introduction," in *Habermas and Modernity*, ed. R. J. Bernstein (Cambridge: Polity Press, 1985), p. 23.

9. Habermas, *The Theory of Communicative Action*, vol. 2, pp. 332–373; and S. K. White, *The Recent Work of Jürgen Habermas* (Cambridge: Cambridge University Press, 1988), chaps. 5 and 6.

10. Habermas, *The Theory of Communicative Action*, vol. 2, p. 355.

11. J. Habermas, *Legitimation Crisis*, Cambridge: Polity Press, 1988; see also D. Held, "Crisis Tendencies, Legitimation and the State," in *Habermas: Critical Debates*, ed. J. B. Thompson and D. Held (Cambridge, Mass.: MIT Press, 1982), pp. 181–195

12. J. Habermas, *Theory and Practice*, London: Heinemann, 1974; T. A. McCarthy, *The Critical Theory of Jürgen Habermas* (Cambridge, Mass.: MIT Press, 1978), pp. 1–15.

13. J. Habermas, "Moral Development and Ego Identity," in *Communication and the Evolution of Society* (Boston: Beacon Press, 1979), pp. 69–94; J. Habermas, *Moral Consciousness and Communicative Action* (Cambridge: Polity Press, 1990), pp. 116–195; J. Habermas, "Justice and Solidarity: On the

Discussion Concerning 'Stage 6'," in *Hermeneutics and Critical Theory in Ethics and Politics*, ed. M. Kelly (Cambridge, Mass.: MIT Press, 1990), pp. 32–52; White, *The Recent Work of Jürgen Habermas*, pp. 58–68.

14. Habermas, *The Theory of Communicative Action*, vol. 2, op. cit., chaps. 6 and 7; see also R. C. Holub, *Jürgen Habermas: Critic in the Public Sphere* (London: Routledge, 1991), pp. 106–132.

15. J. Habermas, *The Philosophical Discourse of Modernity* (Cambridge: Polity Press, 1987); see also Holub, *Jürgen Habermas*, pp. 133–161; J. Habermas, "Modernity versus Postmodernity," *New German Critique*, no. 22, 1981, pp. 3–14.

16. J. Habermas, "New Social Movements," *Telos*, no. 49, 1981, pp. 33–37; J. Cohen, "Strategy or Identity: New Theoretical Paradigms and Contemporary Social Movements," *Social Research*, vol. 52, no. 4, 1985, pp. 663–716. See also C. Offe, "New Social Movements: Challenging the Boundaries of Institutional Politics," *Social Research*, vol. 52, no. 4, 1985, pp. 817–868; L. J. Ray, *Rethinking Critical Theory: Emancipation in the Age of Global Social Movements* (London: Sage, 1993); K.H. Tucker, "Ideology and Social Movements: The Contribution of Habermas," *Sociological Inquiry*, vol. 59, no. 1, pp. 30–47, 1989; Parkin, "Rethinking the Subject," chap. 6, pp. 7–13.

17. J. Habermas, *Towards a Rational Society: Student Protest, Science, and Politics* (Boston: Beacon Press, 1971); see also Holub, *Jürgen Habermas*, pp. 78–105.

18. See J. Haacke, "Theory and Praxis in International Relations: Habermas, Self-Reflection, Rational Argumentation," *Journal of International Studies*, vol. 25, no. 2, pp. 255–289.

19. Habermas, *The Theory of Communicative Action*, vol. 2, op. cit., pp. 374–404.

20. Ibid., p. 361ff.

21. Ibid., pp. 358–361.

22. Ibid., pp. 378–382.

23. Ibid., pp. 386–388.

24. Ibid., p. 388; but see C. F. Alford, "Habermas, Post-Freudian Psychoanalysis and the End of the Individual," *Theory, Culture and Society*, vol. 4, 1987, pp. 3–29.

25. Habermas, *The Theory of Communicative Action*, vol. 2, pp. 363, 395.

26. Ibid., pp. 389–390; see also D. C. Hallin, "The American News Media: A Critical Theory Perspective," in *Critical Theory and Public Life*, ed. J. Forester (Cambridge, Mass.: MIT Press, 1985), pp. 121–146, and the discussion in C. Calhoun, "Introduction," in *Habermas and the Public Sphere*, ed. C. Calhoun (Cambridge, Mass.: MIT Press, 1992), pp. 1–50, here at p. 22.

27. Habermas, *The Theory of Communicative Action*, vol. 2, p. 393; see also J. S. Dryzek, *Discursive Democracy: Politics, Policy, and Political Science* (Cambridge: Cambridge University Press, 1990); White, *The Recent Work of Jürgen Habermas*, pp. 136–144.

28. Habermas, *Legitimation Crisis*, p. 122; J. Habermas, "Struggles for Recognition in Constitutional States," *European Journal of Philosophy*, vol. 1,

no. 2, 1993, pp. 128–155; J. Habermas, "Citizenship and National Identity: Some Reflections on the Future of Europe," *Praxis International*, vol. 12, no. 1, 1992, pp. 1–19.

29. J. Habermas, *Between Facts and Norms: Contributions to a Discourse Theory of Law and Democracy* (Cambridge: Polity Press, 1996); R. Shelly, "Habermas and the Normative Foundations of a Radical Politics," *Thesis Eleven*, no. 35, 1993, pp. 62–83; W. Outhwaite, *Habermas: A Critical Introduction* (Cambridge: Polity Press, 1994), pp. 137–151.

30. Dryzek, *Discursive Democracy*; J. Forester. "Towards a Critical-Empirical Framework for the Analysis of Public Policy," *New Political Science*, Summer 1982, pp. 33–61.

31. S. D. Ealy, *Communication, Speech, and Politics: Habermas and Political Analysis* (Washington, D.C.: University Press of America, 1981).

32. J. D. Wisman, "The Scope and Goals of Economic Science: A Habermasian Perspective," in *Economics and Hermeneutics*, ed. D. Lavoie (London: Routledge, 1991), pp. 113–133.

33. C. Anderson and L. Rouse, "Intervention in Cases of Women Battering: An Application of Symbolic Interactionism and Critical Theory," *Clinical Sociology Review*, vol. 6, 1988, pp. 134–147.

34. For an analysis of interactions between doctor and patient, see E. Mishler, *The Discourse of Medicine: Dialectics of Medical Interviews* (Norwood, N.J.: Ablex, 1984).

35. G. Scambler, "Habermas and the Power of Medical Expertise," in *Sociological Theory and Medical Sociology*, ed. G. Scambler (London: Tavistock, 1987), pp. 165–193.

36. P. Rodwell, "Habermas and the Evaluation of Public Policy" (Ph.D. dissertation, Manchester University, 1990).

37. R. Blaug, "The Distortion of the Face to Face: Communicative Reason and Social Work Practice," *British Journal of Social Work*, vol. 25, no. 4, 1995.

38. T. W. Luke and S. K. White, "Critical Theory, the Informational Revolution, and an Ecological Path to Modernity," in *Critical Theory and Public Life*, ed. J. Forester (Cambridge, Mass.: MIT Press, 1985), pp. 22–56.

39. D. Misgeld, "Education and Cultural Invasion: Critical Social Theory, Education as Instruction, and the 'Pedagogy of the Oppressed'," in *Critical Theory and Public Life*, pp. 77–118; M. R. Welton (ed.), *In Defense of the Lifeworld: Critical Perspectives on Adult Learning* (Albany: State University of New York Press, 1995).

40. Ruane and Todd, "The Application of Critical Theory," p. 536.

41. Ibid., p. 535.

42. R. J. Bernstein, "Introduction," in *Habermas and Modernity*, ed. R. J. Bernstein (Cambridge: Polity Press, 1985), pp. 17, 21; White, *The Recent Work of Jürgen Habermas*, chap. 1.

43. White, *The Recent Work of Jürgen Habermas*, p. 153.

44. D. Kellner, *Critical Theory, Marxism, and Modernity* (Baltimore: John Hopkins University Press, 1989), p. 232.

45. Forester, "Introduction: The Applied Turn in Contemporary Critical Theory," in *Critical Theory and Public Life*, p. xviii.

46. Ruane and Todd, "The Application of Critical Theory," p. 535.

47. Parkin, "Rethinking the Subject," chap. 6, pp. 13, 44.

48. Ruane and Todd, "The Application of Critical Theory," p. 535

49. V. A. Malhotra, "Habermas' Sociological Theory as a Basis for Clinical Practice with Small Groups," *Clinical Sociology Review*, vol. 5, 1987, pp. 181–192; V. A. Malhotra, "Research as Critical Reflection: A Study of Self, Time and Communicative Competency," *Humanity and Society*, vol. 8, 1984, pp. 468–477.

50. J. Forester, "Critical Theory and Planning Practice," in *Critical Theory and Public Life*, pp. 202–230. Parkin rejects Ruane and Todd's assessment of the empirical content of this study in Parkin, "Rethinking the Subject," p. 70 n. 119, and he therefore includes it in his list of empirical studies. However, Ealy's *Communication, Speech, and Politics* (see note 31 above), which Parkin also describes as an example of an empirical study, is, according to our distinction, rather to be viewed as an interpretative piece. The problem for Parkin here is that he uses the phrase "all those who based their work on detailed observations of actually existing concrete interactions" as the division between empirical and interpretative; see "Rethinking the Subject," pp. 44–45. However, "based on" can mean empirical investigation, and it can also mean critical interpretation.

51. R. E. Young, "Critical Theory and Classroom Questioning," *Language and Education*, vol. 1, no. 2, 1987; R. E. Young, "Moral Development, Ego Autonomy, and Questions of Practicality in the Critical Theory of Schooling," *Educational Theory*, vol. 38, no. 4, 1988, pp. 391–404; R. E. Young, *A Critical Theory of Education: Habermas and Our Children's Future* (New York: Wheatsheaf, 1989).

52. Parkin, "Rethinking the Subject," p. 41. This critique is also leveled at the more interpretative work of Anderson and Rouse (see note 33 above). Parkin, at p. 33, is particularly troubled by their lack of analysis of the underlying causes of spousal violence.

53. A. J. Carroll, "Ethics, Critical Theory, and the Inner City" (Ph.D. dissertation, Manchester University, 1993).

54. Malhotra, "Research as Critical Reflection," pp. 468, 470, 475.

55. Malhotra, "Habermas' Sociological Theory," p. 186.

56. Malhotra, "Research as Critical Reflection," p. 469.

57. Parkin treats this at some length in "Rethinking the Subject," pp. 35–40.

58. I. Mitroff and L. V. Blankenship, "On the Methodology of the Holistic Experiment," *Technological Forecasting and Social Change*, vol. 4, 1973. pp. 339–353.

59. See Dryzek's discussion of experimental methodology in *Discursive Democracy*, p. 39

60. Parkin, in "Rethinking the Subject," pp. 51–61, esp. p. 51, suggests that the attempt by social research to "fix meanings" from an "expert point of view" may be inherently power-saturated.

61. Dryzek, *Discursive Democracy*, p. 177.

62. See S. R. Brown, *Political Subjectivity: Applications of Q Methodology in Political Science* (New Haven: Yale University Press, 1980); B. McKeown and

D. Thomas, *Q Methodology* (Newbury Park, Calif.: Sage, 1988); Dryzek, *Discursive Democracy*, pp. 174–188.

63. Dryzek, *Discursive Democracy*, p. 176; it therefore shares certain characteristics with the method of Repertory Grids developed from Kelly's Personal Construct theory, in which the persons who are to fill out the questionnaire first go through a process whereby they construct the questions themselves. See D. Bannister and F. Fransella, *Inquiring Man: The Theory of Personal Constructs* (Harmondsworth, U.K.: Penguin, 1971).

64. Dryzek, *Discursive Democracy*, p. 178.

65. Ibid., p. 180.

66. See, for example, C. Kitzinger, "Introducing and Developing Q as a Feminist Methodology: A Study of Accounts of Lesbianism," in *Feminist Social Psychology: Developing Theory and Practice*, ed. S. Wilkinson (Milton Keynes, U.K.: Open University Press, 1986), pp. 151–172.

67. Dryzek, *Discursive Democracy*, p. 188.

68. J. S. Dryzek and J. Berejikian, "Reconstructive Democratic Theory," *American Political Science Review*, vol. 87, no. 1, 1993, pp. 48–60.

69. Habermas, *Moral Consciousness and Communicative Action*, p. 179.

70. S. Wolin, "Fugitive Democracy," *Constellations*, vol. 1, no. 1, 1994, p. 16.

71. S. Benhabib, "The Methodological Illusions of Modern Political Theory: The Case of Rawls and Habermas," *Neue Hefte fur Pholosophie*, vol. 21, 1982, pp. 47–74, here at 48–49.

72. Ibid., p. 49.

73. See pragmatic rule 3.1 in Habermas's rules of discourse, *Moral Consciousness and Communicative Action*, p. 89.

74. Regarding the use of unanimity by various democratic theories in order to claim legitimacy, see R. P. Wolff, *In Defence of Anarchism* (New York: Harper & Row, 1970), p. 27; B. Manin, "On Legitimacy and Political Deliberation," *Political Theory*, vol. 15, no. 3, 1987, p. 340ff.

75. J. Dunn, *Western Political Theory in the Face of the Future* (Cambridge: Cambridge University Press, 1979), p. 1.

76. See the discussion of realism versus rationalism in G. Sartori, *The Theory of Democracy Revisited*, vol. 1 (Chatham, N.J.: Chatham House, 1987), pp. 39–82: also that in D. Beetham, "Liberal Democracy and the Limits of Democratization," in *Prospects for Democracy: North, South, East, West*, ed. D. Held (Cambridge: Polity Press, 1993).

77. Hence the concern with the possibility of "moral sponginess" in T. Nagel, "What Makes a Political Theory Utopian?" *Social Research*, vol. 56, no. 4, 1989, pp. 903–920, here at p. 914.

78. Benhabib, "The Methodological Illusions of Modern Political Theory," p. 49.

79. Ibid.

80. See J. Elster, "The Market and the Forum: Three Varieties of Political Theory," in *Foundations of Social Choice Theory*, ed. J. Elster and A. Hylland (Cambridge: Cambridge University Press, 1986), pp. 103–132.

81. For this reason, Habermas would fall into Fishkin's fourth category of

democratic theories, for he combines an actual decision situation with a refinement of motivation and preferences. See J. S. Fishkin, *The Dialogue of Justice: Toward a Self-Reflective Society* (New Haven: Yale University Press, 1992), p. 51ff. See, for a discussion of the effect of deliberation on preferences, C. R. Sunstein, "Preferences and Politics," *Philosophy and Public Affairs*, vol. 20, no. 1, 1991, pp. 3–34.

82. Habermas, *Moral Consciousness and Communicative Action*, p. 89

83. McCarthy, *The Critical Theory of Jürgen Habermas*, p. 309.

84. This has been the subject of some misunderstanding, particularly among early commentators such as G. Therborn, "Jürgen Habermas: A New Eclecticism," *New Left Review*, no. 67, 1971, pp. 69–83, and T. Woodiwiss, "Critical Theory and the Capitalist State," *Economy and Society*, vol. 7, 1978, pp. 175–192.

85. Habermas, *Moral Consciousness and Communicative Action*, p. 92

86. See A. Ferrara, "Justice and Identity," *Philosophy and Social Criticism*, vol. 18, no. 3/4, 1992, pp. 333–354. McCarthy, *The Critical Theory of Jürgen Habermas*, p. 309; R. Alexy, "A Theory of Practical Discourse," in *The Communicative Ethics Controversy*, ed. S. Benhabib and F. Dallmayr (Cambridge, Mass.: MIT Press, 1990), pp. 151–192, here at pp. 180–183.

87. Habermas, *Legitimation Crisis*, pp. 111–112; J. Habermas, "A Reply to my Critics," in *Habermas: Critical Debates*, ed. J. B. Thompson and D. Held (Cambridge, Mass.: MIT Press, 1982), pp. 219–283, here at pp. 257–258; Habermas, *Moral Consciousness and Communicative Action*, p. 72; McCarthy, *The Critical Theory of Jürgen Habermas*, p. 314; Dryzek, *Discursive Democracy*, p. 17; D. Ingram, "The Limits and Possibilities of Communicative Ethics for Democratic Theory," *Political Theory*, vol. 21, no. 2, 1993, pp. 294–321, here at p. 302.

88. J. Habermas, *Justification and Application* (Cambridge: Polity Press, 1993), pp. 54–55.

89. Dryzek, *Discursive Democracy*, p. 87.

90. Forester, "Introduction: The Applied Turn in Contemporary Critical Theory," in *Critical Theory and Public Life*, p. xvi.

91. Dryzek, *Discursive Democracy*, p. 87.

92. S. Benhabib, *Situating the Self* (Oxford: Polity Press, 1992), pp. 23–67; M. Passerin d'Entréves, *Modernity, Justice and Community* (Milan: Franco Angeli, 1990), p. 16.

93. Ingram, "The Limits and Possibilities of Communicative Ethics for Democratic Theory," pp. 294–321.

94. A. Wellmer, "Practical Philosophy and the Theory of Society: On the Problem of the Normative Foundations of a Critical Social Science," in *The Communicative Ethics Controversy*, pp. 293–329, here at p. 293; L. J. Ray, *Rethinking Critical Theory* (London: Sage, 1993), p. 37 n. 24.

95. Habermas, *Justification and Application*, p. 36.

96. J. Habermas, *Communication and the Evolution of Society* (Boston: Beacon Press, 1979), p. 183ff.; Ingram, "The Limits and Possibilities of Communicative Ethics for Democratic Theory," p. 311.

97. Habermas, *Moral Consciousness and Communicative Action*, p. 109;

J. Habermas, *The Philosophical Discourse of Modernity* (Cambridge: Polity Press, 1987), p. 322.

98. See, for example, C. C. Gould, "On the Conception of the Common Interest: Between Procedure and Substance," in *Hermeneutics and Critical Theory in Ethics and Politics*, pp. 267–269, and J. Habermas, "Citizenship and National Identity: Some Reflections on the Future of Europe," *Praxis International*, vol. 12, no. 1, 1992, pp. 1–19, here at p. 10.

99. R. Shelly. "Habermas and the Normative Foundations of a Radical Politics," *Thesis Eleven*, no. 35, 1993, pp. 62–83, here at p. 74.

100. As, for example, in J. Cohen. "Discourse Ethics and Civil Society," *Philosophy and Social Criticism*, vol. 14 no. 3/4, 1988, pp. 315–337, here at p. 326.

101. Ingram, "The Limits and Possibilities of Communicative Ethics for Democratic Theory," p. 311; see also Cohen, "Discourse Ethics and Civil Society," p. 324.

102. Cohen, "Discourse Ethics and Civil Society," p. 326.

103. Ibid.

104. K. Baynes, *The Normative Grounds of Social Criticism: Kant, Rawls, and Habermas* (Albany: State University of New York Press, 1992), p. 180, and K. Baynes, "The Liberal/Communitarian Controversy and Communicative Ethics," *Philosophy and Social Criticism*, vol. 14, no. 3/4, 1988, pp. 293–313, here at p. 306.

105. M. Walzer, "A Critique of Philosophical Conversation," in *Hermeneutics and Critical Theory in Ethics and Politics*, pp. 182–196, here at p. 186.

106. R. Shelly, "Habermas and the Normative Foundations of a Radical Politics," p. 75; A. Arato and J. Cohen, *Civil Society and Political Theory* (Cambridge, Mass.: MIT Press, 1992), p. 441.

107. Benhabib, *Situating the Self*, p. 29.

108. Habermas gives his own derivation of basic rights from the discourse principle in *Between Facts and Norms*, pp. 118–131.

109. See A. Ferrara, "A Critique of Habermas's Consensus Theory of Truth," *Philosophy and Social Criticism*, vol. 13. no. 1, 1988, pp. 39–68, here at p. 53; and Benhabib, "The Methodological Illusions of Modern Political Theory," p. 58.

110. S. K. White, "Reason and Authority in Habermas: A Critique of the Critics," *American Political Science Review*, vol. 74, 1980, pp. 1007–1017, p. 1016.

111. Ingram, "The Limits and Possibilities of Communicative Ethics for Democratic Theory," p. 311.

112. Shelly, "Habermas and the Normative Foundations of a Radical Politics," p. 72.

113. J. Habermas, "Struggles for Recognition in Constitutional States," *European Journal of Philosophy*, vol. 1, no. 2, 1993, pp. 128–155, here at p. 139.

114. K. Eder, "Politics and Culture: On the Sociocultural Analysis of Political Participation," in *Cultural-Political Interventions in the Unfinished Project*

of *Enlightenment*, ed. A. Honneth, T. McCarthy, C. Offe, and A. Wellmer (Cambridge, Mass.: MIT Press, 1992), pp. 95–120.

115. A. MacIntyre, *After Virtue* (Notre Dame, Ind.: University of Notre Dame Press, 1981), pp. 66–68; see also Habermas, *Moral Consciousness and Communicative Action*, p. 114.

116. Forester, *Critical Theory and Public Life.*

117. R. Kemp, "Planning, Public Hearings, and the Politics of Discourse," in *Critical Theory and Public Life*, pp. 177–201, here at p. 177.

118. Ibid., p. 196.

119. See McCarthy, *The Critical Theory of Jürgen Habermas*, pp. 288–289; also J. Forester, "A Critical Empirical Framework for the Analysis of Public Policy," *New Political Science*, Summer 1982, pp. 33–61, here at p. 43.

120. The distinction between "grading" and "ranking" values is drawn in P.W. Taylor, *Normative Discourse* (Englewood Cliffs, N.J.: Prentice Hall, 1961).

121. See Ferrara's various discussions of this problem in "On Phronesis," *Praxis International*, vol. 7, no. 3/4, 1987, p. 247; "A Critique of Habermas' Diskursethik," *Telos*, no. 64, 1985, p. 63; and "A Critique of Habermas's Consensus Theory of Truth," p. 75, where he explores an analogous difficulty in scientific inquiry. Generally, Ferrara stresses the importance of *phronēsis* in compensating for this indeterminacy.

122. Dryzek, *Discursive Democracy*, p. 37.

123. A further difficulty with Dryzek's example is that one of the practices it mentions is not democratic at all. The crudest of democratic theories could therefore distinguish between them.

124. Habermas, *Communication and the Evolution of Society*, p. 3.

125. Dryzek, *Discursive Democracy*, p. 87.

126. McCarthy, *The Critical Theory of Jürgen Habermas*, p. 309.

127. A. Wellmer, "Reason, Utopia, and the Dialectic of Enlightenment," in *Habermas and Modernity*, pp. 35–66, here at p. 62.

128. Wellmer, "Practical Philosophy and the Theory of Society," p. 324.

129. Wellmer, "Reason, Utopia and the Dialectic of Enlightenment," p. 61.

130. T. L. Beauchamp, "On Eliminating the Distinction between Applied Ethics and Ethical Theory," *The Monist*, vol. 67, 1984, pp. 514–531, here at p. 519. Benhabib presents a similar criticism in her discussion of O. O'Neill's "dismal choice between triviality or inconsistency," in Benhabib, *Situating the Self*, p. 29.

131. C. Calhoun, "Introduction," in *Habermas and the Public Sphere*, p. 2.

132. J. Habermas, "Further Reflections on the Public Sphere," in *Habermas and the Public Sphere*, pp. 447–448.

133. J. Habermas, *The Structural Transformation of the Public Sphere* (Cambridge: Polity Press, 1989), pp. 24, 27.

134. J. J. Rodger, "On the Degeneration of the Public Sphere," *Political Studies*, vol. 33, 1985, p. 214.

135. It should also be noted that his characterization of the public sphere,

and its historical transformation, has generated a large body of literature that has served to further explicate both the theoretical and sociological implications of the concept. See, for example, Calhoun (ed.), *Habermas and the Public Sphere.*

136. J. Habermas, "The Public Sphere: An Encyclopedia Article," *New German Critique*, no. 3, 1974, p. 49.

137. Rodger, "On the Degeneration of the Public Sphere," p. 200.

138. See N. Fraser, "Rethinking the Public Sphere: A Contribution to the Critique of Actually Existing Democracy," in *Habermas and the Public Sphere*, pp. 109–114.

139. Rodger is interested in the opening of a public sphere within New Social Movements and cites particularly the actionist sociology of Alan Touraine as addressing this issue. See Rodger, "On the Degeneration of the Public Sphere," pp. 211–212.

140. See T. R. Berger, *Northern Frontier, Northern Homeland: Report of the MacKenzie Valley Pipeline Inquiry* (Toronto: Lorimer, 1977).

141. See J. Keane, "Introduction," in *Civil Society and the State*, ed. J. Keane (London: Verso, 1988), pp. 1–32.

142. Shelly, "Habermas and the Normative Foundations of a Radical Politics," p. 75.

143. J. Cohen and A. Arato, *Civil Society and Political Theory* (Cambridge, Mass.: MIT Press, 1992), pp. 429, 434ff.

144. Habermas, *The Theory of Communicative Action*, vol. 2, p. 146ff.

145. K. Baynes, *The Normative Grounds of Social Criticism: Habermas, Kant, Rawls* (Albany: State University of New York, 1992), p. 180.

146. Habermas, "Further Reflections on the Public Sphere," p. 453.

147. Ibid., pp. 436, 443–444; Habermas, *The Philosophical Discourse of Modernity*, p. 363.

148. Habermas, "Further Reflections on the Public Sphere," p. 452; J. Habermas, "Three Models of Democracy," *Constellations*, vol. 1, no. 1, 1994, pp. 1–10, here at pp. 8–9.

149. Habermas, "Further Reflections on the Public Sphere," p. 455.

150. J. Habermas, "The New Obscurity: The Crisis of the Welfare State and the Exhaustion of Utopian Energies," in *The New Conservatism: Cultural Criticism and the Historian's Debate*, ed. S. W. Nicholsen (Cambridge, Mass.: MIT Press, 1989), pp. 48–70, here at p. 64.

151. Ibid., p. 63; Habermas, *The Philosophical Discourse of Modernity*, p. 365.

152. Habermas, *The Philosophical Discourse of Modernity*, pp. 357, 361.

153. Ibid., p. 364.

154. Ibid., p. 365.

155. J. Habermas, "What Theories Can Accomplish—and What They Can't," in *The Past as Future* (Cambridge: Polity Press, 1994), pp. 99–120, here at p. 117.

156. Habermas, *The Philosophical Discourse of Modernity*, pp. 357, 365.

157. Ibid., p. 357.

158. It is precisely this insight that informs Habermasian attempts to

understand New Social Movements, and that we considered as examples of cultural criticism in 3.1 above.

159. J. Habermas, "Towards a Communication-Concept of Rational Collective Will-Formation: A Thought Experiment," *Ratio Juris*, vol. 2, no. 2, 1989, pp. 144–154; Habermas, "Further Reflections on the Public Sphere," p. 449; S. Benhabib, "Deliberative Rationality and Models of Democratic Legitimacy," *Constellations*, vol. 1, no. 1, 1994, pp. 26–52, here at p. 37; Outhwaite, *Habermas: A Critical Introduction* (Cambridge: Polity Press, 1994), chap. 9; Shelly, "Habermas and the Normative Foundations of a Radical Politics."

160. Habermas, *Moral Consciousness and Communicative Action*, p. 114 n. 81.

161. J. Habermas, *Between Facts and Norms: Contributions to a Discourse Theory of Law and Democracy* (Cambridge: Polity Press, 1996).

162. Benhabib, "Deliberative Rationality and Models of Democratic Legitimacy," p. 42; J. Habermas, "Three Models of Democracy," p. 10.

163. Baynes, *The Normative Grounds of Social Criticism*, p. 180; Benhabib, "Deliberative Rationality and Models of Democratic Legitimacy," p. 40.

164. Baynes, *The Normative Grounds of Social Criticism*, p. 180.

165. N. Fraser, "Rethinking the Public Sphere: A Contribution to the Critique of Actually Existing Democracy," in *Habermas and the Public Sphere*, pp. 109–142.

166. J. F. Bohman, "Communication, Ideology, and Democratic Theory," *American Political Science Review*, vol. 84, no. 1, 1990, p. 109.

167. R. J. Bernstein, *The Restructuring of Social and Political Theory* (London: Methuen, 1979), p. 236.

168. S. Benhabib, *Critique, Norm, and Utopia* (New York: Columbia University Press, 1986), p. 353.

169. Baynes, *The Normative Grounds of Social Criticism*, p. 181.

170. See, for example, B. Manin, "On Legitimacy and Political Deliberation," *Political Theory*, vol. 15, no. 3, 1987, pp. 338–368; J. S. Fishkin, *The Dialogue of Justice*; B. R. Barber, *Strong Democracy* (Berkeley: University of California Press, 1984); C. Pateman, *Participation and Democratic Theory* (Cambridge: Cambridge University Press, 1970); D. Held and C. Pollitt (eds.), *New Forms of Democracy* (London: Sage, 1986).

171. For example, C. Mouffe, *The Return of the Political* (London: Verso, 1993).

172. J. Cohen, "Deliberation and Democratic Legitimacy," in *The Good Polity: Normative Analysis of the State*, ed. A. Hamlin and P. Pettit (Oxford: Blackwell, 1991), pp. 17–34, here at p. 30.

173. J. Forester, "Towards a Critical-Empirical Framework for the Analysis of Public Policy"; Forester, "Critical Theory and Planning Practice," in *Critical Theory and Public Life*, p. 205; see also Parkin, "Rethinking the Subject," chap. 6, pp. 6, 23.

174. Habermas, *Moral Consciousness and Communicative Action*, p. 207.

175. Habermas, *Legitimation Crisis*, op. cit., passim.

176. Habermas, *The Philosophical Discourse of Modernity*, p. 363.

177. Habermas, *Moral Consciousness and Communicative Action*, p. 207.

178. See Baynes, *The Normative Grounds of Social Criticism*, p. 180: D. Coole, "Wild Differences and Tamed Others: Postmodernism and Liberal Democracy," *Parallax*, no. 2, February 1996, pp. 23–36; T. McCarthy, "Kantian Contructivism and Reconstructivism: Rawls and Habermas in Dialogue," *Ethics*, vol. 105, 1994, pp. 44–63.

4. METHODOLOGICAL PROBLEMS AND LIMITS TO THEORY

1. See P. Hohendahl's "Foreword" to J. Habermas, *The Past as Future* (Cambridge: Polity Press, 1994), pp. xxiii–xxv.

2. L. J. Ray, *Rethinking Critical Theory* (London: Sage, 1993), pp. 12, 20.

3. Ferrara refers to "the much lamented lack of a Habermasian politics," in "A Critique of Habermas' Diskursethik," *Telos*, no. 64, 1985, pp. 45–74, here at p. 53.

4. See, for a review of his various interventions in the student radical movement, R. C. Holub, *Jürgen Habermas: Critic in the Public Sphere* (London: Routledge, 1991), pp. 78–105.

5. Habermas thus criticises Rawls, both for his monological approach and for his substantive principles of justice. See J. Habermas, *Moral Consciousness and Communicative Action* (Cambridge: Polity Press, 1990), p. 66

6. J. Habermas, *Communication and the Evolution of Society* (Cambridge: Polity Press, 1984), pp. 178–205.

7. Ibid., p. 183.

8. Ibid., pp. 183–185.

9. Ibid., p. 185.

10. Ibid., p. 186.

11. Indeed, they situate Habermas within the grand tradition of attacking Rousseau for something he did not say. Hegel and Marx treated Rousseau with similar roughness, as shown in R. Wokler, "Hegel's Rousseau: The General Will and Civil Society," *Arachne*, no. 8, 1993, pp. 7–45. Habermas's critique is in fact an almost complete mirror image of Hegel's, effectively turning the latter's reading of Rousseau on its head.

12. See Q. Skinner, "The Empirical Theorists of Democracy and Their Critics: A Plague on Both Their Houses," *Political Theory*, vol. 1, no. 3, 1973, pp. 287–306.

13. See A. Wellmer, "Practical Philosophy and the Theory of Society: On the Problem of the Normative Foundations of a Critical Social Science," in *The Communicative Ethics Controversy*, ed. S. Benhabib and F. Dallmayr (Cambridge, Mass.: MIT Press, 1990), pp. 293–329, here at p. 314; see also D. Beetham, "Liberal Democracy and the Limits of Democratization," in *Prospects for Democracy: North, South, East, West*, ed. D. Held (Cambridge: Polity Press, 1993).

14. David Ingram says almost exactly this in "The Limits and Possibilities of Communicative Ethics for Democratic Theory," *Political Theory*, vol. 21, no. 2, 1993, pp. 294–321, here at p. 310ff.

15. Habermas, *Communication and the Evolution of Society*, p. 186.

16. Ibid.

17. In this regard, J. F. Bohman, in "Participating in Enlightenment: Habermas's Cognitivist Interpretation of Democracy," in *Knowledge and Politics: Case Studies in the Relationship between Epistemology and Political Philosophy*, ed. M. Dascal and O. Gruengard (Boulder, Colo.: Westview Press, 1989), pp. 264–289, likens discourse ethics to a theory of knowledge, where what is revealed is the nature of true statements rather than exactly which statements are true. See also Ingram, "The Limits and Possibilities of Communicative Ethics for Democratic Theory," p. 311.

18. Habermas, *Communication and the Evolution of Society*, p. 186.

19. See Skinner, "The Empirical Theorists of Democracy and Their Critics"; Habermas takes this paper as his starting point in the passage we are here discussing.

20. Habermas, *Communication and the Evolution of Society*, pp. 186–187.

21. Skinner, "The Empirical Theorists of Democracy," p. 288.

22. P. Bachrach, *The Theory of Democratic Elitism: A Critique* (Boston: Little, Brown, 1967), p. 20.

23. See, for example, R. A. Dahl, *A Preface to Democratic Theory* (Chicago: University of Chicago Press, 1956), pp. 69–74.

24. Habermas, *Communication and the Evolution of Society*, p. 187.

25. This argument has strong similarities to that advanced by R. P. Wolff in *In Defence of Anarchism* (New York: Harper & Row, 1970), though here the account of the normative ground for legitimacy is quite different.

26. Ibid., p. 187.

27. Ibid.

28. See G. Sartori, *The Theory of Democracy Revisited*, vol. 1 (Chatham, N.J.: Chatham House, 1987), pp. 58–82.

29. See, for example, A. Wellmer, "Reason, Utopia, and the Dialectic of Enlightenment," in *Habermas and Modernity*, ed. R. J. Bernstein (Cambridge: Polity Press, 1985), p. 58.

30. A. Wellmer, *Reason, Emancipation and Utopia* (Unpublished, 1979).

31. J. Habermas, "A Reply to My Critics," in *Habermas: Critical Debates*, ed. J. B. Thompson and D. Held (Cambridge, Mass.: MIT Press, 1982), p. 261. In this same passage, Habermas admits to having, on occasion, used such a "shortcut" himself.

32. See S. K. White, "Reason and Authority in Habermas: A Critique of the Critics," *American Political Science Review*, vol. 74, 1980, pp. 1007–1017, here at p. 1010. White also discusses Spaemann's accusation that Habermas himself violates the negative limit at certain points in his writings. See ibid., p. 1010 n. 4.

33. J. Elster, "The Market and the Forum: Three Varieties of Political Theory," in *Foundations of Social Choice Theory*, ed. J. Elster and A. Hylland (Cambridge: Cambridge University Press, 1986), pp. 103–132.

34. J. Habermas, "Three Models of Democracy," *Constellations*, vol. 1, no. 1, 1994, pp. 1–10.

35. See B. R. Barber, *Strong Democracy* (Berkeley: University of California Press, 1984).

36. See J. J. Mansbridge, *Beyond Adversary Democracy* (New York: Basic Books, 1980).

37. J. S. Fishkin, *The Dialogue of Justice: Toward a Self-Reflective Society* (New Haven: Yale University Press, 1992).

38. J. S. Mill, "Essay on Bentham," in *Utilitarianism and Other Writings*, ed. M. Warnock (New York: Meridian, 1959), pp. 78–125, esp. p. 106; C. Pateman, *Participation and Democratic Theory* (Cambridge: Cambridge University Press, 1970); see also Held's second type of "developmental democracy," outlined in D. Held, *Models of Democracy* (Cambridge: Polity Press, 1987), p. 102.

39. This is the third category of democratic theory outlined in J. Habermas, "Three Models of Democracy."

40. There is a careful discussion of this criticism of Rousseau in J. Cohen. "Reflections on Rousseau: Autonomy and Democracy," *Philosophy and Public Affairs*, vol. 15, no. 3, 1986, pp. 275–297; K. Baynes, in *The Normative Grounds of Social Criticism: Kant, Rawls, and Habermas* (Albany: State University of New York Press, 1992), p. 44, shows his agreement with the criticism, and suggests it leads to a utopian moment in Rousseau's thought.

41. See Habermas, "A Reply to My Critics," p. 261.

42. J. Cohen, "Deliberation and Democratic Legitimacy," in *The Good Polity: Normative Analysis of the State*, p. 34 n. 27.

43. See J.-J. Rousseau, *The Social Contract* (Harmondsworth, U.K.: Penguin, 1968), p. 101; R. Wokler, "Rousseau's Two Concepts of Liberty," in *Lives, Liberties and the Public Good*, ed. G. Feaver and F. Rosen (London: Macmillan, 1987), p. 82; and Cohen, "Reflections on Rousseau: Autonomy and Democracy," p. 289.

44. Outlined in Cohen, "Reflections on Rousseau: Autonomy and Democracy," p. 289.

45. Ibid., p. 290.

46. See the discussion of Rousseau's "democracy without public opinion," in J. Habermas, *The Structural Transformation of the Public Sphere* (Cambridge: Polity Press, 1989), pp. 96–99.

47. Ingram, "The Limits and Possibilities of Communicative Ethics," op. cit.

48. R. Shelly, "Habermas and the Normative Foundations of a Radical Politics," *Thesis Eleven*, no. 35, 1993, pp. 62–83, here at pp. 69–71.

49. Citing B. Manin's important article, "On Legitimacy and Political Deliberation," *Political Theory*, vol. 15, no. 3, 1987, pp. 338–368.

50. Shelly, "Habermas and the Normative Foundations of a Radical Politics," p. 69.

51. J. S. Dryzek, *Discursive Democracy: Politics, Policy, and Political Science* (Cambridge: Cambridge University Press, 1990).

52. Ibid., p. 18.

53. Ibid., p. 20. It is interesting to note the difference here to Arendt's position. She would see the use of deliberative means to solve "social problems" as an inappropriate incursion of politics into questions of administration. See H. Arendt, *The Human Condition* (Chicago: University of Chicago Press, 1958).

54. Dryzek, *Discursive Democracy*, p. 21.

55. J. Dryzek, "Discursive Designs: Critical Theory and Political Institutions," *American Journal of Political Science*, vol. 31, 1987, pp. 656–679, here at p. 664.

56. Dryzek, *Discursive Democracy*, p. 13.

57. S. Benhabib, *Critique, Norm, and Utopia* (New York: Columbia University Press, 1986), p. 298; S. Benhabib, *Situating the Self* (Cambridge: Polity Press, 1992); N. Fraser, "Rethinking the Public Sphere: A Contribution to the Critique of Actually Existing Democracy," in *Habermas and the Public Sphere*, ed. C. Calhoun (Cambridge, Mass.: MIT Press, 1992), pp. 109–142.

58. Dryzek, *Discursive Democracy*, p. 16.

59. See A. MacIntyre, "Does Applied Ethics Rest on a Mistake?" *The Monist*, vol. 67, 1984, pp. 498–513.

60. Dryzek, *Discursive Democracy*, p. 17.

61. J. Habermas, *Communication and the Evolution of Society*, p. 90.

62. Dryzek, *Discursive Democracy*, p. 17.

63. S. K. White, *The Recent Work of Jürgen Habermas* (Cambridge: Cambridge University Press, 1988), p. 70.

64. Ibid., p. 74.

65. Dryzek, "Discursive Designs," p. 665.

66. Dryzek, *Discursive Democracy*, p. 30. Dryzek here refers also to the remarks on utopian blueprints in White, "Reason and Authority in Habermas," pp. 1007–1017.

67. Dryzek, *Discursive Democracy*, p. 30.

68. Dryzek, "Discursive Designs," p. 665.

69. Dryzek, *Discursive Democracy*, p. 32.

70. Dryzek, "Discursive Designs," p. 665.

71. Ibid.

72. Ibid. Notice the similarity between this and other arguments that rely upon the notion of rational agency reviewed in the previous chapter.

73. Dryzek, *Discursive Democracy*, p. 41.

74. R. Fisher and W. Ury, *Getting to Yes* (Boston: Houghton Mifflin, 1981).

75. Dryzek, *Discursive Democracy*, p. 42.

76. Ibid. See also J. Habermas, "A Reply to My Critics," pp. 257–258; and T. McCarthy, "Practical Discourse: On the Relation of Morality to Politics," in *Ideals and Illusions* (Cambridge: Polity Press, 1991), pp. 181–199.

77. See the discussion of such work in section 3.2 in the previous chapter.

78. Dryzek, *Discursive Democracy*, p. 45.

79. Ibid., p. 46.

80. Ibid., p. 54; see, for an excellent discussion of this problem, M. Taylor, *Anarchy and Co-operation* (London: Wiley, 1976).

81. Dryzek, *Discursive Democracy*, p. 55.

82. Ibid., p. 57ff. The assertion that deliberation can in fact increase efficiency of policy output is a common one among deliberative democrats; see my "New Theories of Discursive Democracy: A User's Guide," *Philosophy and Social Criticism*, vol. 22, no. 1, 1996, pp. 49–80, here at p. 55. A good example is that of D. Miller, "Deliberative Democracy and Social Choice," *Political Studies*, vol. 40, special issue, 1992, pp. 54–76.

83. Barber, *Strong Democracy.*

84. Bohman makes this critique of Barber in J. F. Bohman, "Communication, Ideology, and Democratic Theory," *American Political Science Review*, vol. 84, no. 1, 1990, pp. 93–109, here at p. 99.

85. Dryzek, "Discursive Designs," p. 665.

86. See L. Putterman, "Some Behavioural Perspectives on the Dominance of Hierarchical over Democratic Forms of Enterprise," *Journal of Economic Behaviour and Organization*, vol. 3, 1982, pp. 139–160. Such an empirical insight is also the source of the almost overwhelming rhetorical power of Michels's Iron Law of Oligarchy. See R. Michels, *Political Parties* (Glencoe, Ill.: Free Press, 1958), p. 415, and G. Parry, *Political Elites* (London: George Allen and Unwin, 1969), pp. 42–45.

87. J. Elster, "The Market and the Forum," p. 121; J. Elster, *Sour Grapes* (Cambridge: Cambridge University Press, 1983), p. 92.

88. A review of this type of attempted justifications can be found (with some difficulty) in M. Warren, "Democratic Theory and Self-Transformation," *American Political Science Review*, vol. 86, no. 1, 1992, pp. 8–23, though the article does not deal with Elster's counter-argument or with the wide-ranging discussion it has engendered.

89. Habermas, *Communication and the Evolution of Society*, p. 186, emphasis mine.

90. J. Habermas, *Theory and Practice* (London: Heinemann, 1974), p. 32.

91. See the discussion of Habermas's distinction between the function and organization of enlightenment in D. Held, *Introduction to Critical Theory: Horkheimer to Habermas* (Cambridge: Polity Press, 1980), p. 348.

92. S. Benhabib, "Modernity and the Aporias of Critical Theory," *Telos*, no. 49, Autumn 1981, pp. 39–59, here at p. 54.

93. S. Benhabib, "The Utopian Dimension in Communicative Ethics," *New German Critique*, no. 35, 1985, pp. 83–96, here at p. 84.

94. Habermas, "A Reply to My Critics," p. 262.

95. For example, see J. Habermas, *The Theory of Communicative Action*, vol. 1 (Boston: Beacon Press, 1984), pp. 243–253.

96. M. Passerin d'Entrèves, *Modernity, Justice and Community* (Milan: Franco Angeli, 1990), p. 22.

97. Ibid., p. 23.

98. For many critical theorists, the question of means is a diffuse anxiety. Elster provides more definite reasons to be afraid in J. Elster and A. Hylland, *Foundations of Social Choice Theory* (Cambridge: Cambridge University Press, 1986), esp. p. 120.

99. Habermas addresses this when he confronts the counter-Enlightenment tradition and the messianic utopian strand of critical theory. See J. Habermas, "Consciousness-Raising or Redemptive Criticism: The Contemporaneity of Walter Benjamin," *New German Critique*, no. 17, Spring 1979. For a discussion of this encounter, see J. Whitebook, "Saving the Subject: Modernity and the Problem of the Autonomous Individual," *Telos*, no. 50, Winter 1981.

100. Benhabib, "The Utopian Dimension in Communicative Ethics," p. 84.

101. Ibid., pp. 85, 91.

102. A. Wellmer, "Reason, Utopia, and the Dialectic of Enlightenment," in *Habermas and Modernity*, ed. R. J. Bernstein (Cambridge: Polity Press, 1985), pp. 35–66, here at pp. 57–61.

103. Wellmer, "Reason, Utopia, and the Dialectic of Enlightenment," p. 61.

104. Habermas, "A Reply to My Critics," p. 251.

105. R. Beiner, *Political Judgment* (London: Methuen, 1983), p. 7; see also Dryzek's discussion of "comparative evaluation" in *Discursive Democracy*, p. 37.

106. Habermas, *Communication and the Evolution of Society*, p. 186, emphasis mine.

107. Habermas, "A Reply to My Critics," p. 254.

108. S. Benhabib, *Critique, Norm, and Utopia* (New York: Columbia University Press, 1986), p. 323.

109. Ibid.,

110. The question of whether these problems are in part overcome by construing such judgment as reflective rather than determinant is addressed in the next chapter.

111. Habermas, "A Reply to My Critics," p. 253

112. Benhabib, *Critique, Norm, and Utopia*, p. 323

113. D. Ingram, "The Limits and Possibilities of Communicative Ethics for Democratic Theory," p. 297.

114. "Habermas has backed away from regarding consensus as a criterion of truth. He now holds that consensus is a condition of warranted assertibility . . . [for] consensus would be a sign of truth only if we further assumed that all participants possessed complete knowledge of themselves and their world." Ibid., p. 296. Such a revision does indeed move the normative ideal "closer" to reality, yet it still requires a moment of application.

115. S. Cavell, *The Claim of Reason* (Oxford: Oxford University Press, 1982), p. 265.

116. A. Wellmer, *The Persistence of Modernity: Aesthetics, Ethics and Postmodernism* (Cambridge: Polity Press, 1991), p. 200; see also Ingram, "The Limits and Possibilities of Communicative Ethics for Democratic Theory," p. 298.

117. J. Elster, *Solomonic Judgements: Studies in the Limitations of Rationality* (Cambridge: Cambridge University Press, 1989), p. 181.

118. Ibid., pp. 184–187.

119. Ibid., pp. 187–189.

120. Ibid., pp. 189–190.

121. Ibid., pp. 191–194.

122. Ibid., p. 181; see also A. MacIntyre, *After Virtue* (Notre Dame, Ind.: University of Notre Dame Press, 1981), pp. 93–101.

123. Benhabib, *Critique, Norm, and Utopia*, p. 322.

124. See R. C. Holub, *Jürgen Habermas: Critic in the Public Sphere* (London: Routledge, 1991), pp. 49–77; A. Ferrara. "Universalisms: Procedural, Contextual and Prudential," *Philosophy and Social Criticism*, vol. 14, no. 3–4, 1989, pp. 243–269.

125. See S. Benhabib, *Situating the Self* (Cambridge: Polity Press, 1992), p. 125.

126. There are times when he seems to back away from this characterization of judgment. See, for example, Habermas. "A Reply to My Critics," p. 262, and Habermas, *Moral Consciousness and Communicative Action*, p. 182.

127. A. MacIntyre, "Does Applied Ethics Rest on a Mistake?" *The Monist*, vol. 67, 1984, pp. 498–513, here at p. 503.

128. Beauchamp discusses the value of case-based learning in T. L. Beauchamp, "On Eliminating the Distinction between Applied Ethics and Ethical Theory," *The Monist*, vol. 67, 1984, pp. 514–531, here at pp. 524–529.

129. See J. Habermas, *Justification and Application* (Cambridge: Polity Press, 1993), pp. 54–55; and Ferrara's discussion of Apel's formulation of the "principle" by which we should attempt to "reduce as far as possible the gap between the ideal speech situation and the actual communicative contexts," in "A Critique of Habermas' Diskursethik," *Telos*, no. 64, 1985, p. 63 n. 34.

130. This phrase is taken from A. Margalit, "Ideals and Second Bests," in *Philosophy for Education*, ed. S. Fox (Jerusalem: Van Leer Foundation, 1983), pp. 77–90.

131. Wellmer, "Reason, Utopia, and the Dialectic of Enlightenment," p. 61.

132. P. Laslett, "The Face to Face Society," in *Philosophy, Politics and Society*, first series, ed. P. Laslett (Oxford: Basil Blackwell, 1956), pp. 157–184, here at p. 184.

5. HABERMASIAN DIFFICULTIES WITH JUDGMENT

1. J. Habermas, *Justification and Application* (Cambridge: Polity Press, 1993), p. 39.

2. Ibid., p. 38.

3. J. Habermas, *Moral Consciousness and Communicative Action* (Cambridge: Polity Press, 1990), p. 206.

4. Habermas, *Justification and Application*, p. 13.

5. K. Günther, "Impartial Application of Moral and Legal Norms: A Contribution to Discourse Ethics," *Philosophy and Social Criticism*, vol. 4, no. 3/4, 1988, pp. 425–432, here p. 425.

6. S. O'Neill, "Morality, Ethical Life and the Persistence of Universalism," *Theory, Culture and Society*, vol. 11, no. 2, 1994, pp. 129–149, at p. 145.

7. Habermas, *Moral Consciousness and Communicative Action*, p. 206.

8. A. Wellmer, *The Persistence of Modernity: Aesthetics, Ethics and Postmodernism* (Cambridge: Polity Press, 1991), p. 206.

9. Habermas, *Justification and Application*, p. 38; Wellmer, *The Persistence of Modernity*, p. 200.

10. Wellmer, *The Persistence of Modernity*, p. 35; Habermas, *Moral Consciousness and Communicative Action*, p. 206; see also S. Benhabib, "Afterword: Communicative Ethics and Current Controversies in Practical Philosophy," in *The Communicative Ethics Controversy*, ed. S. Benhabib and F.

Dallmayr (Cambridge, Mass.: MIT Press, 1990), pp. 330–369, here p. 334.

11. Habermas, *Moral Consciousness and Communicative Action*, p. 206.

12. Ibid.

13. Habermas, *Justification and Application*, pp. 35–36.

14. Ibid., p. 36.

15. Habermas, *Moral Consciousness and Communicative Action*, p. 206.

16. Habermas, *Justification and Application*, pp. 10, 17; A. Ferrara, "A Critique of Habermas's Consensus Theory of Truth," *Philosophy and Social Criticism*, vol. 13, no. 1, 1988, pp. 54–55; K. Günther, *The Sense of Appropriateness: Application Discourses in Morality and Law* (Albany: State University of New York Press, 1993).

17. K. Günther, "Impartial Application of Moral and Legal Norms: a Contribution to Discourse Ethics," *Philosophy and Social Criticism*, vol. 14, no. 3/4, 1988, pp. 425–432, here at p. 430.

18. As in A. MacIntyre, *A Short History of Ethics* (New York: Macmillan, 1966), p. 8, and R. Beiner, "Do We Need a Philosophical Ethics? Theory, Prudence, and the Primacy of Ethos," *The Philosophical Forum*, vol. 20, no. 3, 1989, pp. 230–243.

19. Günther, *The Sense of Appropriateness*, pp. 73–170.

20. Ibid., pp. 229–245.

21. Habermas, *Justification and Application*, pp. 4–5.

22. Günther, *The Sense of Appropriateness*, pp. 229–239.

23. Ibid., pp. 239–246.

24. Habermas, *Justification and Application*, p. 37.

25. Habermas, *Moral Consciousness and Communicative Action*, p. 206.

26. Günther, "Impartial Application of Moral and Legal Norms," p. 430.

27. Habermas, *Justification and Application*, p. 37; Günther, *The Sense of Appropriateness*, pp. 34–35.

28. Günther, "Impartial Application of Moral and Legal Norms," p. 426; *The Sense of Appropriateness*, pp. 35–40.

29. Habermas, *Justification and Application*, pp. 1–17.

30. A. Ferrara, "On Phronesis," *Praxis International*, vol. 7, no. 3/4, 1987, pp. 246–267, here at p. 248.

31. R. Beiner, *Political Judgment* (London: Methuen, 1983), p. 110.

32. Ibid.

33. Ibid., p. 65.

34. Ibid., p. 97.

35. I. Kant, *Critique of Judgment* (Oxford: Clarendon Press, 1952), section IV; see also S. Benhabib, *Situating the Self* (Cambridge: Polity Press, 1992), p. 130.

36. Habermas, *Justification and Application*, p. 37; see also Günther's discussion of the discovery that, in moral questions, "it depends," in *The Sense of Appropriateness*, pp. 137–155.

37. Habermas, *Moral Consciousness and Communicative Action*, pp. 181–182.

38. Günther, *The Sense of Appropriateness*, passim.

39. A. Ferrara, "Authenticity and the Project of Modernity," *European*

Journal of Philosophy, vol. 2, no. 3, 1994, pp. 241–273, here p. 255, emphasis in original.

40. Habermas, *Moral Consciousness and Communicative Action*, p. 150.

41. S. Benhabib, *Critique, Norm, and Utopia* (New York: Columbia University Press, 1986), p. 323.

42. Benhabib, *Situating the Self*, pp. 148–177.

43. C. Gilligan, *In a Different Voice: Psychological Theory and Women's Development* (Cambridge, Mass.: Harvard University Press, 1982).

44. Benhabib, *Situating the Self*, pp. 158–159.

45. See M. Cooke, "Habermas and Consensus," *European Journal of Philosophy*, vol. 1, no. 3, 1993, pp. 11–13.

46. T. McCarthy, "Practical Discourse: On the Relation of Morality to Politics," in *Ideals and Illusions* (Cambridge: Polity Press, 1991), pp. 181–199.

47. A. Wellmer, *The Persistence of Modernity: Aesthetics, Ethics and Postmodernism* (Cambridge: Polity Press, 1991), p. 155; A. Wellmer, *Ethik und Dialog* (Frankfurt: Suhrkamp, 1986), pp. 61, 64–65; A. Ferrara, "Critical Theory and Its Discontents: Wellmer's Critique of Habermas," *Praxis International*, vol. 9, no. 3, 1989, pp. 305–320, here at p. 305.

48. Wellmer, *The Persistence of Modernity*, p. 155.

49. Benhabib collects the various objections to (U) in terms of it being "either too indeterminate or too complex or too counterfactual," in *Situating the Self*, p. 36; see also J. Keane, *Public Life and Late Capitalism: Towards a Socialist Theory of Democracy* (Cambridge: Cambridge University Press, 1984), p. 190; S. Lukes, "Of Gods and Demons: Habermas and Practical Reason," in *Habermas: Critical Debates*, ed. J. B. Thompson and D. Held (Cambridge, Mass.: MIT Press, 1982), pp. 134–148, and Habermas's comments regarding Lukes's criticisms in "A Reply to My Critics," in *Habermas: Critical Debates*, pp. 219–283, esp. pp. 254–258.

50. Habermas, *Justification and Application*, p. 35; see also McCarthy, *Ideals and Illusions*, pp. 181–199.

51. Ferrara, "Critical Theory and Its Discontents: Wellmer's Critique of Habermas," p. 310.

52. Habermas, *Justification and Application*, p. 35.

53. Ibid.

54. Wellmer, *The Persistence of Modernity*, p. 206: Günther deals at length with Wellmer's objection in *The Sense of Appropriateness*, pp. 45–58.

55. This is how Günther describes Wellmer's position in "Impartial Application of Moral and Legal Norms: A Contribution to Discourse Ethics," p. 426.

56. Ferrara, "A Critique of Habermas's Consensus Theory of Truth," p. 64.

57. This is the argument presented in H. L. Dreyfus and S. E. Dreyfus, "What Is Morality? A Phenomenological Account of the Development of Ethical Expertise," in *Universalism vs. Communitarianism: Contemporary Debates in Ethics*, ed. D. Rasmussen (Cambridge: Polity Press, 1990), pp. 237–264.

58. Benhabib, *Situating the Self*, p. 50.

59. See H. Putnam, *Reason, Truth and History* (Cambridge: Cambridge University Press, 1981).

60. Benhabib, *Situating the Self*, p. 8.

61. Ferrara, "Critical Theory and Its Discontents," p. 312.

62. See J. Keane, "Introduction," in *Civil Society and the State*, ed. J. Keane (London: Verso, 1988), pp. 24–25; S. Benhabib, "The Methodological Illusions of Modern Political Theory: The Case of Rawls and Habermas," *Neue Hefte fur Philosophie*, vol. 21, 1982, pp. 70–72; A. Ferrara, "A Critique of Habermas' Diskursethik," *Telos*, no. 64, 1985, p. 63.

63. Benhabib, *Situating the Self*, p. 53.

64. Ibid. The metaphor was originally Aristotle's, in *Nicomachean Ethics*, in *Basic Works of Aristotle*, ed. R. McKeon (New York: Random House, 1966), 1114b5ff., 1142a25ff., and is repeated by H. G. Gadamer in *Truth and Method* (New York: Seabury Press, 1975); see also Benhabib, *Situating the Self*, p. 135.

65. See Günther, *The Sense of Appropriateness*, p. 50.

66. It has been argued that consensus cannot function as an adequate criterion of validity. See, for example, A. Ferrara, "A Critique of Habermas's Consensus Theory of Truth"; A. Ferrara, "A Critique of Habermas' Diskursethik," *Telos*, no. 64, 1985, pp. 45–74; D. Ingram, "The Limits and Possibilities of Communicative Ethics for Democratic Theory," *Political Theory*, vol. 21, no. 2, 1993, pp. 294–321; see also note 13 in J. Cohen, "Discourse Ethics and Civil Society," *Philosophy and Social Criticism*, vol. 14, no. 3/4, 1988, pp. 334–335.

67. Cooke, "Habermas and Consensus," p. 14; see also J. Cohen, "Discourse Ethics and Civil Society," p. 316.

68. Wellmer, *The Persistence of Modernity*, p. 147.

69. Benhabib, *Situating the Self*, p. 37.

70. Cooke, "Habermas and Consensus," p. 17.

71. Ibid., p. 14; see also Wellmer, *The Persistence of Modernity*, p. 147.

72. J. Rawls, "Kantian Constructivism in Moral Theory. The John Dewey Lectures," *Journal of Philosophy*, vol. 77, 1980, pp. 515–572.

73. Wellmer, *The Persistence of Modernity*, pp. 174–188.

74. Ibid., p. 195.

75. A. Wellmer, *Ethik und Dialog* (Frankfurt: Suhrkamp, 1986), pp. 65–66. This, of course, is not something Habermas would accept; see Ferrara, "Critical Theory and its Discontents: Wellmer's Critique of Habermas," p. 305.

76. Wellmer, *The Persistence of Modernity*, p. 196.

77. Ibid., p. 227.

78. Benhabib, *Situating the Self*, p. 128.

79. Wellmer, *The Persistence of Modernity*, p. 197.

80. See A. MacIntyre, "Does Applied Ethics Rest on a Mistake?" *The Monist*, vol. 67, 1984, pp. 498–513, here at p. 503.

81. R. Beiner, *Political Judgment* (London: Methuen, 1983), p. 24.

82. J. Habermas, "What Theories Can Accomplish—and What They Can't," in *The Past as Future*, ed. M. Haller (Cambridge: Polity Press, 1994), pp. 99–120, here at p.102.

83. Wellmer, *The Persistence of Modernity*, p. 116.

84. S. Benhabib, *Situating the Self*, p. 37ff.

85. Cooke, "Habermas and Consensus," p. 14.

86. Ferrara, "Critical Theory and Its Discontents," pp. 305, 317.

87. Beiner, *Political Judgment*, p. 53.

88. I. Kant, *Critique of Judgment* (Oxford: Clarendon Press, 1952), p. 141.

89. Ibid., p. 51; see also Beiner, *Political Judgment*, p. 37.

90. Kant, *Critique of Judgment*, p. 198.

91. Beiner, *Political Judgment*, p. 43.

92. Ibid., p. 51.

93. Kant, *Critique of Judgment*, p. 198.

94. Ibid., p. 18

95. Ibid., p. 145.

96. Scruton describes it as "lame" in *Kant* (Oxford: Oxford University Press, 1982), p. 83.

97. See H. Arendt, *Between Past and Future* (Harmondsworth, U.K.: Penguin, 1977), p. 219.

98. See M. Passerin d'Entrèves, *The Political Philosophy of Hannah Arendt* (London: Routledge, 1994).

99. R. Makkreel, "Kant and the Interpretation of Nature and History," in *Hermeneutics and Critical Theory in Ethics and Politics*, ed. M. Kelly (Cambridge, Mass.: MIT Press, 1990), pp. 169–181, here at p. 175.

100. Passerin d'Entrèves, *The Political Philosophy of Hannah Arendt*, p. 114.

101. Ibid., p. 113.

102. Ibid., p. 114.

103. Quoted in ibid.

104. Ibid., pp. 114–116.

105. See Passerin d'Entrèves, *The Political Philosophy of Hannah Arendt*, p. 123, for the differences between the Arendtian view of judgment and *phronēsis*.

106. Wellmer, "Hannah Arendt on Judgement: the Unwritten Doctrine of Reason," unpublished manuscript, 1985, pp. 1–28, here at p. 14.

107. Passerin d'Entrèves, *The Political Philosophy of Hannah Arendt*, p. 116.

108. Ibid., p. 117.

109. Ibid., pp. 117–121.

110. Benhabib, *Situating the Self*, p. 137.

111. Ibid.

112. R. Makkreel, "Kant and the Interpretation of Nature and History," in *Hermeneutics and Critical Theory in Ethics and Politics*, p. 173.

113. Passerin d'Entrèves, *The Political Philosophy of Hannah Arendt*, p. 118.

114. Ibid., p. 119.

115. Kant, *Critique of Judgment*, p. 108.

116. Makkreel, "Kant and the Interpretation of Nature and History," p. 174, quoting I. Kant, *Critique of Judgment* (Oxford: Clarendon Press, 1952), pp. 22, 76.

117. Ferrara, "A Critique of Habermas' Diskursethik," p. 69; Makkreel, "Kant and the Interpretation of Nature and History," p. 173.

118. Ferrara, "A Critique of Habermas's Consensus Theory of Truth," p. 62.

119. Beiner, *Political Judgment*, p. 43.

120. Wellmer argues, in "Hannah Arendt on Judgement," pp. 7–16, that she remained bound by Kantian presuppositions, and by so ceding reason to science, resisted the notion of rational argumentation. It is for this reason that Wellmer describes her theory of judgment as a "mythology," p. 9.

121. Beiner, *Political Judgment*, p. 119.

122. Benhabib, *Situating the Self*, p. 134.

123. Ibid., p. 138.

124. See Ferrara, "A Critique of Habermas's Consensus Theory of Truth," p. 62; A. Ferrara, "On Phronesis," *Praxis International*, vol. 7, no. 3/4, 1987, pp. 246–267, here at p. 251.

125. Ferrara, "On Phronesis," p. 251ff.

126. Ferrara., "A Critique of Habermas' Diskursethik," p. 69.

127. See Ferrara, "A Critique of Habermas's Consensus Theory of Truth," p. 60; A. Ferrara, "On Phronesis"; A. Ferrara, "Justice and Judgment" (unpublished), 1992; A. Ferrara, "Justice and Identity," *Philosophy and Social Criticism*, vol. 18, no. 3/4, 1992, pp. 333–354; A. Ferrara, "Postmodern Eudaimonia," *Praxis International*, vol. 11, no. 4, 1992, pp. 387–411.

128. J. Rawls, *A Theory of Justice* (Cambridge, Mass.: Harvard University Press, 1971), pp. 92–93, 407–416.

129. M. Walzer, "A Critique of Philosophical Conversation," in *Hermeneutics and Critical Theory in Ethics and Politics*, ed. M. Kelly (Cambridge, Mass.: MIT Press, 1990), pp. 182–196, here at p. 192.

130. See esp. Ferrara, "A Critique of Habermas's Consensus Theory of Truth," p. 62ff.

131. See the discussion in McCarthy, *Ideals and Illusions*, pp. 181–199.

132. J. Habermas, *Knowledge and Human Interests* (Boston: Beacon, 1968).

133. Ferrara, "On Phronesis," p. 252.

134. Ibid.

135. Ferrara, "Postmodern Eudaimonia," p. 389

136. Ibid., p. 397.

137. Ibid., p. 406.

138. Ibid., pp. 398–406.

139. A. Ferrara, "Authenticity and the Project of Modernity," *European Journal of Philosophy*, vol. 2, no. 3, 1994, pp. 241–273, here at p. 252.

140. See, for example, R. Wollheim, *Sigmund Freud* (Cambridge: Cambridge University Press, 1971); R. Wollheim and J. Hopkins (eds.), *Philosophical Essays on Freud*, Cambridge: Cambridge University Press, 1982; A. Grünbaum, *The Foundations of Psychoanalysis: A Philosophical Critique* (Berkeley: University of California Press, 1984); J. Wisdom, *Philosophy and Psychoanalysis* (Berkeley: University of California Press, 1969).

141. See, for example, C. Bernheimer and C. Kahane (eds.), *In Dora's Case: Freud, Hysteria, Feminism* (London: Virago, 1985); J. Malcolm, *In the Freud Archives* (New York: Vintage Books, 1985).

142. Wellmer, *The Persistence of Modernity*, p. 196.

143. Ibid., pp.196, 199.

144. Ibid., p. 198; Notice Wellmer's attempt here to move away from the "approximation assumption."

145. Ibid., p. 200.

146. Ibid., p. 199

147. Ibid., p. 200

148. Ibid., p. 202.

149. Ibid., p. 200.

150. Ibid., p. 204.

151. Ibid., p. 205.

152. Benhabib, *Situating the Self*, p. 3.

153. Ibid., p. 29.

154. Ibid., pp. 30, 61 n. 48; see also D. J. Moon, "Constrained Discourse and Public Life," *Political Theory*, vol. 19, no. 2, 1991, p. 222.

155. Benhabib, *Situating the Self*, p. 37.

156. Ibid., p. 39.

157. G. Warnke, *Justice and Interpretation* (Cambridge: Polity Press, 1992).

158. O'Neill, "Morality, Ethical Life and the Persistence of Universalism," p. 144.

159. Habermas, *Justification and Application*, p. 39.

160. C. Taylor, *Multiculturalism and "The Politics of Recognition"* (Princeton, N.J.: Princeton University Press, 1992).

161. J. Habermas, *Between Facts and Norms: Contributions to a Discourse Theory of Law and Democracy* (Cambridge: Polity Press, 1996); J. Habermas, "Struggles for Recognition in Constitutional States," *European Journal of Philosophy*, vol. 1, no. 2, 1993, pp. 128–155, here at pp. 139, 144.

162. For example J. Rawls, "Kantian Constructivism in Moral Theory. The John Dewey Lectures," *Journal of Philosophy*, vol. 77, 1980. pp. 515–572, esp. p. 518, and M. Walzer, *Spheres of Justice* (New York: Basic Books, 1983).

163. C. Taylor, *Sources of the Self* (Cambridge: Cambridge University Press, 1989), p. 72.

164. Wellmer, *The Persistence of Modernity*, p. 167.

165. Dreyfus and Dreyfus, "What Is Morality?" p. 239.

166. In ibid., p. 238, Dreyfus and Dreyfus refer to this conflation as the "intellectualist prejudice."

6. DISCURSIVE *PHRONĒSIS* WITH A COGNITIVIST CORE

1. See R. Bambrough, "Universals and Family Resemblances," *Proceedings of the Aristotelian Society*, vol. 61, 1961, pp. 207–222; R. I. Aaron, *The Theory of Universals* (Oxford: Clarendon Press, 1952).

2. L. Wittgenstein, *The Blue and Brown Books* (Oxford: Basil Blackwell, 1958), pp. 17–18.

3. Ibid., p. 18.

4. L. Wittgenstein, *Philosophical Investigations* (New York: Macmillan, 1969), paras. 66, 67.

5. Bambrough, "Universals and Family Resemblances," p. 211.

6. Ibid., p. 207.

7. Wittgenstein, *Philosophical Investigations*, para. 66.

8. See J. Tully, "Wittgenstein and Political Philosophy: Understanding Practices of Critical Reflection," *Political Theory*, vol. 17, no. 2, 1989, pp. 172–204.

9. S. Benhabib, *Situating the Self* (Cambridge: Polity Press, 1992), p. 53.

10. J. Habermas, *Moral Consciousness and Communicative Action* (Cambridge: Polity Press, 1990), p. 88; and J. Habermas, *Justification and Application* (Cambridge: Polity Press, 1993), pp. 31, 54–60; see also A. Ferrara, "A Critique of Habermas's Consensus Theory of Truth," *Philosophy and Social Criticism*, vol. 13, no. 1, 1988, pp. 39–68, here at p. 45.

11. Wittgenstein, *The Blue and Brown Books*, p. 17.

12. It is therefore an example of a position that assumes a developmental view of moral psychology. See M. L. Gross, "The Collective Dimensions of Political Morality," *Political Studies*, vol. 42, no. 1, 1994, pp. 40–61, here at p. 42.

13. Wellmer draws a similar conclusion in A. Wellmer, "Hannah Arendt on Judgement: the Unwritten Doctrine of Reason," unpublished paper, 1985, pp. 1–28.

14. See Ferrara, "A Critique of Habermas's Consensus Theory of Truth," p. 61; J. Keane, "Introduction," in *Civil Society and the State*, ed. J. Keane (London: Verso, 1988), pp. 1–32, here at p. 24.

15. A. Ferrara, "On Phronesis," *Praxis International*, vol. 7, no. 3/4, 1987, pp. 246–267, here at p. 252.

16. A. Ferrara, "A Critique of Habermas's Consensus Theory of Truth," p. 59.

17. Ibid.

18. A. Wellmer, *Ethik und Dialog* (Frankfurt: Suhrkamp, 1986), p. 169.

19. A. Ferrara, "Critical Theory and Its Discontents: Wellmer's Critique of Habermas," *Praxis International*, vol. 9, no. 3, 1989, pp. 305–320, here at p. 310.

20. Wellmer, "Hannah Arendt on Judgement," p. 28.

21. H. L. Dreyfus and S. E. Dreyfus, "What Is Morality? A Phenomenological Account of the Development of Ethical Expertise," in *Universalism vs. Communitarianism*, ed. D. Rasmussen (Cambridge: Polity Press, 1990), pp. 237–264, here at p. 243.

22. Ibid., pp. 240–243.

23. Ibid., p. 264.

24. Somewhat typically, Habermas's fear of such a degeneration leads him to accuse Dreyfus and Dreyfus of "undermining Western society," a charge to which they eagerly accede. See B. Flyvbjerg, "Sustaining Non-Rationalized Practices: Body-Mind, Power and Situational Ethics. An Interview with Hubert and Stuart Dreyfus," *Praxis International*, vol. 11, no. 1, 1991, pp. 93–113, quoted on p. 93.

25. A. Wellmer, *Praktische Philosophie und Theorie der Gesellschaft* (Constance, Germany: Universitätsverlag Konstanz, 1981), pp. 46–47; A.

Wellmer, *Ethik und Dialog* (Frankfurt: Suhrkamp, 1986), pp. 132–133; J. Cohen, "Discourse Ethics and Civil Society," *Philosophy and Social Criticism*, vol. 14, no. 3/4, 1988, pp. 315–337; D. Ingram, "The Limits and Possibilities of Communicative Ethics for Democratic Theory," *Political Theory*, vol. 21, no. 2, 1993, pp. 294–321, here at p. 296.

26. J. Habermas, *Justification and Application*, p. 39.

27. Ibid.

28. A. Wellmer, *The Persistence of Modernity: Aesthetics, Ethics and Post-modernism* (Cambridge: Polity Press, 1991), p. 224.

29. Ibid., p. 233.

30. S. Benhabib, *Situating the Self* (Cambridge: Polity Press, 1992), p. 36.

31. J. F. Bohman, "Communication, Ideology, and Democratic Theory," *American Political Science Review*, vol. 84, no. 1, 1990, pp. 93–109.

32. G. Warnke, *Justice and Interpretation* (Cambridge: Polity Press, 1992); S. O'Neill, "Morality, Ethical Life and the Persistence of Universalism," *Theory, Culture and Society*, vol. 11, no. 2, 1994, pp. 129–149, here at p. 147.

33. Ibid., pp. 11–12.

34. Such as, A. Botwinick, *Wittgenstein, Skepticism and Political Participation* (Lanham, Md.: University Press of America, 1985); P. Bachrach and A. Botwinick, *Power and Empowerment: A Radical Theory of Participatory Democracy* (Philadelphia: Temple University Press, 1992).

35. J. Habermas, *The Theory of Communicative Action*, vol. 1 (Boston: Beacon Press, 1984), p. 287.

36. See T. McCarthy, "Practical Discourse: On the Relation of Morality to Politics," in *Ideals and Illusions* (Cambridge: Polity Press, 1991), pp. 181–199, here at p. 189.

37. J. Habermas, *Moral Consciousness and Communicative Action*, pp. 68–76.

38. J. Habermas, *Legitimation Crisis* (Cambridge: Polity Press, 1976), p. 111.

39. Habermas, *Moral Consciousness and Communicative Action*, p. 72.

40. Ibid.

41. Ibid., p. 73.

42. Ferrara, "Critical Theory and Its Discontents," p. 317.

43. K. Baynes discusses this in terms of "recursive validation" in *The Normative Grounds of Social Criticism: Kant, Rawls, and Habermas* (Albany: State University of New York Press, 1992), p. 1; see also J. Mansbridge, "Using Power, Fighting Power," *Constellations*, vol. 1, no. 1, 1994, pp. 53–73, here at pp. 59, 61.

44. J. Forester, "A Critical Empirical Framework for the Analysis of Public Policy," *New Political Science*, Summer 1982, pp. 33–61, here at p. 56.

45. A. Ferrara, "On Phronesis," *Praxis International*, vol. 7, no. 3/4, 1987, pp. 246–267, here at p. 262.

46. Benhabib, *Situating the Self*, p. 86 n. 18.

47. On this trade-off, see R.A. Dahl, *After the Revolution* (New Haven and London: Yale University Press, 1970); J. Le Grand, "Equity versus Efficiency: The Elusive Trade-Off," *Ethics*, vol. 100, no. 3, 1990, pp. 554–568; G. Sartori,

The Theory of Democracy Revisited, pp. 25–31, 69–72; A. M. Okun, *Equality and Efficiency: The Big Tradeoff* (Washington, D.C.: The Brookings Institution, 1975); J. J. Mansbridge, *Beyond Adversary Democracy* (New York: Basic Books, 1980), pp. 235, 246–247.

48. C. Offe, *Contradictions of the Welare State* (London: Hutchinson, 1984), clarifies the distinction between efficiency and effectiveness. "Marginal gains in efficiency occur," he points out at p. 135, "if the same amount of output can be produced at lower costs. Effectiveness, on the other hand, measures the ability of an organization to achieve its stated goals."

49. J. Habermas, *Between Facts and Norms: Contributions to a Discourse Theory of Law and Democracy* (Cambridge: Polity Press, 1996).

50. See, for Habermas's debate with Luhmann regarding these questions, R. C. Holub, *Jürgen Habermas: Critic in the Public Sphere* (London: Routledge, 1991), pp. 106–132; and Habermas, *Legitimation Crisis*, part 3.

51. J. Cohen, "Discourse Ethics and Civil Society," *Philosophy and Social Criticism*, vol. 14, no. 3/4, 1988, pp. 315–337, here at p. 315.

52. A. Heller, "The Discourse Ethics of Habermas: Critique and Appraisal," *Thesis Eleven*, no. 10/11, 1984, pp. 5–17; Cohen, "Discourse Ethics and Civil Society," p. 318.

53. Benhabib, *Situating the Self*, p. 38.

54. Heller, "The Discourse Ethics of Habermas," p. 9; see also Wellmer, *The Persistence of Modernity*, p. 194, and Ferrara, "Critical Theory and Its Discontents," p. 307.

55. D. Ingram, "The Limits and Possibilities of Communicative Ethics for Democratic Theory," *Political Theory*, vol. 21, no. 2, 1993, pp. 294–321, here at p. 299.

56. A. Wellmer, "Practical Philosophy and the Theory of Society: On the Problem of the Normative Foundations of a Critical Social Science," in *The Communicative Ethics Controversy*, ed. S. Benhabib and F. Dallmayr (Cambridge, Mass.: MIT Press, 1990), pp. 293–329, here at p. 316.

57. See the first five chapters of J.-J. Rousseau, *The Social Contract* (Harmondsworth, U.K.: Penguin, 1968).

58. Entropy entails an increase in disorder, or a tendency of a system, without the input of additional energy, to degenerate into a structureless state. By using the word metaphorically in relation to the concept of legitimacy, I do not assume that illegitimacy is a state of disorder. Rather, the word 'entropic' is used here to describe the tendency of legitimacy to degenerate, to decay into illegitimacy, if it is not in receipt of constant energy input. In this metaphor, energy represents the deliberative input of participants.

59. T. M. Scanlon, "Contractarianism and Utilitarianism," in *Utilitarianism and Beyond*, ed. A. Sen and B. Williams (Cambridge: Cambridge University Press, 1982), pp. 103–128.

60. S. K. White, "Reason and Authority in Habermas: A Critique of the Critics," *American Political Science Review*, vol. 74, 1980, pp. 1007–1017, here at 1017.

61. J. Dryzek, "Discursive Designs: Critical Theory and Political Institutions," *American Journal of Political Science*, vol. 31, 1987, pp. 656–679, esp. p. 665.

62. Heller, "The Discourse Ethics of Habermas," p. 9.

63. Ibid., p. 7.

64. Benhabib, *Situating the Self*, pp. 36–37.

65. Ibid., pp. 37–38.

66. Wellmer, *The Persistence of Modernity*, pp. 196, 199.

67. Ibid., p. 200.

68. See chap. 3 notes, pp. 98–104 above for references.

69. See, for example, Cohen, "Discourse Ethics and Civil Society," p. 325.

70. J. Habermas, *Between Facts and Norms* (Cambridge: Polity Press, 1996), p. 532f.

71. J. Habermas, "Citizenship and National Identity: Some Reflections on the Future of Europe," *Praxis International*, vol. 12, no. 1, 1992, pp. 1–19, here at p. 10.

72. T. H. Marshall, *Citizenship and Social Class, and Other Essays* (Cambridge: Cambridge University Press, 1950), pp. 1–85.

73. Quoted in Habermas, "Citizenship and National Identity," p. 10.

74. Wellmer, *The Persistence of Modernity*, p. 198.

75. Habermas, "Citizenship and National Identity," p. 10.

76. E. P. Thompson's *The Making of the English Working Class* (Harmondsworth, U.K.: Penguin, 1968) details the all consuming and almost endless struggle for constitutional rights, the genuine value of which remains contentious.

77. Benhabib, *Situating the Self*, pp. 32–33.

78. Cohen, "Discourse Ethics and Civil Society," pp. 324–325.

79. Benhabib, *Situating the Self*, p. 3.

80. Ibid., p. 38.

81. Ibid.

82. Ibid., p. 43.

83. O'Neill, "Morality, Ethical Life and the Persistence of Universalism," p. 139.

84. Benhabib, *Situating the Self*, p. 148ff.

85. Habermas, *Moral Consciousness and Communicative Action*, p. 200; see also p. 207, and *Justification and Application*, pp. 67–68.

86. O'Neill, "Morality, Ethical Life and the Persistence of Universalism," passim.

87. J. Keane, *Public Life and Late Capitalism: Towards a Socialist Theory of Democracy* (Cambridge: Cambridge University Press, 1984), p. 153.

88. J. Forester, "A Critical Empirical Framework for the Analysis of Public Policy," *New Political Science*, Summer, 1982, pp. 33–61, here at p. 41; see also pp. 42, 53; A. Parkin, "Rethinking the Subject: Habermas, Critical Theory, and the Challenges of Postmodernism" (Ph.D. dissertation, University of Bradford, 1993), chap. 6, p. 23.

89. R. Post, "The Quandary of Democratic Dialogue," *Ethics*, vol. 103, no. 4, 1993, pp. 654–678.

90. A. Heller, "On Formal Democracy," in *Civil Society and the State: New European Perspectives*, ed. J. Keane (London: Verso, 1988), pp. 129–145.

91. A. Gewirth, *Reason and Morality* (Chicago: Chicago University Press, 1978).

92. J. S. Fishkin, *The Dialogue of Justice: Toward a Self-Reflective Society* (New Haven: Yale University Press, 1992), p. 124ff.

93. L. Doyal and I. Gough, *A Theory of Human Need* (London: Macmillan, 1991).

94. Ferrara, "A Critique of Habermas's Consensus Theory of Truth," p. 62.

95. Habermas, *Faktizität und Geltung*, p. 157, translated by Outhwaite, in *Habermas* (Cambridge: Polity Press, 1994).

96. J. Cohen, "Reflections on Rousseau: Autonomy and Democracy," *Philosophy and Public Affairs*, vol. 15, no. 3, 1986, pp. 275–297, here at p. 294, emphasis mine.

97. S. O'Neill, *Procedure and Substance in Accounts of Justice* (Ph.D. dissertation, University of Glasgow, 1994), chap. 3, p. 286.

98. T. McCarthy shows just how close they have become in, "Kantian Contructivism and Reconstructivism: Rawls and Habermas in Dialogue," *Ethics*, vol. 105, October 1994, pp. 44–63.

99. See, for a review of such positions, D. M. Estlund, "Who's Afraid of Deliberative Democracy? On the Strategic/Deliberative Dichotomy in Recent Constitutional Jurisprudence," *Texas Law Review*, vol. 71, 1993, pp. 1437–1477; R. Blaug, "All Talk? The New Deliberative Theories of Democracy," in *The State of the Academy: New Reflections on Political Studies*, ed. R. Lekhi (London: Network Press, 1995).

7. CHANGING THE OBJECT DOMAIN OF APPLICATION

1. K. Eder, *The New Politics of Class: Social Movements and Cultural Dynamics in Advanced Societies* (London: Sage, 1993), p. 53.

2. See P. Hirst, *Associative Democracy: New Forms of Economic and Social Governance* (Cambridge: Polity Press, 1994); J. Cohen and J. Rogers, "Secondary Associations and Democratic Governance," *Politics and Society*, vol. 20, no. 4, 1992, pp. 393–472.

3. A. Arato and J. Cohen, *Civil Society and Political Theory* (Cambridge, Mass.: MIT Press, 1992); J. Habermas, "Further Reflections on the Public Sphere," in *Habermas and the Public Sphere*, ed. C. Calhoun (Cambridge, Mass.: MIT Press, 1992), pp. 421–461.

4. J. Burnheim, *Is Democracy Possible?* Cambridge: Polity Press, 1985.

5. J. S. Fishkin, *Democracy and Deliberation: New Directions for Democratic Reform* (New Haven: Yale University Press, 1991), p. 81ff.

6. R. Eyerman, "Social Movements and Social Theory," *Sociology*, vol. 18, no. 1, 1984, pp. 71–82; J. Cohen, "Strategy or Identity: New Theoretical Paradigms and Contemporary Social Movements," *Social Research*, vol. 52, 1985, pp. 663–716; Eder, *The New Politics of Class*; L. J. Ray, *Rethinking Critical Theory: Emancipation in the Age of Global Social Movements* (London: Sage, 1993).

7. J. S. Dryzek, *Discursive Democracy: Politics, Policy, and Political Science* (Cambridge: Cambridge University Press, 1990).

8. N. Fraser, "Rethinking the Public Sphere: A Contribution to the Critique of Actually Existing Democracy," in *Habermas and the Public Sphere*, ed. C. Calhoun (Cambridge, Mass.: MIT Press, 1992), pp. 109–142.

9. But see J. J. Mansbridge, "Time, Emotion, and Inequality: Three Problems of Participatory Groups," *Journal of Applied Behavioral Science*, vol. 9, no. 2/3, 1973, pp. 351–368; J. J. Mansbridge, *Beyond Adversary Democracy* (New York: Basic Books, 1980); S. Moscovici and W. Doise, *Conflict and Consensus: A General Theory of Collective Decisions* (London: Sage, 1994); V. A. Malhotra, "Habermas' Sociological Theory as a Basis for Clinical Practice with Small Groups," *Clinical Sociology Review*, vol. 5, 1987, pp. 181–192.

10. See, for example, D. Gauthier, "Constituting Democracy," in *The Idea of Democracy*, ed. D. Copp et al. (Cambridge: Cambridge University Press, 1993), pp. 314–315.

11. See A. Phillips, *Engendering Democracy* (Cambridge: Polity Press, 1991), pp. 92–119.

12. A. Hamilton, J. Madison, and J. Jay, *The Federalist Papers* (New York: Mentor Books, 1961); see also Barber's description of "thin democracy" in *Strong Democracy*, pp. 3–26; and D. Held, *Models of Democracy* (Cambridge: Polity Press, 1987), pp. 61–66.

13. Moscovici and Doise review the work of social psychologists on such questions in *Conflict and Consensus*; see also R. de Board, *The Psychoanalysis of Organisations* (London: Tavistock, 1978).

14. See the remarks on this excessively elevated position in A. Phillips, "Dealing with Difference: A Politics of Ideas or a Politics of Presence?" *Constellations*, vol. 1, no. 1, 1994, pp. 74–91, here at p. 77.

15. A. MacIntyre, "A Partial Response to My Critics," in *After MacIntyre*, ed. J. Horton and S. Mendus (Cambridge: Polity Press, 1994), pp. 283–304, here at p. 302.

16. C. Mouffe, "Radical Democracy: Modern or Postmodern," in *Universal Abandon? The Politics of Postmodernism*, ed. A. Ross (Edinburgh: University of Edinburgh Press, 1988), pp. 31–45, here at p. 41.

17. S. Wolin, "Fugitive Democracy," *Constellations*, vol. 1, no. 1, 1994, pp. 11–25, here at p. 18.

18. We inspected this in terms of the "where" of democracy in chapter 3 above.

19. T. Nagel, "What Makes a Political Theory Utopian?" *Social Research*, vol. 56, no. 4, 1989, pp. 903–920.

20. Wolin, "Fugitive Democracy," p. 18.

21. See also H. Lefebvre, *The Production of Space* (Oxford: Blackwell, 1991).

22. Wolin, "Fugitive Democracy," p. 14.

23. A. Pizzorno, "An Introduction to the Theory of Political Participation," *Social Science Information*, vol. 9, no. 5, 1970, pp. 29–61, here at p. 57; Moscovici and Doise make a similar claim in *Conflict and Consensus*, p. 18, and lament the lack of empirical studies at pp. 36 and 125.

24. Phillips states that feminism has always been attentive to groups, and that the women's movement was effectively a "testing ground" for a participa-

tory politics, in *Engendering Democracy*, pp. 2, 126, 149; see also K. E. Ferguson, *The Feminist Case against Bureaucracy* (Philadelphia: Temple University Press, 1983); C. Sirianni, "Learning Pluralism: Democracy and Diversity in Feminist Organisations," in *Nomos XXXV—Democratic Community* (New York: New York University Press, 1993), pp. 283–312. On "pre-figurative forms," see Phillips, *Engendering Democracy*, p. 113; D. Ingram, "The Limits and Possibilities of Communicative Ethics for Democratic Theory," *Political Theory*, vol. 21, no. 2, 1993, pp. 294–321, here at p. 315.

25. Theorists who do look at such phenomena each have their own favorites. See for Isaac's and Arendt's, J. C. Isaac, "Oases in the Desert: Hannah Arendt on Democratic Politics," *American Political Science Review*, vol. 88, no. 1, 1994, pp. 156–168; L. Goodwyn, "Organizing Democracy: The Limits of Theory and Practice," *Democracy*, vol. 1, no. 1, 1981, pp. 41–60; H. F. Pitkin and S. M. Shumer, "On Participation," *Democracy*, vol. 2, no. 4, 1982, pp. 43–54, here at p. 48.

26. W. H. J. Sewell, *Work and Revolution in France: The Language of Labor from the Old Regime to 1848* (Cambridge: Cambridge University Press, 1980), pp. 92–113.

27. E. P. Thompson, *The Making of the English Working Class* (Harmondsworth, U.K.: Penguin, 1968).

28. D. Burns, *Poll Tax Rebellion* (Stirling, U.K.: AK Press, 1992).

29. Moscovici and Doise, *Conflict and Consensus*, p. 51.

30. Ibid., pp. 48, 60.

31. Ibid., p. 49.

32. Habermas, *Moral Consciousness and Communicative Action*, p. 67.

33. Moscovici and Doise, *Conflict and Consensus*, pp. 49, 54; Dryzek, *Discursive Democracy*, pp. 66, 71; Barber, *Strong Democracy*, p. 135.

34. Phillips, *Engendering Democracy*, p. 121.

35. Ibid., p. 142.

36. Ibid., p. 129. That learning is a side-effect of participation is well documented. Indeed, this effect has often been appealed to in order to legitimize increased participation. See, for references, J. Knight and J. Johnson, "Aggregation and Deliberation: On the Possibility of Democratic Legitimacy," *Political Theory*, vol. 22, no. 2, 1994, pp. 227–296, here at p. 295 n. 62. For a recent example of work on the "therapeutic" effects of user participation in mental health service provision, see V. Lindow, "A Chance for a Change," *Nursing Times*, vol. 89, no. 12, 1993, pp. 33–34.

37. J.-J. Rousseau, *The Social Contract* (Harmondsworth, U.K.: Penguin, 1968), p. 140.

38. Mansbridge, *Beyond Adversary Democracy*, p. 9.

39. A. O. Hirschman, "Social Conflicts as Pillars of Democratic Market Society," *Political Theory*, vol. 22, no. 2, 1994, pp. 203–218, here at pp. 206–211.

40. C. R. Sunstein, "Preferences and Politics," *Philosophy and Public Affairs*, vol. 20, no. 1, 1991, pp. 3–34.

41. Phillips describes a "curve of experience" in which women learned gradually to make their decision-making process as fair as possible. See Phillips, *Engendering Democracy*, p. 162.

42. There is a common misconception of Habermas's position on this matter. While he claims that all discourses "anticipate" a rational ideal of fairness, he nowhere suggests, as some have assumed, that *actual* discourses are rational, cold, and dispassionate. For an example of this assumption, see D. Coole, "Habermas and the Question of Alterity," in *Habermas and the Unfinished Project of Modernity: Critical Essays on the Philosophical Discourse of Modernity*, ed. M. Passerin d'Entrèves and S. Benhabib (Cambridge: Polity Press, 1996).

43. J. Ober, *Mass and Elite in Democratic Athens* (Princeton: Princeton University Press, 1989).

44. Ober cites Isocrates's observation that [male] Athenians tended to "sit around in the shops complaining about the existing political order." Ibid., p. 148.

45. Phillips, *Engendering Democracy*, p. 123.

46. "Sapiential power" remains a differential between individuals. See, for example, the platoon "leader" in Orwell's anarchist patrol, *Homage to Catalonia* (Harmondsworth, U.K.: Penguin, 1938). See also Ober's discussion of the power of the rhetors in Athens, in *Mass and Elite*, pp. 314–320.

47. On ostracism in Athens, see Ober, *Mass and Elite*, pp. 74–74. When the ejection of a particular member really becomes unavoidable, it constitutes a highly dangerous moment in the life cycle of a group.

48. Pizzorno, "An Introduction to the Theory of Political Participation," p. 44ff.

49. Phillips, *Engendering Democracy*, p. 123.

50. Such adversarial posturing, or "othering," can become so marked as to begin to threaten the fairness of the group itself. Whether collective and individual identities in some way necessitate such posturing is a question pursued in contemporary work in psychoanalysis and in explanations of phenomena such as racism. Certainly, in-group/out-group distinctions, or, as Carl Schmitt describes it, "us and them" mentalities, can constitute important components of group identities as well as profoundly exclusionary practices.

51. Phillips, *Engendering Democracy*, p. 118.

52. This is the central empirical issue explored in Moscovici and Doise, *Conflict and Consensus*, passim.

53. J.-P. Sartre, *The Critique of Dialectical Reason* (London: New Left Books, 1976), book ll, chap. 1; Pizzorno, "An Introduction to the Theory of Political Participation," p. 58; Mansbridge, *Beyond Adversary Democracy*, p. 22; Phillips, *Engendering Democracy*, p. 120; Moscovici and Doise, *Conflict and Consensus*, p. 61; Isaac, "Oases in the Desert," pp. 163, 165; J. Habermas, *The Structural Transformation of the Public Sphere* (Cambridge: Polity Press, 1989).

54. A. Melucci, "Social Movements and the Democratization of Everyday Life," in *Civil Society and the State*, ed. J. Keane (London: Verso, 1988), pp. 245–260, here at p. 250, cites "rendering power visible" as one form of symbolic challenge effected by such collective action.

55. Goodwyn, "Organizing Democracy," p. 47; Thompson's, *The Making of the English Working Class* is replete with such examples.

56. See Phillips, *Engendering Democracy*, p. 134, for the problems generated for the women's movement by the "star system."

57. A process described by L. J. Ray in *Rethinking Critical Theory*, p. 74, as one of "repressive modernization." He also draws attention to attempts by the state to "displace public issues into socially isolated sub-cultures," pp. 66–68.

58. Moscovici and Doise, *Conflict and Consensus*, p. 62.

59. See M. Walzer, "A Day in the Life of a Socialist Citizen," in M. Walzer, *Obligations: Essays on Disobedience, War and Citizenship* (Cambridge, Mass.: Harvard University Press, 1970).

60. H. Kohut, *The Analysis of the Self* (New York: International Universities Press, 1971), pp. 128–134; Moscovici and Doise, *Conflict and Consensus*, pp. 42, 61. Whether participants are more likely to be so injured in modernity is a question pursued by R. Sennett in *The Fall of Public Man* (London: Faber and Faber, 1977). For a discussion of related issues, see J. J. Mansbridge, "Time, Emotion, and Inequality," pp. 358–361.

61. See, for example, recent work on participation in housing cooperatives such as J. Birchall, *Building Communities the Co-operative Way* (London: Routledge and Kegan Paul, 1988); Y. Levin and H. Litwin (eds.), *Community and Co-operatives in Participatory Democracy* (London: Gower, 1986).

62. Knight and Johnson, "Aggregation and Deliberation," p. 286.

63. Phillips, *Engendering Democracy*, pp. 130–133.

64. Ibid., p. 145.

65. See Moscovici and Doise, *Conflict and Consensus*, p. 144.

66. Zuckerman highlights this tendency of democratic fora in "The Social Context of Democracy in Massachusetts," *The William and Mary Quarterly*, third series, vol. 25, no. 4, 1968, pp. 523–544.

67. This, for Wolin, is what gives it its "fugitive" character. See also, Lefebvre, *The Production of Space*, p. 416.

68. This is one way of describing what J. G. A. Pocock refers to as the Machiavellian moment in the life of a republic. *The Machiavellian Moment* (Princeton and London: Princeton University Press, 1975).

8. TOWARD A DEMOCRATIC POLITICS

1. Adapted from R. Agger, D. Goldrich, and B. Swanson, *The Rulers and the Ruled* (New York: Wiley, 1958), pp. 40–51, and from Gestalt accounts of the cycle of experience. See, for example, F. Perls, *Gestalt Therapy Verbatim* (Chicago: Real People Press, 1969).

2. The distinction between figure and ground also comes from Gestalt theory, where it is used to explicate the process by which something emerges from the background to become an object of awareness.

3. See J. Mansbridge, "Using Power, Fighting Power," *Constellations*, vol. 1, no. 1, 1994, pp. 53–73. It is precisely when confronted with this fact that postmodern theories of radical democracy break down. Unable, or unwilling, to move beyond the analysis of illegitimacy, they cannot help with the problem of how to maximize the "celebration of difference" in situations where some trade-off between participation and efficiency is inevitable. See my "New Theories of

Discursive Democracy: A User's Guide," *Philosophy and Social Criticism*, vol. 22, no. 1, 1995, pp. 49–80, here at p. 55.

4. J. Habermas, *Moral Consciousness and Communicative Action* (Cambridge: Polity Press, 1990), p. 89.

5. H. L. Dreyfus and S. E. Dreyfus, "What Is Morality? A Phenomenological Account of the Development of Ethical Expertise," in *Universalism vs. Communitarianism*, ed. D. Rasmussen (Cambridge: Polity Press, 1990), pp. 237–264, here at p. 259.

6. L. Goodwyn, "Organizing Democracy: The Limits of Theory and Practice," *Democracy*, vol. 1, no. 1, 1981, pp. 41–60, here at p. 48.

7. See, for example, C. Pateman, *Participation and Democratic Theory* (Cambridge: Cambridge University Press, 1970).

8. See B. Flyvbjerg, "Sustaining Non-Rationalized Practices: Body-Mind, Power and Situational Ethics. An Interview with Hubert and Stuart Dreyfus," *Praxis International*, vol. 11, no. 1, 1991, pp. 93–113, here at pp. 93–94; Dreyfus and Dreyfus, "What Is Morality?" pp. 240–243.

9. Dreyfus and Dreyfus, "What Is Morality?" p. 243.

10. Ibid.

11. K. Baynes criticizes Charles Taylor for his excessive reliance on the moral capacities of individuals in "Liberal Neutrality, Pluralism, and Deliberative Politics," *Praxis International*, vol. 12, no. 1, 1992, pp. 50–69, here at p. 59.

12. See, for example, J. Elster, *Ulysses and the Sirens* (Cambridge: Cambridge University Press, 1979).

13. R. Goodin, "Laundering Preferences," in *Foundations of Rational Choice Theory*, ed. J. Elster (New York: Cambridge University Press, 1986), pp. 75–101.

14. For specific examples of such forms of self-binding, see C. R. Sunstein, "Preferences and Politics," *Philosophy and Public Affairs*, vol. 20, no. 1, 1991, pp. 3–34, and I. McLean, "Forms of Representation and Systems of Voting," in *Political Theory Today*, ed. D. Held (Cambridge: Polity Press, 1991), pp. 172–196.

15. S. Holmes, "Gag Rules, or the Politics of Omission," in *Constitutionalism and Democracy*, ed. J. Elster and R. Slagstad (New York: Cambridge University Press, 1988), pp. 195–240.

16. N. Machiavelli, "The Discourses," in *The Portable Machiavelli*, ed. P. Bondanella and M. Musa (Harmondsworth, U.K.: Penguin, 1979), pp. 167–418.

17. As an example, in the UK, local MIND groups, upon affiliation with the National Association for Mental Health, receive a draft "off the shelf" constitution to be amended and adopted by the local executive committee. The expectation is that after its adoption, the procedural arrangements it stipulates will receive little attention.

18. C. Sunstein, *Democracy and the Problem of Free Speech* (New York: Free Press, 1993).

19. G. Parry, *Political Elites* (London: George Allen and Unwin, 1969), p. 155.

20. K. Eder, *The New Politics of Class: Social Movements and Cultural Dynamics in Advanced Societies* (London: Sage, 1993), pp. 49–60.

21. See Fraser's critique of Habermas's characterization of the family in N. Fraser, "What's Critical about Critical Theory? The Case of Habermas and Gender," *New German Critique*, no. 35, 1985, pp. 97–131.

22. Habermas, *The Philosophical Discourse of Modernity*, p. 364. It is precisely this textural difference that grounds many objections to direct democracy and generates the charge of utopianism. See, for example, G. Sartori, *The Theory of Democracy Revisited*, vol. 1 (Chatham, N.J.: Chatham House, 1987), p. 15.

23. See R. Dahl and E. Tufte, *Size and Democracy* (Stanford: Stanford University Press, 1974).

24. R. Dahl, "Democracy and the Chinese Boxes," in *Frontiers of Democratic Theory*, ed. H. S. Kariel (New York: Harper & Row, 1970), pp. 372–373.

25. See, for example, A. Hamlin and P. Pettit, *The Good Polity: Normative Analysis of the State* (Oxford: Basil Blackwell, 1989). Habermas himself has concentrated increasingly on the normative content of the state, particularly in J. Habermas, *Between Facts and Norms: Contributions to a Discourse Theory of Law and Democracy* (Cambridge: Polity Press, 1996).

26. S. Wolin, "Fugitive Democracy," *Constellations*, vol. 1, no. 1, 1994, pp. 11–25; R. P. Wolff, *In Defence of Anarchism* (New York: Harper & Row, 1970), p. 69ff.; A. MacIntyre, "A Partial Response to My Critics," in *After MacIntyre: Critical Perspectives on the Work of Alasdair MacIntyre*, ed. J. Horton and S. Mendus (Cambridge: Polity Press, 1994), pp. 283–304, here at p. 302ff.

27. Wolin, "Fugitive Democracy," p. 14.

28. Goodwyn, "Organizing Democracy," p. 50.

29. The claim that capitalism is effective as a mode of production appears obvious to those who benefit from it, though such a view requires that many of its costs, now displaced onto other groups and countries, remain invisible.

30. C. Taylor, *Human Agency and Language* (Cambridge: Cambridge University Press, 1985); C. Taylor, *Sources of the Self: The Making of the Modern Identity* (Cambridge: Cambridge University Press, 1989), p. 4.

31. S. Freud, *An Outline of Psychoanalysis* (New York: W.W. Norton 1949), pp. 23–24.

32. J. J. Mansbridge, "Time, Emotion, and Inequality: Three Problems of Participatory Groups," *Journal of Applied Behavioral Science*, vol. 9, no. 2/3, 1973, pp. 351–368, here at p. 358.

33. It is for this reason that R. Fisher and W. Ury see one of the requirements for mediation as the separation of emotional questions from substantive ones, see *Getting to Yes* (Boston: Houghton Mifflin, 1981); Ray also discusses the need to "separate personal concerns and beliefs from the formal procedures through which we reach consensus." L. J. Ray, *Rethinking Critical Theory* (London: Sage, 1993), p. 80.

34. H. Kohut, *The Analysis of the Self* (New York: International Universities Press, 1971), pp. 128–134.

35. Mansbridge, "Time, Emotion, and Inequality," op, cit. p. 359.

36. A. Abdennur, *The Conflict Resolution Syndrome: Volunteerism, Violence and Beyond* (Ottawa: University of Ottawa Press, 1987), p. 53, identifies three kinds of response to conflict: confrontation, reconciliation, and avoidance.

37. Mansbridge, "Time, Emotion, and Inequality," p. 360.

38. See, for example, M. S. Peck, *The Different Drum* (London: Arrow Books, 1987), pp. 106–108.

39. U. Merry and G. Brown, *The Neurotic Behavior of Organizations* (New York: Gardner Press, 1987).

40. This is a central issue in J. G. A. Pocock, *The Machiavellian Moment* (Princeton and London: Princeton University Press, 1975).

41. S. Benhabib, "Deliberative Rationality and Models of Democratic Legitimacy," *Constellations*, vol. 1, no. 1, 1994, pp. 26–52, here at p. 42.

42. J. Habermas, *Communication and the Evolution of Society* (Boston: Beacon Press, 1979), p. 186.

BIBLIOGRAPHY

Aaron, R. I. (1952). *The Theory of Universals*, Oxford: Clarendon Press.

Abdennur, A. (1987). *The Conflict Resolution Syndrome: Volunteerism, Violence and Beyond*. Ottawa: University of Ottawa Press.

Albert, H. (1985). *Treatise on Critical Reason*. Princeton: Princeton University Press.

Alexy, R. (1990). "A Theory of Practical Discourse." In *The Communicative Ethics Controversy*, ed. S. Benhabib and F. Dallmayr. Cambridge, Mass.: MIT Press, pp. 151–192.

Alford, C.F. (1985). *Science and the Revenge of Nature: Marcuse and Habermas*. Gainesville: University of Florida Press.

———. (1987). "Habermas, Post-Freudian Psychoanalysis and the End of the Individual." *Theory, Culture and Society*, vol. 4, pp. 3–29.

Anderson, C. and L. Rouse (1988). "Intervention in Cases of Women Battering: An Application of Symbolic Interactionism and Critical Theory." *Clinical Sociology Review*, vol. 6, pp. 134–147.

Apel, K. O. (1972). "The A Priori of Communication and the Foundation of the Humanities," *Man and World*, vol. 5, pp. 3–37.

———. (1980). *Towards a Transformation of Philosophy*. London: Routledge.

———. (1987). "The Problem of Philosophical Foundations in Light of a Transcendental Pragmatics of Language." In *After Philosophy*, ed. K. Baynes, J. Bohman, and T. McCarthy. Cambridge, Mass.: MIT Press, pp. 250–290.

Arato, A. and J. Cohen (1992). *Civil Society and Political Theory*, Cambridge, Mass.: MIT Press.

Arendt, H. (1958). *The Human Condition*. Chicago: University of Chicago Press.

———. (1961). *Between Past and Future*. Harmondsworth, U.K.: Penguin.

———. (1963). *On Revolution*. Harmondsworth, U.K.: Penguin.

———. (1972). *Crises of the Republic*. New York: Harcourt Brace Jovanovich.

———. (1982). "Lectures on Kant's Political Philosophy." In *Lectures on Kant's Political Philosophy*. ed. R. Beiner. Brighton, U.K.: Harvester Press, pp. 7–78.

Aristotle. (1962). *Nicomachean Ethics*. New York: Bobbs-Merrill.

Austin, J. L. (1962). *How to Do Things with Words*. Cambridge, Mass.: Harvard University Press.

Bachrach, P. (1967). *The Theory of Democratic Elitism: A Critique*. Boston: Little, Brown.

Bachrach, P. and A. Botwinick (1992). *Power and Empowerment: A Radical Theory of Participatory Democracy*. Philadelphia: Temple University Press.

Baier, K. (1965). *The Moral Point of View*. New York: Random House.

Bambrough, R. (1961). "Universals and Family Resemblances." *Proceedings of the Aristotelian Society*, vol. 61, pp. 207–222.

Bannister, D. and F. Fransella (1971). *Inquiring Man: The Theory of Personal Constructs*. Harmondsworth, U.K.: Penguin.

Barber, B. R. (1984). *Strong Democracy: Participatory Politics for a New Age*. Berkeley: University of California Press.

Baynes, K. (1988). "The Liberal/Communitarian Controversy and Communicative Ethics." *Philosophy and Social Criticism*, vol. 14, pp. 293–313.

———. (1989). "Rational Reconstruction and Social Criticism: Habermas's Model of Interpretive Social Science." *The Philosophical Forum*, vol. 21, no. 1/2, pp. 122–145.

———. (1992a). "Liberal Neutrality, Pluralism, and Deliberative Politics." *Praxis International*, vol. 12, pp. 50–69.

———. (1992b). *The Normative Grounds of Social Criticism: Kant, Rawls, and Habermas*. Albany: State University of New York Press.

Beauchamp, T. L. (1984). "On Eliminating the Distinction between Applied Ethics and Ethical Theory." *The Monist*, vol. 67, pp. 514–531.

Beetham, D. (1993). "Liberal Democracy and the Limits of Democratization." In *Prospects for Democracy: North, South, East, West*, ed. D. Held. Cambridge: Polity Press.

Beiner, R. (1983). *Political Judgment*. London: Methuen.

———. "On the Disunity of Theory and Practice." *Praxis International*, vol. 7, pp. 25–34.

———. (1989). "Do We Need a Philosophical Ethics? Theory, Prudence, and the Primacy of Ethos." *The Philosophical Forum*, vol. 20, no. 3, pp. 230–243.

Benhabib, S. (1981). "Modernity and the Aporias of Critical Theory." *Telos*, no. 49, pp. 39–59.

———. (1982). "The Methodological Illusions of Modern Political Theory: The Case of Rawls and Habermas." *Neue Hefte fur Philosophie*, vol. 21, pp. 47–74.

———. (1985). "The Utopian Dimension in Communicative Ethics." *New German Critique*, no. 35, pp. 83–96.

———. (1986). *Critique, Norm, and Utopia*. New York: Columbia University Press.

———. (1989). "Liberal Dialogue versus a Critical Theory of Discursive Legitimation." In *Liberalism and the Moral Life*, ed. N. L. Rosenblum. Cambridge, Mass.: Harvard University Press, pp. 143–156.

———. (1992). *Situating the Self*. Cambridge: Polity Press.

———. (1994a). "Democracy and Difference: Reflections on the Metapolitics of Lyotard and Derrida." *The Journal of Political Philosophy*, vol. 2, no. 1, pp. 1–23.

———. (1994b). "Deliberative Rationality and Models of Democratic Legitimacy." *Constellations*, vol. 1, no. 1, pp. 26–52.

Benhabib, S. and F. Dallmayr, eds. (1990). *The Communicative Ethics Controversy*. Cambridge, Mass.: MIT Press.

Bernheimer, C. and C. Kahane, eds. (1985). *In Dora's Case: Freud, Hysteria, Feminism*. London: Virago.

Bernstein, R. J. (1979). *The Restructuring of Social and Political Theory*. London: Methuen.

———. (1983). *Beyond Objectivism and Relativism: Science, Hermeneutics, and Praxis*. Philadelphia: University of Pennsylvania Press.

———, ed. (1985). *Habermas and Modernity*. Cambridge: Polity Press.

Bernstien, R. (1991). *The New Constellation*. Cambridge: Polity Press.

Birchall, J. (1988). *Building Communities the Co-operative Way*. London: Routledge and Kegan Paul.

Blaug, R. (1995). "The Distortion of the Face to Face: Communicative Reason and Social Work Practice." *British Journal of Social Work*, vol. 25, no. 4, pp. 423–439.

———. (1996). "New Theories of Discursive Democracy: A User's Guide." *Philosophy and Social Criticism*, vol. 22, no. 1.

de Board, R. (1978). *The Psychoanalysis of Organisations*. London: Tavistock.

Bohman, J. F. (1989a). "Participating in Enlightenment: Habermas's Cognitivist Interpretation of Democracy." In *Knowledge and Politics: Case Studies in the Relationship between Epistemology and Political Philosophy*, ed. M. Dascal and O. Gruengard. Boulder, Colo.: Westview Press, pp. 264–289.

———. (1989b). "'System' and 'Lifeworld': Habermas and the Problem of Holism." *Philosophy and Social Criticism*, vol. 15, pp. 381–401.

———. (1990). "Communication, Ideology, and Democratic Theory." *American Political Science Review*, vol. 84, pp. 93–109.

Botwinick, A. (1985). *Wittgenstein, Skepticism and Political Participation*. Washington, D.C.: University Press of America.

Bowles, S., H. Gintis, and B. Gustafsson, eds. (1993). *Markets and Democracy: Participation, Accountability and Efficiency*. Cambridge: Cambridge University Press.

Brand, A. (1990). *The Force of Reason*. London: Allen & Unwin.

Breiner, P. (1989). "Democratic Autonomy, Political Ethics, and Moral Luck." *Political Theory*, vol. 17, pp. 550–574.

Brown, S. R. (1980). *Political Subjectivity: Applications of Q Methodology in Political Science*. New Haven: Yale University Press.

Burke, E. (1968). "Strategies of Citizen Participation." *Journal of the American Institute of Planners*, vol. 34, no. 5, pp. 287–293.

Burnheim, J. (1985). *Is Democracy Possible?* Cambridge: Polity Press.

Burns, D. (1992). *Poll Tax Rebellion*. Stirling, U.K.: AK Press.

Calhoun, C., ed. (1992). *Habermas and the Public Sphere*. Cambridge, Mass.: MIT Press.

Carroll A. J. (1993). *Ethics, Critical Theory and the Inner City*. Ph.D. dissertation, Manchester University.

Chambers, S. (1996). *Reasonable Democracy*. Ithaca: Cornell University Press.

Christiano, T. (1990). "Freedom, Consensus, and Equality in Collective Decision Making." *Ethics*, vol. 101, pp. 151–181.

Cohen, J. (1986a). "An Epistemic Conception of Democracy." *Ethics*, vol. 97, pp. 26–38.

———. (1986b). "Reflections on Rousseau: Autonomy and Democracy." *Philosophy and Public Affairs*, vol. 15, no. 3, pp. 275–297.

——. (1991). "Deliberation and Democratic Legitimacy." In *The Good Polity: Normative Analysis of the State*, ed. A. Hamlin and P. Pettit. Oxford: Basil Blackwell, pp. 17–34.

Cohen, J. and J. Rogers (1992). "Secondary Associations and Democratic Governance." *Politics and Society*, vol. 20, pp. 393–472.

Cohen, Jean. (1979). "Why More Political Theory?" *Telos*, no. 40, pp. 70–94.

——. (1985). "Strategy or Identity: New Theoretical Paradigms and Contemporary Social Movements." *Social Research*, vol. 52, pp. 663–716.

——. (1988). "Discourse Ethics and Civil Society." *Philosophy and Social Criticism*, vol. 14, no. 3/4, pp. 315–337.

Cooke, M. (1993). "Habermas and Consensus." *European Journal of Philosophy*, vol. 1, no. 3, pp. 1–20.

Coole, D. (1996a). "Habermas and the Question of Alterity." In *Habermas and the Unfinished Project of Modernity: Critical Essays on the Philosophical Discourse of Modernity*, ed. M. Passerin d'Entrèves and S. Benhabib. Cambridge: Polity Press.

——. (1996). "Wild Differences and Tamed Others: Postmodernism and Liberal Democracy." *Parallax*, no. 2, February, pp. 23–36.

Dahl, R.A. (1956). *A Preface to Democratic Theory*. Chicago: University of Chicago Press.

——. (1970a). *After the Revolution*. New Haven and London: Yale University Press.

——. (1970b). "Democracy and the Chinese Boxes." In *Frontiers of Democratic Theory*, ed. H. S. Kariel. New York: Harper & Row, pp. 372–373.

——. (1989). *Democracy and Its Critics*. New Haven and London: Yale University Press.

Dahl, R. and E. Tufte (1974). *Size and Democracy*. Stanford: Stanford University Press.

Dews, P., ed. (1986). *Habermas, Autonomy and Solidarity: Interviews with Jurgen Habermas*. London: Verso.

Doyal, L. and I. Gough (1991). *A Theory of Human Need*. London: Macmillan.

Dreyfus, H. L. and S. E. Dreyfus (1990). "What Is Morality? A Phenomenological Account of the Development of Ethical Expertise." In *Universalism vs. Communitarianism*, ed. D. Rasmussen. Cambridge: Polity Press, pp. 237–264.

Dryzek, J. S. (1987). "Discursive Designs: Critical Theory and Political Institutions." *American Journal of Political Science*, vol. 31, pp. 656–679.

——. (1990). *Discursive Democracy: Politics, Policy, and Political Science*. Cambridge: Cambridge University Press.

Dryzek, J. S. and J. Berejikian (1993). "Reconstructive Democratic Theory." *American Political Science Review*, vol. 87, no. 1, pp. 48–60.

Duncan, G. and S. Lukes (1963). "The New Democracy." *Political Studies*, vol. 11, pp. 156–177.

Dunn, J. (1979). *Western Political Theory in the Face of the Future*. Cambridge: Cambridge University Press.

Dworkin, R. (1977). *Taking Rights Seriously*. Cambridge, Mass.: Harvard University Press.

Ealy, S. D. (1981). *Communication, Speech, and Politics: Habermas and Political Analysis*. Washington, D.C.: University Press of America.

Eckersley, R. (1990). "Habermas and Green Political Thought: Two Roads Diverging." *Theory and Society*, vol. 19, pp. 739–776.

Eder, K. (1990). "The Rise of Counter-culture Movements against Modernity: Nature as a New Field of Class Struggle." *Theory, Culture and Society*, vol. 7, pp. 21–47.

———. (1992). "Politics and Culture: On the Sociocultural Analysis of Political Participation." In *Cultural-Political Interventions in the Unfinished Project of Enlightenment*, ed. A. Honneth, T. McCarthy, C. Offe, and A. Wellmer. Cambridge, Mass.: MIT Press, pp. 95–120.

———. (1993). *The New Politics of Class: Social Movements and Cultural Dynamics in Advanced Societies*. London: Sage.

Elster, J. (1979). *Ulysses and the Sirens*. Cambridge: Cambridge University Press.

———. (1983). *Sour Grapes*. Cambridge: Cambridge University Press.

———. (1986). "The Market and the Forum: Three Varieties of Political Theory." In *Foundations of Social Choice Theory*, ed. J. Elster and A. Hylland. Cambridge: Cambridge University Press, pp. 103–132.

———. (1989). *Solomonic Judgements: Studies in the Limitations of Rationality*. Cambridge: Cambridge University Press.

Estlund, D. M. (1993). "Who's Afraid of Deliberative Democracy? On the Strategic/Deliberative Dichotomy in Recent Constitutional Jurisprudence." *Texas Law Review*, vol. 71, pp. 1437–1477.

Eyerman, R. (1984). "Social Movements and Social Theory." *Sociology*, vol. 18, no. 1, pp. 71–82.

Fay, B. (1988). *Social Theory and Political Practice*. London: Unwin Hyman.

Ferguson, K. E. (1983). *The Feminist Case against Bureaucracy*. Philadelphia: Temple University Press.

Ferrara, A. (1985). "A Critique of Habermas' Diskursethik." *Telos*, no. 64, pp. 45–74.

———. (1987). "On Phronesis." *Praxis International*, vol. 7, no. 3/4, pp. 246–267.

———. (1988). "A Critique of Habermas's Consensus Theory of Truth." *Philosophy and Social Criticism*, vol. 13, no. 1, pp. 39–67.

———. (1989a). "Critical Theory and Its Discontents: Wellmer's Critique of Habermas." *Praxis International*, vol. 9, no. 3, pp. 305–320.

———. (1989b). "Universalisms: Procedural, Contextual and Prudential." *Philosophy and Social Criticism*, vol. 14, no. 3/4, pp. 243–269.

———. (1992a). "Justice and Identity." *Philosophy and Social Criticism*, vol. 18, no. 3/4, pp. 333–354.

———. (1992b). "Justice and Judgment." Unpublished paper.

———. (1992c). "Postmodern Eudaimonia." *Praxis International*, vol. 11, no. 4, pp. 387–411.

———. (1994). "Authenticity and the Project of Modernity." *European Journal of Philosophy*, vol. 2, no. 3, pp. 241–273.

Fischer, F. (1985). "Critical Evaluation of Public Policy: A Methodological Case

Study." In *Critical Theory and Public Life*, ed. J. Forester. Cambridge, Mass.: MIT Press, pp. 231–257.

Fisher, R. and W. Ury (1981). *Getting to Yes*. Boston: Houghton Mifflin.

Fishkin, J. S. (1991). *Democracy and Deliberation: New Directions for Democratic Reform*. New Haven: Yale University Press.

———. (1992). *The Dialogue of Justice: Toward a Self-Reflective Society*. New Haven: Yale University Press.

Flyvbjerg, B. (1991). "Sustaining Non-Rationalized Practices: Body-Mind, Power and Situational Ethics. An Interview with Hubert and Stuart Dreyfus." *Praxis International*, vol. 11, no. 1, pp. 93–113.

Forester, J. (1982). "A Critical Empirical Framework for the Analysis of Public Policy." *New Political Science*, Summer, pp. 33–61.

———. (1985). "Critical Theory and Planning Practice." In *Critical Theory and Public Life*, ed. J. Forester. Cambridge, Mass.: MIT Press, pp. 202–230.

Forester, J. ed., (1985). *Critical Theory and Public Life*. Cambridge, Mass.: MIT Press.

Fraser, N. (1985). "What's Critical about Critical Theory? The Case of Habermas and Gender." *New German Critique*, no. 35, pp. 97–131.

———. (1986). "Toward a Discourse Ethic of Solidarity." *Praxis International*, vol. 5, no. 4, pp. 425–429.

———. (1992). "Rethinking the Public Sphere: A Contribution to the Critique of Actually Existing Democracy." In *Habermas and the Public Sphere*, ed. C. Calhoun. Cambridge, Mass.: MIT Press, pp. 109–142.

Freud, S. (1949). *An Outline of Psychoanalysis*. New York: W. W. Norton.

Gadamer, H. (1975). *Truth and Method*. New York: Seabury Press.

Gale, R. P. (1986). "Social Movements and the State: The Environmental Movement, Countermovement, and Government Agencies." *Sociological Perspectives*, vol. 29, pp. 202–240.

Gerth, H. H. and C. Wright Mills, eds. (1946). *From Max Weber: Essays in Sociology*. New York: Oxford University Press.

Geuss, R. (1981). *The Idea of a Critical Theory*. London and New York: Cambridge University Press.

Gewirth, A. (1978). *Reason and Morality*. Chicago: University of Chicago Press.

———. (1982). *Human Rights*. Chicago: University of Chicago Press.

Gilligan, C. (1982). *In a Different Voice: Psychological Theory and Women's Development*. Cambridge, Mass.: Harvard University Press.

Goodin, R. and J. Dryzek (1980). "Rational Participation: The Politics of Relative Power." *British Journal of Political Science*, vol. 10, pp. 273–292.

Goodwyn, L. (1981). "Organizing Democracy: The Limits of Theory and Practice." *Democracy*, vol. 1, no. 1, pp. 41–60.

Gould, C. C. (1988). *Rethinking Democracy: Freedom and Social Cooperation in Politics, Economy, and Society*. Cambridge: Cambridge University Press.

———. (1990). "On the Conception of the Common Interest: Between Procedure and Substance." In *Hermeneutics and Critical Theory in Ethics and Politics*, ed. M. Kelly. Cambridge, Mass.: MIT Press, pp. 253–273.

Grahame, P. (1985). "Criticalness, Pragmatics, and Everyday Life: Consumer Literacy as Critical Practice." In *Critical Theory and Public Life*, ed. J.

Forester. Cambridge, Mass.: MIT Press, pp. 147–174.

Gross, M. L. (1994). "The Collective Dimensions of Political Morality." *Political Studies*, vol. 42, no. 1, pp. 40–61.

Grünbaum, A. (1984). *The Foundations of Psychoanalysis: A Philosophical Critique*. Berkeley: University of California Press.

Günther, K. (1988). "Impartial Application of Moral and Legal Norms: A Contribution to Discourse Ethics." *Philosophy and Social Criticism*, vol. 14, no. 3/4, pp. 425–432.

———. (1993). *The Sense of Appropriateness: Application Discourses in Morality and Law*. Albany: State University of New York Press.

Gutmann, A. (1985). "Communitarian Critics of Liberalism." *Philosophy and Public Affairs*, vol. 14, pp. 308–322.

Habermas, J. (1968). *Knowledge and Human Interests*. Boston: Beacon Press.

———. (1970). "Towards a Theory of Communicative Competence." *Inquiry*, vol. 13, pp. 360–375.

———. (1971). *Towards a Rational Society: Student Protest, Science, and Politics*. London: Heinemann.

———. (1974a). "The Public Sphere: An Encyclopedia Article." *New German Critique*, no. 3, pp. 49–55.

———. (1974b). *Theory and Practice*. London: Heinemann.

———. (1975). "Towards a Reconstruction of Historical Materialism." *Theory and Society*, vol. 2, pp. 287–300.

———. (1976). *Legitimation Crisis*. Cambridge: Polity Press.

———. (1979). "Consciousness-Raising or Redemptive Criticism—The Contemporaneity of Walter Benjamin." *New German Critique*, no. 17, pp. 30–59.

———. (1980). "On the German-Jewish Heritage." *Telos*, no. 44, pp. 127–131.

———. (1981a). "The Dialectic of Rationalization: An Interview with Jurgen Habermas." *Telos*, no. 49, pp. 1–12.

———. (1981b). "Modernity versus Postmodernism." *New German Critique*, no. 22, pp. 3–14.

———. (1981c). "New Social Movements." *Telos*, no. 49, pp. 33–37.

———. (1982). "A Reply to My Critics." In *Habermas: Critical Debates*, ed. J. B. Thompson and D. Held. Cambridge, Mass.: MIT Press, pp. 219–283.

———. (1984). *The Theory of Communicative Action*, vol. 1. Boston: Beacon Press.

———. (1985a). "A Philosophico-Political Profile." *New Left Review*, no. 151, pp. 75–105.

———. (1985b). "Questions and Counterquestions." In *Habermas and Modernity*, ed. R. J. Bernstein. Cambridge: Polity Press, pp. 192–216.

———. (1986). *Autonomy and Solidarity: Interviews*. London: Verso.

———. (1987a). *The Philosophical Discourse of Modernity*. Cambridge: Polity Press.

———. (1987c). *The Theory of Communicative Action*, vol. 2. Boston: Beacon Press.

———. (1989a). "The New Obscurity: The Crisis of the Welfare State and the Exhaustion of Utopian Energies." In *The New Conservatism: Cultural Criti-*

cism and the Historians' Debate, ed. S. W. Nicholsen. Cambridge, Mass.: MIT Press, pp. 48–70.

———. (1989b). *The Structural Transformation of the Public Sphere.* Cambridge: Polity Press.

———. (1989c). "Towards a Communication-Concept of Rational Collective Will-Formation: A Thought Experiment." *Ratio Juris*, vol. 2, pp. 144–154.

———. (1990a). "Justice and Solidarity: On the Discussion Concerning 'Stage 6'." In *Hermeneutics and Critical Theory in Ethics and Politics*, ed. M. Kelly. Cambridge, Mass.: MIT Press, pp. 32–52.

———. (1990b). *Moral Consciousness and Communicative Action.* Cambridge: Polity Press.

———. (1991a). *Communication and the Evolution of Society.* Boston: Beacon Press.

———. (1991b). *New Conservatism: Cultural Criticism and the Historians' Debate.* Cambridge, Mass.: MIT Press.

———. (1992a). "Citizenship and National Identity: Some Reflections on the Future of Europe." *Praxis International*, vol. 12, no. 1, pp. 1–19.

———. (1992c). "Further Reflections on the Public Sphere." In *Habermas and the Public Sphere*, ed. C. Calhoun. Cambridge, Mass.: MIT Press, pp. 421–461.

———. (1993a). *Justification and Application.* Cambridge: Polity Press.

———. (1993b). "Struggles for Recognition in Constitutional States." *European Journal of Philosophy*, vol. 1, no. 2, pp. 128–155.

———. (1994a). "Human Rights and Popular Sovereignty: The Liberal and Republican Versions." *Ratio Juris*, vol. 7, no. 1, pp. 1–13.

———. (1994b). *The Past as Future.* Cambridge: Polity Press.

———. (1994c). "Three Models of Democracy." *Constellations*, vol. 1, no. 1, pp. 1–10.

———. (1996). *Between Facts and Norms: Contributions to a Discourse Theory of Law and Democracy.* Cambridge: Polity Press.

Hallin, D. C. (1985). "The American News Media: A Critical Theory Perspective." In *Critical Theory and Public Life*, ed. J. Forester. Cambridge, Mass.: MIT Press, pp. 121–146.

Hamilton, A., J. Madison, and J. Jay (1961). *The Federalist Papers.* New York: Mentor Books.

Hamlin, A. and P. Pettit (1989). *The Good Polity: Normative Analysis of the State.* Oxford: Basil Blackwell.

Hegel, G. W. F. (1967). *Philosophy of Right.* New York: Oxford University Press.

———. (1977). *The Phenomenology of Spirit.* Oxford: Oxford University Press.

Held, D. (1980). *Introduction to Critical Theory: Horkheimer to Habermas.* Cambridge: Polity Press.

———. (1982). "Crisis Tendencies, Legitimation and the State." In *Habermas: Critical Debates*, ed. J. B. Thompson and D. Held. Cambridge, Mass.: MIT Press, pp. 181–195.

———. (1987). *Models of Democracy.* Cambridge: Polity Press.

Held, D. ed., (1991). *Political Theory Today.* Cambridge: Polity Press.

Held, D. and C. Pollitt, eds. (1986). *New Forms of Democracy.* London: Sage.

Heller, A. (1984). "The Discourse Ethics of Habermas: Critique and Appraisal." *Thesis Eleven*, no. 10/11, pp. 5–17.

Herman, B. (1985). "The Practice of Moral Judgment." *Journal of Philosophy*, vol. 82, no. 8, pp. 416–420.

Herzog, D. (1985). *Without Foundations: Justification in Political Theory*. Ithaca: Cornell University Press.

Hirschman, A. O. (1994). "Social Conflicts as Pillars of Democratic Market Society." *Political Theory*, vol. 22, no. 2, pp. 203–218.

Hirst, P. (1994). *Associative Democracy: New Forms of Economic and Social Governance*. Cambridge: Polity Press.

Hobbes, T. (1958). *Leviathan*. New York: Bobbs-Merrill.

Holden, B. (1988). "New Directions in Democratic Theory." *Political Studies*, vol. 36, pp. 324–333.

Holmes, S. (1988). "Gag Rules and the Politics of Omission." In *Constitutionalism and Democracy*, ed. J. Elster and R. Slagstad. Cambridge: Cambridge University Press.

Holub, R. C. (1991). *Jürgen Habermas: Critic in the Public Sphere*. London: Routledge.

Honig, B. (1991). "Declarations of Independence: Arendt and Derrida on the Problem of Founding a Republic." *American Political Science Review*, vol. 85, no. 1, pp. 97–113.

Honneth, A. (1992). "Integrity and Disrespect: Principles of a Conception of Morality Based on a Theory of Recognition." *Political Theory*, vol. 20, no. 2, pp. 187–201.

———. (1994). "The Social Dynamics of Disrespect." *Constellations*, vol. 1, no. 2, pp. 255–269.

Horkheimer, M. (1947). *The Eclipse of Reason*. New York: Continuum.

Horkheimer, M. and T. Adorno (1972). *The Dialectic of Enlightenment*. New York: Seabury Press.

Howard, R. (1974). "A Politics in Search of the Political." *Theory and Society*, vol. 1, pp. 271–306.

Ingram, D. (1993). "The Limits and Possibilities of Communicative Ethics for Democratic Theory." *Political Theory*, vol. 21, no. 2, pp. 294–321.

Isaac, J. C. (1994). "Oases in the Desert: Hannah Arendt on Democratic Politics." *American Political Science Review*, vol. 88, no. 1, pp. 156–168.

Jay, M. (1992). "The Debate over Performative Contradiction: Habermas versus the Poststructuralists." In *Philosophical Interventions in the Unfinished Project of Enlightenment*, ed. A. Honneth, M. McCarthy, and A. Wellmer. Cambridge, Mass.: MIT Press, pp. 261–279.

Johnson, J. (1991). "Habermas on Strategic and Communicative Action." *Political Theory*, vol. 19, no. 2, pp. 181–201.

———. (1993). "Is Talk Really Cheap? Prompting Conversation between Critical Theory and Rational Choice." *American Political Science Review*, vol. 87, no. 1, pp. 74–86.

Kant, I. (1952). *Critique of Judgment*. Oxford: Clarendon Press.

———. (1964). *Groundwork of the Metaphysics of Morals*. New York: Harper & Row.

———. (1965). *Critique of Pure Reason*. New York: St. Martin's Press.

———. (1983). "Perpetual Peace." In *Kant's Political Writings*, ed. H. Reiss. Cambridge: Cambridge University Press,

Keane, J. (1984). *Public Life and Late Capitalism: Towards a Socialist Theory of Democracy*. Cambridge: Cambridge University Press.

Keane, J., ed. (1988a). *Civil Society and the State*. London: Verso.

———. (1988b). *Democracy and Civil Society*. London: Verso.

Kellner, D. (1989). *Critical Theory, Marxism, and Modernity*. Baltimore: Johns Hopkins University Press.

Kellner, D. and R. Roderick (1981). "Recent Literature on Critical Theory." *New German Critique*, no. 23, pp. 141–170.

Kelly, M., ed. (1990). *Hermeneutics and Critical Theory in Ethics and Politics*. Cambridge, Mass.: MIT Press.

Kemp, R. (1985). "Planning, Public Hearings, and the Politics of Discourse." In *Critical Theory and Public Life*, ed. J. Forester. Cambridge, Mass.: MIT Press, pp. 177–201.

Kitzinger, C. (1986). "Introducing and Developing Q as a Feminist Methodology: A Study of Accounts of Lesbianism." In *Feminist Social Psychology: Developing Theory and Practice*, ed. S. Wilkinson. Milton Keynes, U.K.: Open University Press, pp. 151–172.

Knight, J. and J. Johnson (1994). "Aggregation and Deliberation: On the Possibility of Democratic Legitimacy." *Political Theory*, vol. 22, no. 2, pp. 277–296.

Kohut, H. (1971). *The Analysis of the Self*. New York: International Universities Press.

Korsgaard, C. M. (1986). "Skepticism about Practical Reason." *Journal of Philosophy*, vol. 83, no. 1, pp. 5–25.

Kuflik, A. (1979). "Morality and Compromise." In *Compromise in Ethics, Law and Politics*, ed. J. R. Pennock and J. W. Chapman. New York: New York University Press,

Kymlicka, W. and W. Nelson (1994). "Return of the Citizen: A Survey of Recent Work on Citizenship Theory." *Ethics*, vol. 104, pp. 352–381.

Laslett, P. (1956). "The Face to Face Society." In *Philosophy, Polititcs and Society*, first series, ed. P. Laslett. Oxford: Basil Blackwell.

Laursen, J. C. (1986). "The Subversive Kant: The Vocabulary of 'Public' and 'Publicity'." *Political Theory*, vol. 14, no. 4, pp. 584–603.

Lefebvre, H. (1994). *The Production of Space*. Oxford: Basil Blackwell.

Le Grand, J. (1990). "Equity versus Efficiency: The Elusive Trade-Off." *Ethics*, vol. 100, pp. 554–568.

Leonard, S.T. (1990). *Critical Theory in Political Practice*. Princeton: Princeton University Press.

Levin, Y. and H. Litwin, eds. (1986). *Community and Co-operatives in Participatory Democracy*. London: Gower.

Lindow, V. (1993). "A Chance for a Change." *Nursing Times*, vol. 89, no. 12, pp. 33–34.

Lipsey, R. G. and K. Lancaster (1956–57). "The General Theory of the Second-Best." *Review of Economic Studies*, vol. 24, pp. 11–32.

Livy. (1960). *The Early History of Rome*. Harmondsworth, U.K.: Penguin.

Lobkowicz, N. (1967). *Theory and Practice: History of a Concept from Aristotle to Marx*. Notre Dame, Ind.: University of Notre Dame Press.

Locke, J. (1952). *The Second Treatise of Government*. Indianapolis: Bobbs-Merrill.

Lofgren, L. B. (1984). "The Self in a Small Group: A Comparison of the Theories of Bion and Kohut." In *Kohut's Legacy: Contributions to Self Psychology*, ed. P. E. Stepansky and A. Goldberg. Hillsdale, N.J.: The Analytic Press, pp. 203–213.

Luban, D. (1985). "Bargaining and Compromise: Recent Work on Negotiation and Informal Justice." *Philosophy and Public Affairs*, vol. 14, no. 4, pp. 397–416.

Lukacs, G. (1971). *History and Class Consciousness*. London: Merlin Press.

Luke T. W. and S. K. White (1985). "Critical Theory, the Informational Revolution, and an Ecological Path to Modernity." In *Critical Theory and Public Life*, ed. J. Forester. Cambridge, Mass.: MIT Press, pp. 22–56.

Lukes, S. (1982). "Of Gods and Demons: Habermas and Practical Reason." In *Habermas: Critical Debates*, ed. J. B. Thompson and D. Held. Cambridge, Mass.: MIT Press, pp. 134–148.

———. (1991). "Equality and Liberty: Must They Conflict?" In *Political Theory Today*, ed. D. Held. Cambridge: Polity Press, pp. 48–66.

Lyotard, J.-F. (1984). *The Postmodern Condition: A Report on Knowledge*. Minneapolis: University of Minnesota Press.

Lyotard, J.-F. and J.-L. Thébaud (1985). *Just Gaming*. Manchester, U.K.: Manchester University Press.

Machiavelli, N. (1979a). "The Discourses." In *The Portable Machiavelli*, ed. P. Bondanella and M. Musa. Harmondsworth, U.K.: Penguin, pp. 167–418.

MacIntyre, A. (1966). *A Short History of Ethics*. New York: Macmillan.

———. (1981). *After Virtue*. Notre Dame, Ind.: University of Notre Dame Press.

———. (1984). "Does Applied Ethics Rest on a Mistake?" *The Monist*, vol. 67, pp. 498–513.

Mackie, J. L. (1977). *Ethics—Inventing Right and Wrong*. New York: Penguin.

Makkreel, R. (1990). "Kant and the Interpretation of Nature and History." In *Hermeneutics and Critical Theory in Ethics and Politics*, ed. M. Kelly. Cambridge, Mass.: MIT Press, pp. 169–181.

Malcolm, J. (1985). *In the Freud Archives*. New York: Vintage Books.

Malhotra, V. A. (1984). "Research as Critical Reflection: A Study of Self, Time and Communicative Competency." *Humanity and Society*, vol. 8, pp. 468–477.

———. (1987). "Habermas' Sociological Theory as a Basis for Clinical Practice with Small Groups." *Clinical Sociology Review*, vol. 5, pp. 181–192.

Manin, B. (1987). "On Legitimacy and Political Deliberation." *Political Theory*, vol. 15, no. 3, pp. 338–368.

Mansbridge, J. J. (1973). "Time, Emotion, and Inequality: Three Problems of Participatory Groups." *Journal of Applied Behavioral Science*, vol. 9, no. 2/3, pp. 351–368.

———. (1980). *Beyond Adversary Democracy*. New York: Basic Books.

———. (1994). "Using Power, Fighting Power." *Constellations*, vol. 1, no. 1, pp. 53–73.

Margalit, A. (1983). "Ideals and Second Bests." In *Philosophy for Education*, ed. S. Fox. Jerusalem: Van Leer Foundation, pp. 77–90.

Marx, K. (1963). "The Critique of Hegel's Philosophy of Right." In *Early Writings*, ed. T. B. Bottomore. Harmondsworth, U.K.: Penguin.

Matustík, M. J. (1993). *Postnational Identity: Critical Theory and Existential Philosophy in Habermas, Kierkegarrd, and Havel*. New York: Guildford Press.

McCarthy, T. A. (1978). *The Critical Theory of Jürgen Habermas*. Cambridge, Mass.: MIT Press.

———. (1982). "Rationality and Relativism: Habermas's 'Overcoming' of Hermeneutics." In *Habermas: Critical Debates*, ed. J. B. Thompson and D. Held. Cambridge, Mass.: MIT Press, pp. 57–78.

———. (1990). "The Politics of the Ineffable: Derrida's Deconstruction." In *Hermeneutics and Critical Theory in Ethics and Politics*, ed. M. Kelly. Cambridge, Mass.: MIT Press, pp. 146–168.

———. (1991). "Practical Discourse: On the Relation of Morality to Politics." In *Ideals and Illusions*. Cambridge: Polity Press, pp. 181–199.

———. (1994). "Kantian Contructivism and Reconstructivism: Rawls and Habermas in Dialogue." *Ethics*, vol. 105, pp. 44–63.

McKeown, B. and D. Thomas (1988). *Q Methodology*. Newbury Park, Calif.: Sage.

McLean, I. (1991). "Forms of Representation and Systems of Voting." In *Political Theory Today*, ed. D. Held. Cambridge: Polity Press.

Mead, G. H. (1934). *Mind, Self, and Society*. Chicago: University of Chicago Press.

Melucci, A. (1988). "Social Movements and the Democratization of Everyday Life." In *Civil Society and the State*, ed. J. Keane. London: Verso, pp. 245–260.

———. (1989). *Nomads of the Present: Social Movements and Individual Needs in Contemporary Society*. London: Hutchinson Radius.

Mendelson, J. (1979). "The Habermas-Gadamer Debate." *New German Critique*, no. 18, pp. 44–73.

Merry, U. and G. Brown. (1987). *The Neurotic Behavior of Organizations*. New York: Gardner Press.

Michels, R. (1958). *Political Parties: A Sociological Study of the Oligarchical Tendencies of Modern Democracy*. Glencoe, Ill.: Free Press.

Milbrath, L. W. (1965). *Political Participation: How and Why Do People Get Involved in Politics?* Chicago: Rand McNally.

Mill, J. S. (1859). "Essay on Bentham." In *Utilitarianism and Other Writings*, ed. M. Warnock. New York: Meridian, pp. 78–125.

Miller, D. (1992). "Deliberative Democracy and Social Choice." *Political Studies*, vol. 40, Special Issue, pp. 54–67.

Misgeld, D. (1985). "Education and Cultural Invasion: Critical Social Theory, Education as Instruction, and the 'Pedagogy of the Oppressed'." In *Critical*

Theory and Public Life, ed. J. Forester. Cambridge, Mass.: MIT Press, pp. 77–118.

Mishler, E. (1984). *The Discourse of Medicine: Dialectics of Medical Interviews*. Norwood, N.J.: Ablex.

Mitroff, I. and L. V. Blankenship (1973). "On the Methodology of the Holistic Experiment." *Technological Forecasting and Social Change*, vol. 4, pp. 339–353.

Moon, D. J. (1991). "Constrained Discourse and Public Life." *Political Theory*, vol. 19, no. 2, pp. 202–229.

Moscovici, S. and W. Doise (1994). *Conflict and Consensus: A General Theory of Collective Decisions*. London: Sage.

Mouffe, C. (1988). "Radical Democracy: Modern or Postmodern." In *Universal Abandon? The Politics of Postmodernism*, ed. A. Ross. Edinburgh: University of Edinburgh Press, pp. 31–45.

Nagel, T. (1989). "What Makes a Political Theory Utopian?" *Social Research*, vol. 56, no. 4, pp. 903–920.

Natchez, P. (1985). *Images of Voting/Visions of Democracy*. New York: Basic Books.

Ober, J. (1989). *Mass and Elite in Democratic Athens*. Princeton: Princeton University Press.

Offe, C. (1984). *Contradictions of the Welfare State*. London: Hutchinson.

——. (1985). "New Social Movements: Challenging the Boundaries of Institutional Politics." *Social Research*, vol. 52, no. 4, pp. 817–868.

——. (1992). "Bindings, Shackles, Brakes: On Self-Limitation Strategies." In *Cultural-Political Interventions in the Unfinished Project of Enlightenment*, ed. A. Honneth, T. McCarthy, C. Offe and A. Wellmer. Cambridge, Mass.: MIT Press, pp. 63–94.

Offe, C. and U. K. Preuss (1991). "Democratic Institutions and Moral Resources." In *Political Theory Today*, ed. D. Held. Cambridge: Polity Press, pp. 143–171.

O'Hagan, T. (1987). "On Hegel's Critique of Kant's Moral and Political Philosophy." In *Hegel's Critique of Kant*, ed. S. Priest. Oxford: Clarendon Press, pp. 135–160.

Okun, A. M. (1975). *Equality and Efficiency: The Big Tradeoff*. Washington, D.C.: The Brookings Insitution.

O'Neill, J. (1987). "Decolonization and the Ideal Speech Community: Some Issues in the Theory and Practice of Communicative Competence." In *Critical Theory and Public Life*, ed. J. Forester. Cambridge, Mass.: MIT Press, pp. 57–76.

O'Neill, O. (1986). "The Public Use of Reason." *Political Theory*, vol. 14, pp. 523–551.

O'Neill, S. (1994). "Morality, Ethical Life and the Persistence of Universalism." *Theory, Culture and Society*, vol. 11, no. 2, pp. 129–149.

Outhwaite, W. (1994). *Habermas: A Critical Introduction*. Cambridge: Polity Press.

Parkin, A. (1993). *Rethinking the Subject: Habermas, Critical Theory, and the Challenges of Postmodernism*. Ph.D. dissertation, University of Bradford.

Parry, G. (1969). *Political Elites*. London: George Allen and Unwin.

Passerin d'Entrèves, M. (1988). "Aristotle or Burke? Some Comments on H. Shnädelbach's 'What Is Neo-Aristotelianism?'" *Praxis International*, vol. 7, no. 3/4, pp. 238–245.

———. (1990). *Modernity, Justice and Community*. Milan: Franco Angeli.

———. (1994). *The Political Philosophy of Hannah Arendt*. London: Routledge.

Passerin d'Entrèves, M. and S. Benhabib, eds. (1996). *Habermas and the Unfinished Project of Modernity: Critical Essays on The Philosophical Discourse of Modernity*. Cambridge: Polity Press.

Pateman, C. (1970). *Participation and Democratic Theory*. Cambridge: Cambridge University Press.

Phillips, A. (1991). *Engendering Democracy*. Cambridge: Polity Press.

———. (1994). "Dealing with Difference: A Politics of Ideas or a Politics of Presence?" *Constellations*, vol. 1, no. 1, pp. 74–91.

Pitkin, H. F. and S. M. Shumer (1982). "On Participation." *Democracy*, vol. 2, no. 4, pp. 43–54.

Pizzorno, A. (1970). "An Introduction to the Theory of Political Participation." *Social Science Information*, vol. 9, no. 5, pp. 29–61.

Pocock, J. G. A. (1975). *The Machiavellian Moment*. Princeton: Princeton University Press.

Poguntke, T. (1992). "Unconventional Participation in Party Politics: The Experience of the German Greens." *Political Studies*, vol. 40, pp. 239–254.

Putnam, H. (1981). *Reason, Truth and History*. Cambridge: Cambridge University Press.

Putterman, L. (1982). "Some Behavioural Perspectives on the Dominance of Hierarchical over Democratic Forms of Enterprise." *Journal of Economic Behaviour and Organization*, vol. 3, pp. 139–160.

Radin, M. J. (1986). "Risk-of-Error Rules and Non-Ideal Justification." *Nomos*, vol. 28, pp. 33–48.

Rasmussen, D. M. (1990). *Reading Habermas*. Oxford: Basil Blackwell.

Rawls, J. (1971). *A Theory of Justice*. Cambridge, Mass.: Harvard University Press.

———. (1980). "Kantian Constructivism in Moral Theory. The John Dewey Lectures." *Journal of Philosophy*, vol. 77, pp. 515–572.

———. (1993). *Political Liberalism*. New York: Columbia University Press.

Ray, L. J. (1993). *Rethinking Critical Theory: Emancipation in the Age of Global Social Movements*. London: Sage.

Rehg, W. (1991). "Discourse and the Moral Point of View: Deriving a Dialogic Principle of Universalization." *Inquiry*, vol. 34, pp. 27–48.

Ripstein, A. (1987). "Foundationalism in Political Theory." *Philosophy and Public Affairs*, vol. 16, no. 2, pp. 115–137.

———. (1994). "Universal and General Wills: Hegel and Rousseau." *Political Theory*, vol. 22, no. 4, pp. 444–467.

Rodger, J. J. (1985). "On the Degeneration of the Public Sphere." *Political Studies*, vol. 33, pp. 203–217.

Rodwell, P. (1990). *Habermas and the Evaluation of Public Policy*. Ph.D. dissertation, Manchester University.

Rorty, R. (1980). "A Discussion." *Review of Metaphysics*, vol. 34, no. 1, pp. 51–52.

Rousseau, J. J. (1968). *The Social Contract*. Harmondsworth, U.K.: Penguin.

Ruane, J. and J. Todd (1988). "The Application of Critical Theory." *Political Studies*, vol. 36, pp. 533–538.

Rubinstein, D. (1981). *Marx and Wittgenstein: Social Praxis and Social Explanation*. London: Routledge.

Ryle, G. (1945). "Knowing How and Knowing That." *Proceedings of the Aristotelian Society*, vol. 66, pp. 1–16.

Sandel, M. J. (1982). *Liberalism and the Limits of Justice*. Cambridge: Cambridge University Press.

——— . (1984). "The Procedural Republic and the Unencumbered Self." *Political Theory*, vol. 12. no.1, pp. 81–96.

Sandole, D. J. D. and H. van der Merwe (1993). *Conflict Resolution Theory and Practice: Integration and Application*. Manchester, U.K.: Manchester University Press.

Sartori, G. (1987). *The Theory of Democracy Revisited*, vol. 1. Chatham, N.J.: Chatham House.

Sartre, J.-P. (1976). *Critique of Dialectical Reason*. London: New Left Books.

Scanlon, T. M. (1982). "Contractarianism and Utilitarianism." In *Utilitarianism and Beyond*, ed. A. Sen and B. Williams. Cambridge: Cambridge University Press, pp. 103–128.

Schutz, A. (1967). *The Phenomenology of the Social World*. Evanston, Ill.: Northwestern University Press.

Sciulli, D. (1986). "Voluntaristic Action as a Distinct Concept: Theoretical Foundations of Societal Constitutionalism." *American Sociological Review*, vol. 51, pp. 743–766.

Scruton, R. (1982). *Kant*. Oxford: Oxford University Press.

Searle, J. (1969). *Speech Acts: An Essay in the Philosophy of Language*. New York: Cambridge University Press.

Sen, A. and B. Williams, eds. (1982). *Utilitarianism and Beyond*. Cambridge: Cambridge University Press.

Sennett, R. (1977). *The Fall of Public Man*. London: Faber and Faber.

Sensat, J. (1979). *Habermas and Marxism*. Beverly Hills, Calif.: Sage.

Sewell, W. H. J. (1980). *Work and Revolution in France: The Language of Labor from the Old Regime to 1848*. Cambridge: Cambridge University Press.

Shelly, R. (1993). "Habermas and the Normative Foundations of a Radical Politics." *Thesis Eleven*, no. 35, pp. 62–83.

Sirianni, C. (1993). "Learning Pluralism: Democracy and Diversity in Feminist Organisations." In *Nomos*, vol. 35. New York: New York University Press, pp. 283–312.

Skinner, Q. (1973). "The Empirical Theorists of Democracy and Their Critics: A Plague on Both Their Houses." *Political Theory*, vol. 1, no. 3, pp. 287–306.

——— . (1982). "Habermas's Reformation." *New York Review of Books*, October 7, pp. 35–38.

Steinberger, P. (1993). *The Concept of Political Judgment*. Chicago: University of Chicago Press.

Stern, P. (1989). "On the Relation between Autonomy and Ethical Community: Hegel's Critique of Kantian Morality." *Praxis International*, vol. 9, no. 3, pp. 234–248.

Strydom, P. (1990). "Metacritical Observations on a Reductive Approach to Critical Theory: Ruane and Todd's 'The Application of Critical Theory'." *Political Studies*, vol. 38, pp. 534–542.

Sunstein, C. R. (1991). "Preferences and Politics." *Philosophy and Public Affairs*, vol. 20, no. 1, pp. 3–34.

———. (1993). *Democracy and the Problem of Free Speech*. New York: Free Press.

Taylor, C. (1985). *Human Agency and Language*. Cambridge: Cambridge University Press.

———. (1989a). "Cross-Purposes: The Liberal-Communitarian Debate." In *Liberalism and the Moral Life*, ed. N. L. Rosenblum. Cambridge, Mass.: Harvard University Press, pp. 159–182.

———. (1989b). *Sources of the Self: The Making of the Modern Identity*. Cambridge: Cambridge University Press.

Taylor, P. W. (1961). *Normative Discourse*. Englewood Cliffs, N.J.: Prentice Hall.

Therborn, G. (1971). "Jürgen Habermas: A New Eclecticism." *New Left Review*, no. 67, pp. 69–83.

Thompson, E. P. (1968). *The Making of the English Working Class*. Harmondsworth, U.K.: Penguin.

Thompson, J. B. (1982). "Universal Pragmatics." In *Habermas: Critical Debates*, ed. J. B. Thompson and D. Held. Cambridge, Mass.: MIT Press, pp. 116–133.

Thucydides (1982). *The Peloponnesian War*. Harmondsworth, U.K.: Penguin.

Tucker, K. H. (1989). "Ideology and Social Movements: The Contribution of Habermas." *Sociological Inquiry*, vol. 59, pp. 30–47.

Tully, J. (1989). "Wittgenstein and Political Philosophy: Understanding Practices of Critical Reflection." *Political Theory*, vol. 17, no. 1, pp. 172–204.

Unger, R. M. (1987). *False Necessity: Anti-Necessitarian Social Theory in the Service of Radical Democracy*. Cambridge: Cambridge University Press.

Verba, S. (1961). *Small Groups and Political Behaviour*. Princeton: Princeton University Press.

Vetlesen, A. J. (1994). *Perception, Empathy, and Judgment: An Inquiry into the Preconditions of Moral Performance*. University Park: Pennsylvania State University Press.

Villa, D. A. (1992). "Beyond Good and Evil: Arendt, Nietzsche, and the Aestheticization of Political Action." *Political Theory*, vol. 20, no. 2, pp. 274–308.

Walker, B. (1992). "Habermas and Pluralist Political Theory." *Philosophy and Social Criticism*, vol. 18, no. 1, pp. 81–102.

Walzer, M. (1970). "A Day in the Life of a Socialist Citizen." In *Obligations: Essays on Disobedience, War and Citizenship*. Cambridge, Mass.: Harvard University Press, pp. 229–238.

Walzer, M. (1973). "Political Action: The Problem of Dirty Hands." *Philosophy and Public Affairs*, vol. 2, no. 2, p. 175.

————. (1983). *Spheres of Justice*. New York: Basic Books.

————. (1984). "Liberalism and the Art of Separation." *Political Theory*, vol. 12, no. 3, pp. 315–330.

Warren, M. (1992). "Democratic Theory and Self-Transformation." *American Political Science Review*, vol. 86, pp. 8–23.

Watt, A. J. (1975). "Transcendental Arguments and Moral Principles." *Philosophical Quarterly*, vol. 25.

Weber, M. (1949). "Objectivity in Social Science and Social Policy." In Methodology of the Social Sciences, ed. E. A. Shils and H. A. Finch. New York: Free Press, pp. 49–112.

Wellmer, A. (1976). "Communication and Emancipation: Reflections on the 'Linguistic Turn' in Critical Theory." In *On Critical Theory*, ed. J. O'Neill. New York: Seabury Press.

————. (1981). *Praktische Philosophie und Theorie der Gesellschaft*. Constance, Germany: Universitätsverlag Konstanz.

————. (1985). "Reason, Utopia, and the Dialectic of Enlightenment." In *Habermas and Modernity*, ed. R. J. Bernstein. Cambridge: Polity Press, pp. 35–66.

————. (1986). *Ethik und Dialog*. Frankfurt: Suhrkamp.

————. (1990a). "Models of Freedom in the Modern World." In *Hermeneutics and Critical Theory in Ethics and Politics*, ed. M. Kelly. Cambridge, Mass.: MIT Press, pp. 227–252.

————. (1990b). "Practical Philosophy and the Theory of Society: On the Problem of the Normative Foundations of a Critical Social Science." In *The Communicative Ethics Controversy*, ed. S. Benhabib and F. Dallmayr. Cambridge, Mass.: MIT Press, pp. 293–329.

————. (1991). *The Persistence of Modernity: Aesthetics, Ethics and Postmodernism*. Cambridge: Polity Press.

————. (1995). "Hannah Arendt on Judgement: the Unwritten Doctrine of Reason." Unpublished paper, pp. 1–28.

Welton, R. W., ed. (1995). *In Defense of the Lifeworld: Critical Perspectives on Adult Learning*. Albany: State University of New York Press.

White, S. K. (1980). "Reason and Authority in Habermas: A Critique of the Critics." *American Political Science Review*, vol. 74, pp. 1007–1017.

————. (1982). "On the Normative Structure of Action: Gewirth and Habermas." *The Review of Politics*, vol. 44, pp. 282–301.

————. (1983). "The Normative Basis of Critical Theory." *Polity*, vol. 16, pp. 150–164.

————. (1984). "Habermas' Communicative Ethics and the Development of Moral Consciousness." *Philosophy and Social Criticism*, vol. 10, pp. 41–62.

————. (1988). *The Recent Work of Jürgen Habermas*. Cambridge: Cambridge University Press.

————. (1991). *Political Theory and Postmodernism*. Cambridge: Cambridge University Press.

Whitebook, J. (1979). "The Problem of Nature in Habermas." *Telos*, no. 40, pp. 41–69.

———. (1981). "Saving the Subject: Modernity and the Problem of the Autonomous Individual." *Telos*, no. 50.

———. (1985). "Reason and Happiness: Some Psychoanalytic Themes in Critical Theory." In *Habermas and Modernity*, ed. R. J. Bernstein. Cambridge: Polity Press, pp. 140–160.

Wildavsky, A. (1987). "Choosing Preferences by Constructing Institutions: A Cultural Theory of Preference Formation." *American Political Science Review*, vol. 81, pp. 3–21.

Williams, B. (1985). *Ethics and the Limits of Philosophy*. London: Fontana.

Wisdom, J. (1969). *Philosophy and Psychoanalysis*. Berkeley: University of California Press.

Wisman, J. D. (1991). "The Scope and Goals of Economic Science: A Habermasian Perspective." In *Economics and Hermeneutics*, ed. D. Lavoie. London: Routledge, pp. 113–133.

Wittgenstein, L. (1953). *Philosophical Investigations*. Oxford: Basil Blackwell.

———. (1958). *The Blue and Brown Books*. Oxford: Basil Blackwell.

Wokler, R. (1993). "Hegel's Rousseau: The General Will and Civil Society." *Arachne*, no. 8, pp. 7–45.

Wolff, R. P. (1970). *In Defense of Anarchism*. New York: Harper & Row.

———. (1973). *The Autonomy of Reason: A Commentary on Kant's Groundwork of the Metaphysics of Morals*. New York: Harper & Row.

———. (1977). *Understanding Rawls*. Princeton: Princeton University Press.

Wolin, S. (1982). "What Revolutionary Action Means Today." *Democracy*, vol. 2, no. 4, pp. 17–28.

———. (1994). "Fugitive Democracy." *Constellations*, vol. 1, no. 1, pp. 11–25.

Wollheim, R. (1971). *Sigmund Freud*. Cambridge: Cambridge University Press.

Wollheim, R. and J. Hopkins, eds. (1982). *Philosophical Essays on Freud*. Cambridge: Cambridge University Press.

Woodiwiss, T. (1978). "Critical Theory and the Capitalist State." *Economy and Society*, vol. 7, pp. 175–192.

Young, I. M. (1981). "Towards a Critical Theory of Justice." *Social Theory and Practice*, vol. 7, pp. 279–302.

———. (1989). "Polity and Group Difference: A Critique of the Ideal of Universal Citizenship." *Ethics*, vol. 99, pp. 250–274.

Young, R. E. (1987). "Critical Theory and Classroom Questioning." *Language and Education*, vol. 1, no. 2.

———. (1988). "Moral Development, Ego Autonomy, and Questions of Practicality in the Critical Theory of Schooling." *Educational Theory*, vol. 38, no. 4, pp. 391–404.

———. (1989). *A Critical Theory of Education: Habermas and Our Children's Future*. New York: Wheatsheaf.

Zald, M. N. and J. D. McCarthy, eds. (1985). *Social Movements in Organizational Society: Resource Mobilization, Conflict and Institutionalization*. New Brunswick, N.J.: Transaction Books.

Zuckerman, M. (1968). "The Social Context of Democracy in Massachusetts." *William and Mary Quarterly*, vol. 25, third series, pp. 523–544.

INDEX